D0122567

TRUST

Inc.

Strategies for Building Your
Company's Most Valuable Asset

TRUST
Inc.
Strategies for Building Your Company's Most Valuable Asset

Editor:
BARBARA BROOKS KIMMEL

Publisher
NEXT DECADE, INC.

NEXT DECADE

ISBN: 978-1-93-291936-3

e-ISBN: 978-1-93-291937-6

Library of Congress Cataloging-in-Publication Data

Trust Inc. : strategies for building your company's most valuable asset / [edited by] Barbara Brooks Kimmel.
     pages cm
Summary: "More than 30 leading experts share their insights on the impact of trust on business success in this handbook on organizational trust. Through case studies--including Apple's new leadership--stories, and solutions, these experts present a holistic perspective that encompasses the role of all stakeholders, not just leaders, in advancing trust and trustworthiness within organizations. Among the contributors are Ben Boyd of Edelman, Randy Conley of Ken Blanchard Companies, Stephen M. R. Covey of CoveyLink, Amy Lyman of the Great Places to Work Institute, and Bob Vanourek of Triple Crown Leadership"-- Provided by publisher.
ISBN 978-1-932919-36-3 (hardback)
1. Trust. 2. Business ethics. 3. Corporate culture. 4. Corporate image.
5. Organizational behavior. I. Kimmel, Barbara Brooks.
 HF5387.T78 2014
 658.3'145--dc23   2013028496

Next Decade books are available at special quantity discounts to use as premium and sales promotions or for use in corporate training programs. To contact a representative, please e-mail us at info@nextdecade.com.

Cover and interior design by Andrew Hahn, verso6.com

To my sons, Dan and Seth
who inspired me to compile this book.

The future of trust is in your hands.

Contents

Foreword...1
  By Timothy J. McClimon

Preface...5
  By Barbara Brooks Kimmel

Introduction..7
  By Ken Blanchard

Section I: Why Trust Matters 11

The Business Case for Trust..13
  By Barbara Brooks Kimmel and Charles H. Green

What Does a Trustworthy Company Look Like?.................................25
  By Peter Firestein

Brand Trust is the Foundation to Brand Loyalty................................33
  By Jim Gregory

Choosing Candor: The Language of Trust...41
  By L.J. Rittenhouse

Making Your Values "Real" to Enable Trust
(The Common Denominator in an Uncommon Business World)................49
  By Jeff Thomson

Section II: Trust in Practice 57

In Apple We Trust?..59
  By Cynthia Figge

Four Lock Box...67
  By John Gerzema

Trust: The Great Economic Game-Changer...71
  By Robert Porter Lynch

You Can't Take 164 Years of Trust for Granted...................................81
  By Deb Mills-Scofield

Section III: Trustworthy Leadership 89

The ABCDs of Leading with Trust..91
  By Randy Conley

Leading Out in Extending Trust..97
  By Stephen M.R. Covey and Greg Link

Leading *from* the Heart: Build Your Business by Attaining Trust 103
By *Lolly Daskal*

Leading with Trust: Learning from Mistakes 109
By *Amy Lyman*

Ethical Leader as Ethics Coach 117
By *Chris MacDonald, Ph.D.*

The Four C's of Trust 123
By *John Spence*

Stewards Build Trust 129
By *Bob and Gregg Vanourek*

Section IV: Building Trustworthy Teams 137

Practicing Trustworthy Behaviors 139
By *William Benner*

Building the Trust Muscle:
In Our Companies, In our Teams, In Ourselves 147
By *Mary C. Gentile, PhD*

You Can't Take Trust for Granted 153
By *James M. Kouzes and Barry Z. Posner*

Creating Thriving Organizations—
The Bedrock of Trust and Reputation 159
By *Brian Moriarty*

Reinforcing Candor Builds Trust and Transparency 167
By *Bob Whipple*

Section V: Restoring Trust 175

Five Strategies to Maximize The Power of Trust 177
By *Patricia Aburdene*

Trust, Emotion and Corporate Reputation 185
By *Linda Locke*

Building Trust is Tougher Than Ever: A Trust Manifesto for Leaders 193
By *James E. Lukaszewski*

Rebuilding Trust in the Financial Markets 201
By *Davia Temin*

Section VI: A New Paradigm for
Organizational Trust 211

Brave Leadership Builds Trust in the New World 213
By *Ben Boyd*

Why Trust is Our Future's Most Vital Resource 221
  By Eric Lowitt

From CSR to Corporate Social Innovation 227
  By Philip Mirvis

Capitalism and High Trust:
Leveraging Social Worlds as Intangible Assets.. 235
  By Steven N. Pyser, J.D.

Conclusion: Creating a Positive Deviance of Trust 243
  By Robert Easton

Appendix 247

APPENDIX A 249
  Global Experts Define Organizational Trust/Trustworthiness

APPENDIX B 261
  Examples of Vision and Values Statements

APPENDIX C 267
  Call to Action

Index 271

Foreword

By Timothy J. McClimon

I admit, sometimes it's hard to find a corporation's heart. But the idea of corporations giving back to their communities certainly isn't a new one.

Alexander Graham Bell, who founded Bell Telephone Company, which later became AT&T, began his career by teaching the hearing impaired, which led directly to the invention of the telephone. He also founded the voluntary association, Telephone Pioneers of America, which still exists today. My own company, American Express, was founded in 1850 and made its first grant to aid victims of the Boston Fire in 1872. We conducted our first employee giving campaign in 1885 by encouraging employees to give their pennies to help build the pedestal for the Statue of Liberty.

In short, historically companies have given from the heart. This kind of corporate largess, while cherished by some, has been derided by others. In the most famous criticism, Milton Friedman wrote: "Few trends could so thoroughly undermine the very foundations of our free society as the acceptance by corporate officials of a social responsibility other than to make as much money for their shareholders as possible."

Today, corporate social responsibility- some people call it "corporate citizenship" or "sustainability" or "social investing"—has come to mean operating a company so that it meets or exceeds the ethical, legal, commercial and public expectations society has of business. Long-term trustworthiness and integrity trump short-term profits and public relations gimmicks.

I think this approach is especially important now in an era of transparency, widespread social media platforms and 24-hour news channels. As we all know, there are no secrets any more, and there are also no one-off wins. Companies that are held up as the most socially responsible have embraced the ideals of good governance, transparency, being environmentally friendly, treating their employees well, and creating products and services that are high quality and fairly priced.

A number of social investors have listed the following six practices that they look for in socially responsible companies:

- Good corporate citizenship demonstrated through innovative and generous giving
- Good diversity practices with respect to women and minorities in management positions and on the board
- Employee investments through profit-sharing and strong retirement programs
- Environmentally friendly policies that recycle, prevent pollution, and respect the environment
- Concern for human rights and fair treatment of employees especially in less-developed countries
- Concern about producing safe and useful products, and a commitment to research and development.

Call it having a heart and a brain.

At American Express, we strive to bring to life the corporate value of good citizenship by supporting communities in ways that enhance our reputation with employees, customers, business partners, and other stakeholders. Today, we are focused on building the capacity of nonprofit organizations to preserve their communities, develop effective leaders, and utilize volunteers and advocates through our three themes of Historic Preservation, Leadership Development and Community Service. Some of our contributions I'm most proud of are:

- Over the past 35 years, we have contributed more than $50 million to help preserve nearly 500 iconic historic sites in all corners of the globe, including The Temple of Hercules in Rome to the Palace of Fine Arts in Mexico City.
- Over 10,000 emerging nonprofit leaders worldwide have benefitted from professional development programs that we have sponsored over the past six years—including our own American Express Leadership Academy.

- And our effort to build the capacity of organizations also extends to mobilizing our own employees as volunteers and advocates for causes in their communities. Through our Serve2Gether Consulting program, in just one three-month period last year, 80 American Express employees donated over $300,000 in consulting services to nonprofit organizations in the New York area.

So, I think we've all come a long way from focusing on what companies give—to what companies do—but equally important is why they do it. What motivates a company to be a responsible citizen and a responsible business—and whether they are transparent about these motivations—I believe is just as important as what they give or what they do. People want to know what drives a company to act the way it does. And, they want to understand the motivations and the thinking behind the initiation of programs, products and services.

At American Express, we are driven by our Blue Box Values—a set of eight values that the 60,000 employees of American Express pledge to live—and work—by each day. This might sound corny to some, but we're quite serious about it. Values like Integrity, Teamwork, Respect for People, Quality, and Good Citizenship provide the foundation for the development of our products and services, and the operations of our business—including products like our Bluebird Card, a product that helps provide much-needed banking services for the unbanked and under-banked, while still providing a profit to American Express.

Customer Commitment
We develop relationships that make a positive difference in our customer's lives.

Quality
We provide outstanding products and unsurpassed service that, together, deliver premium value to our customers.

Integrity
We uphold the highest standards of integrity in all of our actions.

Teamwork
We work together, across boundries, to meet the needs of our customers and to help the company win.

Respect for People
We value our people, encourage their development and reward their performance.

Good Citizenship
We are good citizens in communities in which we live and work.

A Will to Win
We exhibit a strong will to win in the marketplace and in every aspect of our business.

Personal Accountability
We are personally accountable for delivering on our commitments.

Now, despite what some activists seem to think, there's nothing wrong with profits—corporations are after all for-profit organizations—and there's nothing wrong with ensuring that any action that a company takes is being done to advance its own business interests.

While the past five years have been challenging ones for many companies, I sense a growing interest in looking forward rather than backward now. As the economy continues to show improvement, many eyes are now on what ideas and innovations will drive growth and sustainability for the coming years, which gives companies—and their employees—license to think different.

What will the future socially responsible business look like?

It will look like IBM or FedEx or Starbucks or Microsoft or American Express or one of the thousands of small businesses or start-up companies that are good citizens in their communities. These companies will be admired because they focus on business results, but do it in a way that is beneficial to their employees and to the global community as well as their owners and shareholders.

Alice Korngold, a consultant and frequent contributor to Fast Company, calls this approach, "Corporate Global Vision." She describes it as: Envisioning and achieving the greater potential for both the company and the world by affirming the interdependence of corporate success with the health and prosperity of the planet and its people.

So, in the future let's stay focused on our business interests, but let's have a heart too.

Or, as they say in "Friday Night Lights" football:

"Clear Eyes, Full Hearts, Can't Lose."

Timothy J. McClimon
President, America Express Foundation

Extract from a speech given at Rutgers Business School Institute for Ethical Leadership

Ethics in Action: A Conference on Corporate Social Responsibility
April 19, 2013

Preface

By Barbara Brooks Kimmel

It's my honor to have served as editor for *Trust Inc.: Strategies for Building Your Company's Most Valuable Asset.*

My mission in compiling these essays was to find knowledgeable and well-known experts to contribute their unique perspective on six organizational trust topics: Why Trust Matters, Trust in Practice, Trustworthy Leadership, Building Trustworthy Teams, Restoring Trust and A New Paradigm for Organizational Trust—all in one text.

We set this ambitious goal for one reason: to give you the most comprehensive and current information on what many global leaders consider the issue of the decade—trust. It's our hope that we've captured the best theories, advice and solutions. And that you'll share what you learn with your colleagues, teams and organizations.

Each contributor has written in his or her own voice and style, but they all come to the same conclusion—**trust works.** The essays contained in Trust Inc. describe better ways to do business and improve the odds for long term success and sustainability. Regardless of whether the reader is the owner of a small startup or the CEO of a Fortune 500 company, this book will provide lessons in how to infuse trust into any organization and reap the resulting rewards.

I would like to thank the thirty-plus contributors who took time out of their busy schedules to write these outstanding essays and collaborate on this important project. I would also like to thank Ken Blanchard for contributing the Introduction, following the publication of his own book on trust, *Trust Works: Four Keys to Building Lasting Relationships.* We're grateful as well to Tim McClimon,

President of the American Express Foundation, whose recent, heartfelt and highly inspirational speech is reproduced, in part, as our Foreword.

The founding of Trust Across America—Trust Around the World in 2009 represented the beginning of a new professional journey. Our work encompasses the challenges of organizational trust across cultural and generational boundaries, for-profit and not-for-profit organizations, government institutions, academia and the media. It's going to take a substantial collaborative effort to bring trust back to the heart of how we live and work. We believe this book is an important step towards that vision.

I hope you will join us in our global Campaign for Trust.

Barbara Kimmel
Executive Director
Trust Across America—Trust Around the World

Introduction

By Ken Blanchard

These days there's a lot of talk about trust, and even more talk about the lack of it. Without trust, people give up on relationships and leave organizations; cynicism reigns, progress grinds to a halt, and self-interest trumps the common good. But in a trusting environment, people feel free to move faster, risk more, and give their all. They don't feel the need to protect themselves or hold back the way they might in a less trusting environment. Creativity flourishes, productivity rises, barriers are overcome, and relationships deepen.

But trust is a delicate thing. It often takes a long time to build—and yet you can blow it in a minute. One incident of behaving inconsistently with someone else's perception of trustworthy behavior can cause that person to pull away from you. You see, trust is in the eye of the beholder. What seems to be fine behavior to you could actually be eroding the trust of those around you.

Because we see trust through our own filters, we need to learn as much as we can about the subject—particularly about how we can build and sustain trust in our organizations. That's what this book is all about. Some of the finest thought leaders in the field have been gathered to focus on trust topics such as:

How trust inspires commitment in employees

The disease of distrust

Do you practice trustworthy behaviors?

How candor encourages trust

Trust-driven collaboration

Conscious capitalism

Trust and reputational crisis

Take the lead by being the first to trust

Is your business worthy of trust?

Increasingly, smart organizations are taking steps to build and support a high-trust culture as a way to ignite individual and organizational performance. Wise leaders in these companies understand that amazing things can be accomplished within an atmosphere of trust.

The insights you gain from this book will enrich your life and the lives of your colleagues. Read it, absorb it, and practice it—and before you know it, you will be building a climate of trust in your organization.

Ken Blanchard
Coauthor, *The One Minute Manager®* and *Trust Works!*

Section I:

Why Trust Matters

The Business Case for Trust

By Barbara Brooks Kimmel and Charles H. Green

Trustworthiness—once exemplified by a simple firm handshake—is a business value that has suffered erosion. We see this in how the public has grown increasingly cynical about corporate behavior—with good reason. The PR firm Edelman found in a recent "Trust Barometer" survey that trust, transparency, and honest business practices influence corporate reputation *more than* the quality of products and services or financial performance.[1] And yet, scandals and bad behavior continue to pile up. Our view is that a company seriously interested in its reputation must increasingly focus not just on "business performance" as it is traditionally understood, but on being seen as trustworthy too.

We believe there is an important, material business case for trust. This doesn't mean that trust isn't or shouldn't be justified on moral or societal grounds. Of course it should. But trust makes for good business as well. This essay will put forth the business case for trust by exploring the gap between low- and high-trust organizations' performance. We will also offer a framework for assessing corporate trustworthiness, and point the way toward strategies for creating a trust-enhancing business model.

First, let's look at the costs of low trust.

How low trust affects stakeholder outcomes

Low Trust in Society. Business operates in a social context; because of that, low trust in society-at-large costs business. Indirect examples include the TSA airport security program ($5.3 billion[2], not to mention the impact on tens of millions of business travelers), and the criminal justice system ($167 billion in 2004). Both of these examples are funded by taxes on individuals and business.

---

1   Argenti, Lytton-Hitchins and Verity, Booz & Co., *Strategy & Business* Issue 61, Winter 2010
2   Consolidated Appropriations Act, 2012; US PUBLIC LAW 112–74—DEC. 23, 2011

Businesses also shoulder direct tangible losses from crime ($105 billion)[3], where they are often the victims.

A more obvious social cost for business is the cost of regulation. Economist Clyde Wayne Crews[4] releases an annual report entitled "The Ten Thousand Commandments" that tallies federal regulations and their costs. In 2010, the federal government spent $55.4 billion dollars funding federal agencies and enforcing existing regulation. In 2013, *The Washington Post* reported that "the federal government imposed an estimated $216 billion in regulatory costs on the economy (in 2012), nearly double its previous record."

Doing business in a low-trust environment is costly. Whether or not you believe that companies can, or should directly impact social conditions, one thing is clear. In aggregate, business bears a lot of weight for the cost of low-trust in our society.

Low Trust in Business Practices. Social costs on business, however, are just the tip of the iceberg. Far bigger costs are exacted by simple business practices. Consider the need for detailed financial audits. The Big 4 accounting firms' aggregate global revenue is $110 billion[5], of which about one quarter is made up of audits in the U.S.

Consider lawyers: there are over 1.2 million licensed attorneys in the United States, more per capita than in 28 of 29 countries (Greece being the 29th)[6]. The cost of the tort litigation system alone in the United States is over $250 billion[7]—or 2% of GDP[8]. It's estimated that tort reform in health care alone could trim medical costs by 27 percent.

All these are examples of transaction costs: costs we incur to protect or gain (we hope) larger economies of scale, markets, or hierarchies. Transaction costs add no value to the economy *per se*; they just foster favorable market conditions so that other economic factors (e.g. markets, scale economies) can add value. But there comes a

---

3 Criminal Justice in America, George Cole and Christopher Smith, 2007
4 of the Competitive Enterprise Institute, a non-profit public policy organization dedicated, in part, to advancing the cause of limited government
5 http://en.wikipedia.org/wiki/Big_Four_(audit_firms)
6 http://en.wikipedia.org/wiki/Attorneys_in_the_United_States
7 http://www.forbes.com/sites/mattkibbe/2012/01/19/americas-ongoing-tort-litigation-nightmare/
8 Matt Kibbe, "America's Ongoing Litigation Nightmare," Forbes, January 19, 2012

point at which the addition of more non-value-adding transaction costs ceases to be positive and becomes burdensome. It's clear to us today that we are well past this point. A *Harvard Business Review* article from 8 years ago (*Collaboration Rules* by Philip Evans and Bob Wolf, July 2005) suggests that *nearly 50%* of the U.S. non-governmental GDP was, as of 2005, comprised of transaction costs. Imagine the impact of redirecting even a small proportion of these monies to value-adding actions.

Their research goes on to say that, in such an economy, the most productive investments are often not those that increase scale or volume, but those *that reduce transaction costs*. And the most viable strategy for reducing massive transaction costs? Trust.

Low Trust and Employee Disengagement. Disengagement occurs when people put in just enough effort to avoid getting fired but don't contribute their talent, creativity, energy or passion. In economic terms, they under-perform. Gallup's research[9] places 71 percent of U.S. workers as either not engaged or actively disengaged. The price tag of disengagement is $350 billion a year[10]. That roughly approximates the annual combined revenue of Apple, General Motors and General Electric.

According to *The Economist*, 84 percent of senior leaders say disengaged employees are considered one of the biggest threats facing their business. However, only 12 percent of them reported doing anything about this problem.[11]

What does disengagement have to do with trust? Everything. In a Deloitte LLP ethics and workplace survey[12], the top three reasons given for employees planning to seek a new job were:

- A loss of *trust* in their employer based on decisions made during the Great Recession (48 percent);
- A lack of *transparency* in leadership communication (46 percent); and
- Being treated *unfairly* or *unethically* by employers over the last 18 to 24 months (40 percent).

9   Gallup.com 2011/10/28 "Majority of American Workers Not Engaged in their Jobs"
10   Gallup Business Journal, 2002/4/15 "The High Cost of Disengaged Employees"
11   The Economist Intelligence Unit Limited 2010
12   Deloitte LLP, 2010 Ethics and Workplace Survey

A lack of trust in the employer is at the heart of each of these reasons. To the extent that plans to find a new job are a proxy for disengagement, the case is clear. Lack of trust drives away employees.

In discussing the survey, Deloitte LLP Board Chairman Sharon Allen notes:

> *Regardless of the economic environment, business leaders should be mindful of the significant impact that trust in the workplace and transparent communication can have on talent management and retention strategies. By establishing a values-based culture, organizations can cultivate the trust necessary to reduce turnover and mitigate unethical behavior.*

The survey also provides some interesting data on the business case for organizational trust. When asked to rate the top two items most positively affected when an employee trusts his or her employer, employed U.S. adults made the following top rankings:

- Morale (55%);
- Team building and collaboration (39%);
- Productivity and profitability (36%);
- Ethical decision making (35%); and
- Willingness to stay with the company (32%).

As Mary Gentile eloquently states later in this book, "Very often the most visible, most costly challenges to the public trust in business are fairly predictable: deceptive marketing practices; falsified earnings reporting; failure in safety compliance; lack of consistency in employee relations; and so on."

In other words, the ability to manage the costs of low trust –whether arising from society, from business practices, or from management practices—is to a great extent *within the control* of the corporation. And yet, it is largely not being done—with sadly predictable results.

How high trust improves stakeholder outcomes

That's the bad news about how low trust impacts business performance. Here's the compelling evidence for the positive results from trust.

Shareholders: In *Fortune Magazine's* "100 Best Companies to Work For," trust comprises 60 percent of the criteria and is the "primary defining characteristic," according to a study by Russell Investment Group. The companies in the list earned over *four times* the returns of the broader market over the prior seven years.

Think about that. Trust is identified as highly correlated with fourfold returns.

In a Towers Watson study on employee engagement, those organizations that have high employee engagement (which is driven by high trust), have higher revenue growth, lower costs of goods sold, and lowers sales, general and administrative expenses[13].

In a forthcoming book titled *Trusted to Lead*, author, trust expert and essay contributor to this book, Robert Porter Lynch, points to three industries—airlines, automobiles, and steel—where the high-trust companies are the clear competitive winners.

Lynch also conducted a survey of 2,650 senior managers, asking them to quantify the effect of high or low trust on 17 dimensions of performance. These include innovation, productivity, procurement, planning and coordination. The average results across all dimensions ranged over *50 percent* in each direction.

Customers: The positively correlated relationship between trust and buying behavior, while complex, is well understood and the subject of literally thousands of research cases. So rather than citing statistics, we suggest the (U.S. -based) reader merely observe their own reactions to these words:

> Johnson & Johnson/Tylenol
> Walter Cronkite
> IBM

What comes to mind? Most people will easily note the strong emotional connection between the brand's trust connotation and the company's market performance.

---

13   2012 Global Workforce Study, Engagement at Risk: Driving Strong Performance in a Volatile Global Environment

Employees: A sincere interest in the well-being of another, whether customer or employee, is one of the defining characteristics of a trust-based relationship.

As leadership guru Warren Bennis says, "Trust is the lubrication that makes it possible for organizations to work."[14] In *Closing the Engagement Gap*[15], author Julie Gebauer identifies the number-one item driving employee engagement worldwide as "Senior management's sincere interest in employee well-being."

Suppliers, distributors and other partners: And finally, a Warwick Business School[16] study shows that partnering relationships based on trust experience a dividend of **up to 40 percent** of the contract.

That's it for a quick review of the cost of low trust, and the benefits of high trust. It's a strong business case. Now let's turn to action. As Frank Sonnenberg states in his book *Managing with a Conscience*, "If businesses are to thrive in the global marketplace, trust must be more than something that is talked about; it must be at the core of everything that is done."

A framework for assessing trustworthiness

We often hear, "Trustworthy business is important to our company, but we don't know where to start." So where DO companies start? One approach is to start by defining the level of corporate trustworthiness in a way that is measurable.

It's eminently clear to us, and the hundreds of business colleagues we've engaged with over the past two decades, that a lack of consensus around how to define and measure trustworthiness represents a still-unmet business need. That's why Trust Across America–Trust Around the World (TAA-TAW) created a framework to give stakeholders apple-to-apple metrics to define and compare organizational trustworthiness.

Says Executive Director, Barbara Kimmel, "After years of dialogue to get clear on definitions, TAA-TAW chose five quantitative markers, or indicators, of

---

14 http://www.brainyquote.com/quotes/quotes/w/warrengbe384360.html

15 Gebauer, Julie; Lowman, Don (2008-12-24). Closing the Engagement Gap: How Great Companies Unlock Employee Potential for Superior Results (p. 13). Penguin Group. Kindle Edition.

16 Cullen, Sara and Willcocks, Leslie P. (2004)IT outsourcing: carving the right strategy. General management review, 2004 (Jan-Mar). pp. 1-6.

trustworthy business. They are: **F**inancial stability and strength, **A**ccounting conservativeness, **C**orporate governance, **T**ransparency, and **S**ustainability, to which we assigned the acronym FACTS®. This particular framework for defining corporate trustworthiness, we believe, generates the broadest consensus about which factors to include. And, it has the virtue of being quantifiable."

In 2008, TAA-TAW started identifying data sources to populate this framework by aggregating dozens of data points that allow for financial and non-financial definitions of trustworthiness, and are available in data series form. As a result, today TAA-TAW can provide trust rankings and reports for over 2000 U.S. publicly traded companies, as well as making industry and sector comparisons and performing benchmarking studies.

Here's what the FACTS Framework looks like:

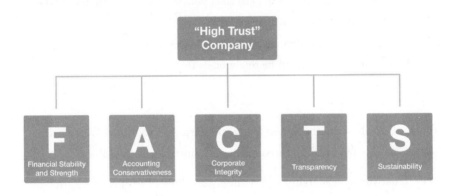

TAA-TAW completed the Framework in 2010 and began to review the performance of its tracked companies. Surprisingly (or perhaps not, depending on your viewpoint) it appears so far that perfection—at least from a "trustworthiness" standpoint—does not (yet) exist. In fact, over the past three years, no company has yet scored over 90 percent.

So far in this essay, we have talked about the business value of trust, and about an approach to defining and measuring the presence or absence of trustworthiness. While it's beyond the scope of this essay to lay out a definitive roadmap for implementation of trust initiatives, we'd like to end by broadly addressing this critical issue.

Trustworthiness in Action

Generally speaking, initiatives for improving the levels of trust in organizations can be classified into the following categories (many of which you'll see throughout this book):

Principles: Adoption of a values-level set of principles by which trust can be applied and delivered in specific situations. One example is the Federal Express *Purple Promise.*

Practices: Training for individuals in practicing and leading with trustworthiness in their behaviors and interactions. Examples are listening practices, feedback, and idea sessions.

Policies and Procedures: Ways of doing things that translate the principles above into organized group behavior. Examples of this are the structure of meetings, transparency of personnel policies, and how customer and supplier relationships are managed.

Protocols: Consciously defined activities, gestures and vocabulary for top leadership that help them be role models for trustworthy behavior.

Touching on all of the above, and to get you started on your own program, here is our own Top Ten list for how companies can increase trustworthiness:

#1 **Trustworthy leadership**—Very simply, a culture of trust cannot exist with an untrustworthy leader. Trustworthy behavior must start at the top and flow down through every manager in an organization.

#2 **Transformation**—Productivity and execution begin when the CEO creates a set of values and goals that are shared, accepted and adopted by all stakeholders. CEOs should regularly address all stakeholders about the steps being taken to build trustworthy behavior within the organization. Trust should not be confused with compliance. Being "legal" is not synonymous with being trustworthy.

#3 **Tools**—There are many trust tools CEOs can use to build trust with their internal and external stakeholders. These run the gamut from metrics and assessments to online surveys. The results may be surprisingly good, or just the opposite. And if they are the latter, and really bad, it's time to get busy. And maybe time to add a Chief Trust Officer to the C-Suite.

#4   Treatment- The Golden Rule says to "treat others the way you want to be treated." This certainly holds true for trust. The CEO that extends trust to his or her stakeholders is more likely to have it returned. Trust fundamentally works by a series of reciprocating actions between the trustor and the trusted.

#5   Teamwork—Teamwork leads to better decisions and better outcomes. Teams create trust, and trust creates teams. Breaking down silos, and in particular exhibiting trustworthy behavior in the C-Suite, should be on every CEO's priority list.

#6   Talk—Your stakeholders need to know what steps you are taking to build a trustworthy organization. Quarterly numbers are no longer the be all and end all. In fact, evidence is mounting that a trustworthy culture and "good numbers" go hand in hand. As mentioned earlier, long-term trustworthy behavior is *more* profitable—every quarter—than short-term changes that don't last.

#7   Truth—Truth-telling is at the core of trust. Any CEO who wants to build a trustworthy organization must have an extremely comfortable relationship with the truth. No company is perfect and it's not necessary to air all the dirty laundry—just don't lie about it or intentionally mislead. In times of crisis, a habit of truth telling yields particularly good returns. The absence of such habits can be disastrous.

#8   Time—Building a culture of trustworthy business does not happen overnight. It takes time, maybe even years—but not decades. The CEO who invests the time to educate himself or herself about how to build trust with teams and stakeholders—then develops a plan, communicates and implements it—will be rewarded with greater stakeholder trust. When a slip up occurs, those who "banked" trust will recover faster.

#9   Transparency—Merriam Webster defines "transparent" as visibility or accessibility of information, especially with business practices. Any CEO who thinks he or she can still hide behind a veil of secrecy need only spend a few minutes on social media reading what their stakeholders are saying. In today's world, transparency is no longer the risk—opacity has become the risk. Transparency must exist inside and outside the company. Communications and social media have roles to play here, but the fundamental is that transparency positively helps build trust.

#10 Thoughtful—Not all stakeholders need to know the company's trade secrets, or what the CEO had for dinner. But if your company is serious about increasing trustworthiness, consider engaging all your stakeholders in rich, thoughtful conversations. Don't approach them as constituencies to be maneuvered, managed or massaged. Instead, view them as vital contributors to a better organization by letting them into the conversation. To be a thoughtful company with a thoughtful strategy, trust the stakeholders to be thoughtful.

Being trustworthy is about doing business *differently*. That's not a platitude; it's a concept championed by Michael Porter (arguably the world's expert on competitive strategy, and no stranger to profit drivers) in his seminal 2011 *Harvard Business Review* essay, "Creating Shared Value: How to reinvent capitalism."[17] Perhaps the biggest difference in making business trustworthy is to practice putting trust, truth, and stakeholders first—and profit second. We know that this is a unconventional mindset. But one of the powerful by-products of behaving this way is that—paradoxically—profits end up *higher*, not lower, than if profit maximization had been the goal. We call that managing for trust, not profits. And for anyone still doubting its efficacy, we refer you back to Part 1. There is a business case for trust. Trust works.

---

17 Porter, Michael E. and Kramer, Mark, (2011, January), Creating Shared Value, Harvard Business Review

Barbara Brooks Kimmel

Barbara Brooks Kimmel is Cofounder and Executive Director of Trust Across America— Trust Around the World, the global leader in information, standards and data, and the "Who's Who" of organizational trust. As social innovators, the program's mission is to help enhance trustworthy behavior in organizations. Barbara creates, often through strategic partnerships, tools to foster organizational trust, programs to showcase top thought leaders, and research on trustworthy organizations. She also facilitates the growing Alliance of Trustworthy Business Experts, a group of global thought leaders who are collaborating to advance the cause. Barbara is also the President of Next Decade, Inc an award- winning communications and publishing firm. In 2012 Barbara was named one of "25 Women who are Changing the World" *by Good Business International. She is a graduate of Lafayette College and has an MBA from Bernard M. Baruch Graduate School of Business at the City University of New York.*

Charles H. Green

Charles H. Green is an author, speaker and world expert on trust-based relationships and sales in complex businesses. Founder and CEO of Trusted Advisor Associates, he is co-author of the classic The Trusted Advisor *and its practical follow-up,* The Trusted Advisor Fieldbook, *and author of* Trust-based Selling.

Charles works with complex organizations to improve trust in sales, internal trust between organizations, and trusted advisor relationships with external clients and customers. Charles spent 20 years in management consulting. He majored in philosophy (Columbia), and has an MBA (Harvard). A widely sought-after speaker, he has published articles in Harvard Business Review, Directorship Magazine, Management Consulting News, CPA Journal, American Lawyer, Businessweek, Forbes.com, Investments and Wealth Monitor, and Commercial Lending Review, and is a contributing editor at RainToday.com.

What Does a Trustworthy Company Look Like?

By Peter Firestein

There isn't a more paradoxical concept in business today than trust. Everybody believes in it, and everybody decries its scarcity. Are we simply deceiving ourselves that trust—in real business in the real world—actually matters?

We are, at the very least, troubled by the need to reconcile contradictory pressures we face in business. Even if you're a CEO who believes in building trust as an authentic business practice, you're not going to be there to do it for very long unless your stock price is rising. In the event that it doesn't, a stronger competitor will likely take control of the company and send you off—if your own board hasn't done it first. So, while you're there, you're going to do whatever is necessary to please the capital markets—particularly equity investors—whose time horizons for making judgments on companies are notoriously short.

So, how much capital are you going to divert to initiatives that build trust? What's the business argument for doing it? After all, BP and the other companies vilified in the Deepwater Horizon disaster (most notably Transocean and Halliburton) are, for the most part, doing well enough to reward their investors today. Johnson & Johnson, which originated the notion of corporate trustworthiness 70 years ago, has in recent years suffered allegations of deceptive practices. Yet, its happy investors continue to see significant rises in share price. It seems there are not enough people mad at J&J—for trying to keep a carcinogenic ingredient in baby shampoo, for surreptitiously supporting an organization that promotes one of its anti-depressants, for hesitating too long to recall a faulty hip implant—to put much of a dent in sales. It's hard to make a case against the argument—which appears rampant in the pharmaceutical industry—that fines and legal settlements are a rational (and tax-deductible) cost of doing business. Could one not say the same for banking?

J&J, however, makes the best case against such cynicism. Long ago, in 1943, the company introduced its famed Credo that spelled out its responsibilities to doctors, nurses, patients, and employees. Today, J&J persistently ranks among the top five most trustworthy US companies. In 2012, most likely because of the series of adverse events just mentioned, it fell to as low as 7th in a closely watched poll. In 2013, the company is back among the top five. The momentum of trust J&J built over the decades gave the company the reputational stability it needed to weather a rough period with very little wear and tear. AIG, on the other hand, which has not only paid all of its $182 billion TARP money back to the Government, but has given taxpayers a $22.7 billion profit, still ranks last out of 60 companies measured. Most people still identify it as one of the companies that nearly brought down the system, not as the company that performed exceptionally well in keeping its promises. It would seem, then, that the persistent development of a reputation for trustworthy conduct serves a company's long-term interests. And, when lost, it takes more or less as long to recover.

How do you know a trustworthy company when you see one?

By far the best assessment of whether a company is worthy of trust lies in an answer to the question: "Who trusts it?"

- A trusted company's shares trade at a premium to its competitors' based on investors' expectations of strong performance in the future. This expectation, itself, is a matter of belief in customers' trust in its products, lenders' trust in its judgment, and regulators' trust in its practices.
- When unwanted events occur, a trusted company receives the benefit of the doubt until the facts can be established. It is not assumed to be in the wrong.
- A trusted company attracts the best available employees, helping to ensure that it will continue to hold the trust of stakeholders into the next generation.
- A trusted company's practices and strategies are adopted by other companies wishing to emulate its success. Those strategies enter the curricula of business schools to be studied and adapted.
- Concentration on the continued worthiness of a trusted company is

spread evenly across all levels of the company's hierarchy. Maintaining and strengthening trust in the company is a career-long preoccupation of virtually everyone who works there.

What a Trustworthy Company Knows:

Any company intent on building trust among investors, customers, and other stakeholders can make considerable progress by understanding and implementing a few fundamental concepts:

1. To earn trust, you must trust. A company that regards the larger world with suspicion—feels victimized by journalists or misunderstood by investors, analysts and NGOs—is unlikely to offer the kind of transparency that leads to trust. The best way to engender trust in others is to offer your own. Perhaps the most effective use of this point of view lies in engaging one's opponents in dialogue.

2. You must trust yourself. An internal company culture of trust is essential not only to build trust from outsiders, but simply to function well as an organization. You must trust your colleagues sufficiently to share information. You must trust that your communications will be received and used as they are intended. The absence of such trust, alone, can qualify a company as dysfunctional.

3. You cannot edit trust. An organization is trusted as much as its least trusted area. The company with less-than-effective customer service is not generally regarded as likely to offer the best products. Investors and analysts are unlikely to regard a CEO's utterances as credible if the company's standards of financial disclosure are weak or lacking in transparency.

4. You cannot disguise untrustworthy behavior in a collaborative world. The interconnectedness of the world means failures of trust have more profound and far-reaching effects than ever before. Virtually every complex device—from a handheld phone to an airliner—is assembled from parts converging from an extended supply chain that can contain dozens of distinct links. The importance of cooperation is intensified by the need to minimize inventory cost through just-in-time delivery techniques. These are essential if a manufacturer like Apple is to remain competitive. Long before its famous problems with lithium-ion batteries, the Boeing 787 Dreamliner faced years of delays because parts from distant locations failed to match up.

5. Holding on to trust is worth breaking the paradigm: Once trust slips, there is no lasso to bring it back. Most breakdowns in trust result from a loss of hope when experience exposes the true character of a manufacturer, employer or government.

A small democratization in China:

The Chinese Government came face-to-face with a collapse in trust when riots erupted at one of the giant Foxconn plants that manufacture products for Apple and many other consumer electronics companies. The riots followed a series of worker suicides and accompanied an emerging story—within China and elsewhere—of abusive working conditions in Foxconn's gigantic installations. The Government's desperate need to restore some basic level of trust among the workers, whose growing taste for insurrection put a fright into the country's leadership, brought about changes that are probably unprecedented in China's ancient history. It responded to the crisis by allowing truly free elections of union representatives. Elections would not have been the Government's first choice, but the need for stability brought about a change that had never been part of its DNA.

An intriguing aspect of the Foxconn story is the power of the narrative of workers' suicides. Twenty-three suicides over three years sounds frightening until you realize that they occurred among a worker population that, during this time, reached approximately 930,000. In fact, this rate of suicide is lower than the rest of China and, according to the *Financial Times,* of every one of the 50 US states. But the durability of the narrative of the Foxconn suicides served to objectify the profound resentment over conditions in the company's factories. Foxconn installed anti-jumping nets around its buildings, but they had little effect. For many, the suicides described the reality at Foxconn, rendering irrelevant the ratio of their actual number to the larger worker population.

Corporate execs cast themselves against type in the great Wall St. pantomime:

Credibility is the great stealth factor in corporate managers' communication with Wall Street. CEOs and investor relations directors do not typically question their own credibility. But investors and equity analysts, who decide what their companies are worth through the price they're willing to pay for shares, think about management credibility all the time. They believe their livelihoods depend on the degree to which they can believe what companies tell them.

For this reason, Wall St. can punish a company's stock price 3-5% for missing analysts' earnings estimates by 1%. The reason for this is the uncertainty caused by the miss. Some large institutional investors do not value stocks on their earnings, but on the earnings' relation to analysts' estimates. It is, of course, impossible to forecast a company's earnings within so fine a margin. But if analysts were to admit that, they would bring the entire analyst profession into question. So, if the company meets or exceeds expectations, analysts reward the company not because of its strong performance so much as its affirmation of their own wisdom. There is no more powerful narrative on Wall St. than the defense of intellectual turf.

Company managements have figured this out, and they are becoming humble. Managers whose primal instinct is to talk their companies up—to try to convince the "Street" why they're worth more than the current stock price would indicate— have taken to talking their stocks down instead. But it's not about the company's financial performance. It's about arousing trust by matching or beating expectations in a Wall St. environment where the analysts and investors make the rules.

Seven strategies for building trust and reputation:

(Adapted from my book, *CRISIS OF CHARACTER—Building Corporate Reputation in the Age of Skepticism.*

1. **Establish your values.** A country can't run without a constitution, nor can a corporation without a company-wide agreement on principles. There are no off-the-shelf value systems that are worth anything. They must be particular to the company's character. So, they must be built by consensus from the ground up—then disseminated and habitually reinforced.

2. **See yourself through stakeholders' eyes.** An understanding of how customers, partners, investors and others see you is essential in building trust. Dedicated listening through surveys, perception studies, and direct engagement delivers information that is unavailable by any other means.

3. **Define your company's landscape.** Mapping techniques that group stakeholders according to shared interests maximize the efficiency of trust-based initiatives. If, for example, certain NGOs, local communities, and investors are all interested in your environmental impact, emphasizing that information in communications should increase trust across a number of different constituencies.

4. **Build your reputation from the inside out.** Structure the entire company for trust. Analyze internal processes for their contribution to the perception of trustworthiness. For example, establish a vertical internal communications channel that goes from top to bottom and is sufficiently democratic for any voice to be heard.

5. **Tell your corporate story in terms of your obligations.** Communications about the company—even in press releases—should imply a convergence of business strategies and values. Recognize that communication, by itself, can't change anything. But it can be framed to depict the company's intent—and therefore its character—as well as its long-term vision.

6. **Prepare for crisis.** Any company of sufficient size will face a crisis some day. This is a given. It could involve considerable civic hardship for which the company is responsible. It could involve loss of life. The company's immediate response can either increase the level of trust it receives, or collapse it. The best approach any company can take to a crisis is to shape the terms of the story before the media gets the chance. This may constitute its only opportunity to obtain fairness. To carry this out, it must have been creative enough in advance to prepare a systematic, but flexible, response plan that addresses a crisis whose nature it has no way of anticipating.

7. **Strong governance is the glue that holds the company together.** Responsibility for establishing trust in the organization resides ultimately with the board. Just as the board provides a check on the trustworthiness of management, so the board should have internal checks on its own trustworthiness. A board that bears the look of trust is one that is non-homogenous. It is diverse in gender, in areas of expertise, and, often, in ethnicity. In other words, the board that makes final decisions about the company should look as much as possible like the world in which the company is attempting to operate.

Conclusion:

It is impossible to build trust through strategy and technique alone. Achieving success requires an authentic belief that the company cannot ultimately succeed at the expense of its stakeholders—and that it's a very poor business decision to try.

Peter Firestein

Peter Firestein is President of Global Strategic Communications, Inc., a New York advisory firm that helps corporate managements build institutional reputations and offers in-depth intelligence on investor thinking. He is author of the book, "CRISIS OF CHARACTER—Building Corporate Reputation in the Age of the Skepticism" and originator of the Open Perception Study™. Peter has been a guest contributor to the New York Times online, the Conference Board Review, the Journal of the American Management Association, Corporate Secretary Magazine, and many other publications. He has written a regular column on corporate reputation in the Management section of Bloomberg/Businessweek.com. He is an international Keynote speaker and has served as a guest commentator on Bloomberg Television and Radio, the BBC World Service, NPR, Fox Business, and many other media venues. He is a graduate of Stanford University.

Brand Trust is the Foundation to Brand Loyalty

By Jim Gregory

Trust is a vital component of every successful business transaction, which grows when expectations are consistently met or exceeded. Branding is the conscious management of the elements that build trust. Trust elements go far beyond a simple interaction between customers and purchases. Trust is part of every public and corporate interaction, including: the hiring process, corporate investments, supplying the company with goods or services, local operations and media coverage. Without trust, the company will cease to function.

Marketing professionals generally think of brand building as nothing more than a combination of product/service packaging, public relations and advertising. In reality, the effort needed to build a trusted brand touches every aspect of a business. You can't just claim to be trustworthy; you must act and behave accordingly. Building brand loyalty through trustworthy behavior motivates audiences to continually select your brand over competitors, improving financial performance. Brand loyalty can also bolster your company's performance through economic shifts, public relations gaffes and even significant management changes.

Build brand trust by aligning your business processes, company culture and communications with your corporate brand strategy. When these aspects radiate a clear and consistent message of what kind of company you are and what audiences can expect of you, trust builds, customers return repeatedly and corporate performance improves.

Leverage your touch points

Audience interactions with your company and brand come through "touch points." With direct touch points, such as a consumer using your product, talking with customer service or reading an advertisement, you control the message. With indirect touch points such as a prospect hearing someone else's review of your services or reading an editorial written about you, you have no control over the message about your brand.

Both direct and indirect touch points are opportunities to gain "trust points", which are a measure of favorability. If consumer experience is positive and consistent with expectations, a trust point is earned. If the interaction is negative or misaligned with expectations, cognitive dissonance sets in and an opportunity to build brand loyalty is lost.

For every audience member, internal or external, your brand is experienced through three main channels: How you run operations and deliver your offerings, the personality of your organization and your proactive outreach.

Your brand supports the touch points, which span across all, through your business process, culture and communications. Align these channels to best leverage your touch points.

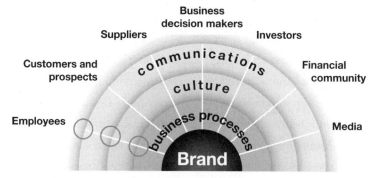

Figure 1: Where you earn trust points

The more thorough your communications strategy is, the more consistent and aligned your messages in the market will be. A one-size-fits most message isn't going to be as effective as a message that can adapt to different constituents. You need to manage your brand experiences to be relevant to the specific audience while staying true to who you are. The goal is to have everyone—regardless of audience category—to have the same idea of the "big picture" of what your brand stands for. If you are actively putting your message out into the market, it will become the dominant voice about your brand and well-aligned brand communications are easier and more cost-effective to amplify.

Build a trust point bank account

Human nature has us remembering negative experiences more clearly than positive ones. A consumer can have several positive experiences with a brand and not mention a word to anyone, but if they perceive that a brand has wronged them, they will repeat that story over and over. Negative experiences build brand barriers, which takes great effort to overcome. A well-managed brand can help you avoid crises and recover quickly should a crisis arise. Every brand interaction helps grow a cache of goodwill, creating brand loyalty. We like to think of this as a "trust point bank account." Every positive experience counts as a deposit. Every negative experience is a withdrawal.

Build up your trust point balance by maintaining consistent contact with your customer. Whether you transact with your customers once a year or on a daily basis, paying attention to your relationship with them is a vital part of brand management. Communication builds top-of-mind familiarity with consumers for their own purchase decisions and also facilitates word-of-mouth referrals.

Once you have a cushion in your bank account, you will begin to see the return on your brand investment. Brand loyalty will grow and a form of "brand insurance" will be developed. With a positive "bank account" balance, even if a negative experience does occur, your reputation will not be irreparably marred and your constituents will give you the benefit of the doubt to resolve any issues that occurred.

How to measure brand trust

We see the measure of brand trust demonstrated every day in our Corporate Branding Index®. We have tracked 1000 companies continuously over time among a business decision-making audience of VPs of major corporations. We conduct 10,000 telephone interviews per year to generate Familiarity and Favorability scores, and we model that information against corporate financial performance. We believe the Favorability scores represent brand trust and is the way to track your brand trust deposits and withdrawals. While any company can create its own benchmark tracking system, our approach has been in place for over twenty years and gives us the historical trend data to fully understand how brand investment leads to corporate performance. Our long-established models clearly tie brand trust into brand value.

Case studies of how brand trust works

We've taken three examples from our database that demonstrate the point of how Favorability equates to brand trust.

Apple is well known as an innovative company with a loyal customer base. The company is marketing-savvy and continuously striving to bring new innovative products to market. Look how Apple has grown both Familiarity and Favorability over time.

Familiarity and Favorability 2000—2012: Apple

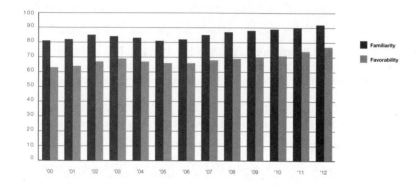

Continuous brand engagement and consumer interaction can really pay off over time. Apple has consistently grown their brand's favorability for six years straight.

BP went through a classic image crisis with the Gulf oil spill in 2010. You can see how Favorability declined precipitously from the high in 2009 to a low in 2011. The crisis isn't over yet but BP has shown improvement in Favorability in 2012.

Familiarity and Favorability 2000—2012: BP

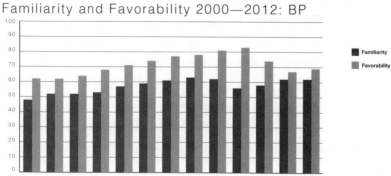

Trust can be lost in very little time if an event strikes a strong enough chord among consumers and investors. BP lost the equivalent of six year's worth of brand building over the course of just two years.

AIG was at ground zero in the financial crisis of 2008-2009. You can see the dramatic decline of Favorability, which has since rebounded to levels of where the company was in 2000.

Familiarity and Favorability 2000—2012: AIG

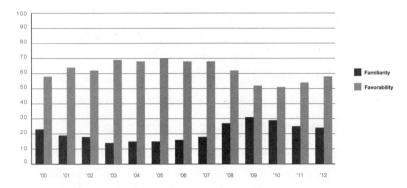

Rebuilding trust after a crisis takes considerably more effort than initial favorability inducing efforts. AIG has spent three hard years to curb their decline, and work towards replenishing their trust points bank account with customers.

Start building trust from the very beginning

So, how can you build up your trust point bank account? Trust points are founded on the first impression and can be won or lost with every following engagement. When building your brand strategy, outline all of the opportunities for audiences to interact with your brand. Trace these interactions through the sales process from awareness, to understanding, to interest, to purchase, to use and ultimately to preference/loyalty. Match your goals and objectives against this brand touch points map, identifying the areas of greatest influence and drawing upon this knowledge to enhance your communications strategy.

Ask yourself a few key questions. Where is a potential audience's first interaction most likely to be? What kind of information does the audience seek at that time and how can they most readily digest it? What do they need to know to make a purchase? Once they have become a first-time customer, what do they need to evolve into a repeat customer?

This plan should define your direct communications with customers and also influence decisions in all operational areas. Decisions such as how to staff your organization, which suppliers to use and how products/services will be delivered must reinforce your brand. Use employee engagement and brand training to ensure that your brand message is understood internally and being communicated appropriately externally. Alignment and predictability from department to department is critical for building reputational trust.

Establish a benchmark measurement of your brand to better understand the return on your branding investment. You will discover where trust points are being earned today and will be able to identify areas of opportunity to gain more trust points in the future. Set up a system to track and evaluate the efforts over time to determine what's effective, what needs refinement and what can be cut.

Speak in common business language

Build trust in your brand to create a premium value for the company through both revenue improvement as well as stock performance. It is commonly accepted that a valuable brand makes a company more valuable. But it is rare for a company to take the time to quantify exactly what the optimal amount of resources and investment should be for the brand. Allocations are typically set based on last year's budget, not on projected ROI. CoreBrand's research has shown that approximately 70% of budgets are chronically underfunded—and 10% are actually overfunded and wasting resources.

Currently, Generally Accepted Accounting Principles (GAAP) don't account for brand value on the balance sheet. Brand is typically not measured, valued or budgeted for in the same way as other corporate investments. For many corporate decision makers, if you can't measure it, there is no argument for investing in it. And without the common language of return-on-investment, marketing is relegated to being viewed as an expense rather than an investment.

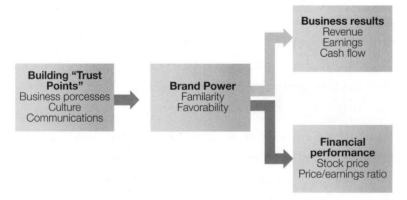

Figure 2: CoreBrand's research has proven the impact of brand on financial performance.

Instead of insisting the company see things from marketing's point of view, speak and behave more on par with other areas of operations. Using terms and metrics that are commonly accepted will earn brand trust points internally among executives. It is crucial that senior management use brand valuation to set budgets and evaluate the success of marketing efforts. Marketing budgets should be determined in the same manner as other budgets within a company—based on projected return, not gut feeling.

Methodical benchmarking and tracking hold brand building successes and failures are accountable, allowing for refinement of outreach strategies. When a brand is properly funded and the brand managers know with certainty how to influence their audiences effectively, trust can more easily be cultivated.

Educate your brand stewards

Your employees should be well informed as to what they're selling, what they're endorsing, what their company stands for and what their role is in the company's success. An employee's body language and demeanor matter immensely when interacting with a prospect. But you have to earn trust points with your employees first, before they can go into the market and earn trust points from your audiences.

There are many obvious things that employees care about such as their compensation, hours and working conditions. But they also care deeply about a sense of purpose, belonging and understanding. Engage with your employees and reward them in brand-aligned ways so they fully understand your brand, and can self-define brand-appropriate.

Upfront investment in training and engagement lowers employee turnover rates, creates greater self-regulation/management and encourages a generally happier workforce. When it comes to building trust points with customers, quality trumps quantity. Your employees aren't just your most valuable assets, they are your most valuable brand stewards.

Nurture trust through branding

No one will argue that trust can only be earned, not demanded. For a business, your brand is your most powerful tool in earning that trust. Each positive interaction with your brand through your business processes, culture or communications creates an opportunity to build favorability, gain a trust point and build your goodwill bank account. A solid brand strategy supported by all aspects of your business—operationally and culturally—is the key to methodically building and sustaining trust.

Jim Gregory
Founder and CEO of CoreBrand, LLC.

With over 35 years of experience in advertising and branding, Jim is a leading expert on corporate brand valuation and management. Most notable of the tools that Jim has created is the Corporate Branding Index® (CBI), a quantitative research vehicle that has continuously tracked the reputation and financial performance of 1000 companies across 54 industries since 1990. CoreBrand clients use the CBI to compare their brands with industry peers and understand how communications can impact corporate perception and performance, including stock price and revenue growth. Jim is a published author and frequent speaker on the topic of the financial benefits of communications and brand management. He is also a founding member of the Marketing Accountability Standards Advisory Council (MASAC) and is a member of the Marketing Accountability Standards Board (MASB).

Choosing Candor: The Language of Trust

By L.J. Rittenhouse

After the horrific 9/11 attacks in New York and Washington, D.C. Berkshire Hathaway CEO Warren Buffett sent a letter to his managers. He reaffirmed important business fundamentals to restore their confidence in the future. Admitting that terrorism risk had not been factored into Berkshire's insurance premium pricing, he expected Berkshire would face significant losses. At the same time, he assumed their Fort Knox balance sheet would cover these.

Buffett described how trust in the nation's security systems and post-Enron business institutions had been damaged. He exhorted his managers to follow this rule: "Avoid business involving moral risk." Why? Buffett explained, "No matter what the rate, you can't write good contracts with bad people. While most policyholders and clients are honorable and ethical, doing business with the few exceptions is usually expensive."

How can we know if we are avoiding moral risk? Buffett's communications over a 40-year career offer clues: When he examines the writings of a potential partner or executive, he asks: 'Are the words he or she uses accurate and candid or are they meaningless, or even, misleading? Can I trust the word of this individual? Can I take his promises to the bank? The story below also offers guidance:

Transforming Talk

Investors are gathered in a hotel meeting room to listen to presentations from two prominent utility company CEOs, as well as a widely followed industry analyst and a respected portfolio manager.

The two CEOs speak first. Each shows Power Point slides to explain their strategies and why investors should expect "a bright future" from investing in their companies. As they speak, people in the audience read their Blackberries and unfold *Wall Street Journals* to catch up on news. Whatever these executives are saying, the audience isn't buying it.

Then the sell-side financial analyst takes the podium. He makes a startling introduction, "At the end of this presentation, I *may not* have many friends left in the audience." Suddenly, Blackberries are dropped and newspapers stop rustling. The atmosphere is changed. People sit straighter. They focus on the speaker.

The analyst turns to address the two CEOs seated on the dais. He describes the disappointing losses their companies have sustained from troubled, non-core businesses. These results, he believes, raise questions about their ability to manage risks in non-utility enterprises. He similarly challenges their efforts to successfully navigate industry deregulation.

When he sits down, a buzz grows in the audience as if bees have swarmed into the room. Imagine the conversations and questions: What prompted this analyst's chutzpah? His frustration seems real. Were the CEOs insulted or inspired by his candor? It is hard to say.

Then the portfolio manager comes to the podium. He manages billions of dollars of investments held in individual retirement funds. Clearing his throat, he begins: "When I'm finished, I *know* I won't have any friends left in the audience." Now people are galvanized. What is as *he* going to say? Describing a recent meeting with investors in his utility funds, he relates how it turned ugly.

In a market swooning for dot.com speculative investments, his funds were underwater. Investors voice their dissatisfaction and anger. One retiree, with hands "the size of meat loaves" demands to know, "Why should I invest in utilities when I could become rich investing in technology companies?" Such a vivid description makes it possible to imagine this straight-talking retiree aggressively waving his beefy hands in the air.

Then the speaker pivots. Stepping into the shoes of this retiree, he turns to the CEOs and asks, "Why do you deserve this investor's capital, his savings from a lifetime of hard work?" The executives, startled by this question, offer canned responses.

Over dinner that night, people from the audience dissect all four of the morning presentations. Everyone agrees it was hard to remember what the CEOs said. Anchored in their comfort zones, they had not strayed far. Their remarks were predictable—and forgettable. They failed to connect with the audience.

The third speaker, the sell-side analyst, could not be dismissed so easily. He had connected with the audience, but his remarks were remembered more for their tone and less for their content. He had made an impact, but not a meaningful difference.

The fourth speaker, however, not only had connected with the audience, he also made them care about this connection. His message stuck. Just about everyone at the table could recite what he had said. He inspired them to debate the important questions that were raised.

How long did this portfolio manager's message stick? Several weeks later, an investor who had been at that dinner attended another conference where one of the CEOs from that earlier presentation spoke. He was startled to hear this same CEO try to answer questions that had been raised on behalf of the frustrated retiree: the man with meat loaf-sized hands. The CEO even referred to the prior conference. In other words, that portfolio manager had conveyed his message so effectively that this executive was still engaged in the conversation. He trusted the truth in the portfolio manager's story and felt compelled to respond. The portfolio manager's speech had changed this CEO's behavior.

Moral and Ethical Communications

In fact, the portfolio manager's speech met Buffett's morality test. Wikipedia states that the word "morality" comes "from the Latin word *moralitas* meaning "manner, character, proper behavior." Morality differentiates "good or right" intentions, decisions, and actions from those that are 'bad' (or wrong)." The portfolio manager infused qualities into the conversation that day that had been missing: investor behavior, character and how these CEOs were serving their owners and other stakeholders. His word choices revealed his underlying morality and commitment to ethical behavior.

From 2002 to 2012, my company, Rittenhouse Rankings, has analyzed over a thousand shareholder letters to find the ethical and moral word choices made by CEOs to affirm their promises and reveal underlying commitments.

Over this period, only four percent of the CEOs in our survey have used the words "moral" or "morality" in their shareholder communications. Fifty-two percent have used the words "ethical" or "ethics". Of course, merely using these words is not a reliable measure of trustworthy behavior. Rittenhouse Rankings also looks for actions described in a communication or the word choices made by a speaker that will engage or confuse the audience.

We systematically analyze CEO words using standardized protocols and point values that allow us to measure both positive and negative candor. We total these point values and then rank order companies based on degrees of candor. Correlating these rankings with stock price performance over the past seven years, we have found that the companies highest-ranked in candor, on average, out-performed those ranked lowest, and also the S&P 500.

The portfolio manager described above sets a gold standard in executive communications. In fact, the differences in the executive, analyst and portfolio manager's conversations are illustrated in the model below as "Just Talk", "Real Talk" and "Transforming Talk". Each type of communication is differentiated by five elements, including the: 1) parts of our anatomy used to communicate; 2) time perspective; 3) speaker's experience; 4) listener's experience and 5) expected outcome.

Three Levels of Business Conversations

	Anatomy Employed	Time Focus	Speaker Experience	Listener Experience	Expected Outcome
Just Talk (Blah-Blah)	Mouth/Eyes/ Left Brain	Past	Monologue/ Talk At Justify	Anesthetized Gain facts and information	Make Talk Show Up Inform
Real Talk (Transparency)	Mouth/Eyes/ Left Brain/ Ears	Past and Present-	Dialogue/ Talk with & Listen Explain/ Teach/ Educate	Listens/Pays Attention Gain context and importance	Support a Position Make a Point Sell
Transforming Talk (Candor)	Mouth/Eyes/ Left Brain/ Ears/Right Brain and Heart	Past, Present and Future-	Story & Drama/Talk & Experience Motivate/ Inspire/ Imagine	Connects Energetically Gains relevance, meaning and commitment	Share Experience Make a Difference Attract

Speakers who engage in "Just Talk" use their mouths and the analytical, rational left part of their brain. Such communications are designed to be more like monologues than dialogues. Typically, the speaker is focused on the past and less on the present. The speaker may be standing before an audience, but he or she is not fully present—nor is the audience. While the speaker's purpose is to inform the audience, the experience of being talked at leaves listeners in an anesthetized state. This kind of communication might also be called "the business as usual" standard.

In contrast, "Real Talk" communication engages not only the mouth and the rational, analytic left side of the brain, but also the ears. In this instance, the speaker listens as well as speaks and appears transparent. The speaker creates a dialogue and references the present as well as the past. Open to the experience of the moment, he or she connects more energetically with the audience. In Real Talk communications, the listener is informed and educated about a particular position or point of view. Often, the listener can be persuaded or even "sold" on the speaker's position.

"Transforming Talk" involves all of the body parts in Real Talk and also taps the creative, intuitive, emotional right side of the brain and the heart where courage, empathy and wisdom reside. Transforming Talk reaches into the past, present, and imagines the future. Transforming Talk has a narrative structure with a beginning, a middle, and end. Like a good story, it weaves together ideas that show how we are connected, rather than focus on what separates us. It is candid and moral. Speakers, who empathically step out of their own experience into the experience of their audience, create compelling communications with staying power. These have the power to transform those who listen.

Consider that "Candor" is sometimes used to define "Transparency." Rittenhouse Rankings, however, views these two standards differently. The dictionary definition of Candor, like the word candle, it is derived from *candere*, a Latin word meaning "to illuminate." Candor is defined as "the quality of being honest and straight-forward in attitude and speech and having the ability to make judgments free from discrimination or dishonesty." Leaders who adopt a candor standard choose to shine light into dark places. By choosing to trust and be trusted, they are more likely to run long-term, sustainable businesses.

Transparency, on the other hand, is derived from the Latin word *parere* meaning "to show through". Concerned with "how things appear," transparency describes communications that are free from guile; that can be seen through. Transparent communications inform, educate and teach others, but they do not necessarily build trust.[1] They are not likely to transform others.

Consider the following examples from shareholder letters published in 2012. Each illustrates one of the three kinds of communication modalities.

Just Talk: AMD 2011 Shareholder Letter Introduction

> *AMD enters 2012 firmly focused on becoming a solid execution engine, while positioning ourselves to take advantage of growth opportunities driven by a fundamental shift in the computing ecosystem.*

---

1   Rittenhouse L.J., *Investing Between the Lines*. New York: McGraw Hill, 2012, p. 91

Real Talk: Lockheed Martin 2011 Shareholder Letter Introduction

This is a milestone year for Lockheed Martin: our 100th anniversary. Our company's success over the past century is due to the exceptional character and ingenuity of the hundreds of thousands of people who have walked through the doors of our heritage companies. As this remarkable enterprise begins its second century, we and our customers face unprecedented global security challenges and an uncertain economic environment.

Transforming Talk: Eaton Corporation 2011 Shareholder Letter Introduction

In 1911, young entrepreneur Joseph Oriel Eaton staked his future on a transformational axle for the fledgling U.S. trucking industry. He bet upon a megatrend—that the transportation industry would become a hallmark of American industry and our economy. And he was right.

Candor as a Competitive Advantage

The significance of transforming communication is obvious. Delivering thoughts that make a difference can be a critical competitive advantage. When we clearly communicate, others are more likely to understand this and trust what we say. Execution is more focused, precise and accurate. Decision-making is wiser and better informed. Yet few of us are truly effective, trust-building communicators.

Much can be learned about the quality of corporate leadership and integrity of the corporate culture from analyzing corporate communications based on standards of candor. Is there a real world impact from studying corporate candor? Consider that about a year after these letters were published, AMD's stock had dropped 58 percent, Lockheed's stock was up 6 percent and Eaton's stock had climbed 175 percent.

Not many investors realize that Principle #12 in the Berkshire Hathaway Owner's Manual sets out Warren Buffett's candor commitment to owners:

We will be candid in our reporting to you, emphasizing the pluses and minuses important in appraising business value. Our guideline is to tell you the business facts that we would want to know if our positions were reversed. We owe you no less...we also believe candor benefits us as managers: The CEO who misleads others in public may eventually mislead himself in private.

In other words, Buffett describes a fundamental moral code: the Golden Rule. He intends to treat his owners as he wants to be treated if their positions were reversed.

As businesses increase their influence over global economic, political and social agendas, the principles, values and communications of their leaders gain increasing importance. Leaders committed to candor will make a positive and sustainable difference with investors, customers, employees and all stakeholders. They will create and build trust.

Laura (L.J.) Rittenhouse

Laura (L.J.) Rittenhouse, is a trust expert, financial strategist and innovation coach to the FORTUNE 20. A former investment banker, Rittenhouse is the author of the, Investing Between the Lines: How to Make Smarter Decisions by Decoding CEO Communications *[McGraw-Hill Jan. 2013], recommended in Warren Buffett's 2013 shareholder letter, as well as* Buffett's Bites *[2010].*

Laura is President of Rittenhouse Rankings, Inc., an advisory firm that counsels executives on integrating financial strategies with building trust. The annual Rittenhouse Rankings Corporate and Culture Candor survey measures organizational trustworthiness to reveal investment potential and links candor with market performance.

Making Your Values "Real" to Enable Trust (The Common Denominator in an Uncommon Business World)

By Jeff Thomson

The reputation of—and trust in—corporate leaders has taken a public pummeling over the last couple decades. We've witnessed colossal scandals involving hundreds of executives in each case: the accounting scandal of 2001; the stock options backdating scandal of 2005; the sub-prime mortgage scandal of 2008; not to mention the countless more "trivial" scandals lucky enough (for them) to escape headlining national news for months on end. No surprise then that in a Gallup poll rating the perceived ethical standards of people in various professions ranked business executives just a few notches higher than lawyers and car salesmen. As an executive myself, the comparison is a punch in the gut. The illegal and unethical behavior of a few has tainted the trust of the masses. And rightly so.

Aaron Beam, first chief financial officer of HealthSouth—among the largest healthcare and rehabilitation providers in the nation today—is one of these storied leaders who fell down the proverbial slippery slope, one of the fall guys of CEO Richard Scrushy, with whom he co-founded the company, and his elaborate and persuasive "cook the books" scheme. In short: Beam started the company from scrap, raised enough venture capital to take it public in two years, became an instant millionaire, watched Wall Street make it its darling, was convinced to help fudge earnings numbers with the promise "We'll make it up next quarter," found himself embroiled in fraud, landed in prison, ended up with almost nothing left but some shreds of dignity.

Beam isn't particularly well known, but his story is memorable, mostly because it could apply to any number of corporate executives whose moral compass is led astray by the promise of profit. Just a few years ago, Beam was a man whose estate grounds once boasted a regulation size football field; today, he mows lawns for a living. Karma? Sure, but more importantly, it's a cautionary tale in trust with a lesson for all.

Trust Requires Risk, Creates Values

Corporate scandals—Enron, WorldCom, HealthSouth—and the Sarbanes-Oxley legislation that resulted, have forced companies to self-examine and—reflect while elevating the role of risk management. Executives face greater account-ability than ever before and they're making more concerted efforts to identify potential exposures, how they can be prevented and how their companies can most effectively handle any situation they may face. Reviewing internal processes and controls is only the beginning. Delving much deeper, executives—me and many of my peers included—are increasingly probing the "inner core"; what our companies stand for and how we do business.

After all, in highly publicized downfalls, while processes may have failed or were perhaps non-existent to stop corporate abuses, executive misbehavior arose primarily from bad judgment or lapse of integrity, leading to the manipulation of company resources and deception of stakeholders. Rules upon rules are created to manage behavior. Too little effort, however, is made to identify the values underlying that behavior. And at the heart of these values is trust.

Living a set of admirable values isn't easy in today's bottom-line driven business world. Trust must be made "real" and earned every day. Words come cheap; actions are at a premium. At IMA (Institute of Management Accountants), we have long referred to this as "creating value through values." In other words, achieving great outcomes requires a genuine and ingrained culture of trust, respect and the like. Having a set of core values serving as organizational guideposts to appropriate business behavior is foundational to vulnerability-based trust (in essence, the willingness of people to abandon their pride and their fear, to sacrifice their egos for the collective good of the team). It requires fierce conversations and plenty of them to make trust, ethics and values tangible.

Making Trust Tangible

How do you make your organizational values real and foundational to building trust, organizational health, and creating great business outcomes? Two very simple suggestions:

> *The CEO, not a committee or consultant, must set the core values. Why? Tone at the top. Genuine, authentic and sustained exemplary behaviors are required and should be expected from the leader and the leadership team.*

> *While the CEO must make a substantial effort in drafting the core values, it's critical to remember it's not a dictatorship and you must get weigh-in before achieving buy-in from multiple and diverse stakeholders. At IMA, after I created our initial core values, my leadership team provided input (not blinded; one week) and then all of our global staff weighed in (confidential/blinded to HR; one month). We considered the collective input and then finalized for all global staff. Some period of time later, our volunteer leaders (IMA is a not-for-profit membership association) tweaked the core values and adopted them as well.*

Importantly, the goal in the process is not solely tone at the top; it's tone throughout the organization, one that will survive beyond the current management team and is a table stake for being a part of the organization. Staff and stakeholders know phonies when they see them, and so the leader and leadership team are indeed in a fish bowl with their behaviors always being observed and reflected upon. At their core, the leader and team must believe not only that living the values is the right thing to do from a social virtue perspective, but that it will lead to profitable business outcomes for stakeholders. After all, these are the people who will help educate and reeducate, enforce and reinforce their support of the values and their importance to each employee's responsibilities.

Of course, the values must account for plenty of "gray" when it comes to human behavior. One person's aggressiveness may be another person's assertiveness. One person's view of the "customer comes first" may mean the customer is literally always right; another's may be that listening and engaging in constructive contention with the customer is the path to a lasting solution—and relationship. Without this specific conversation, however, how would you or the organization know what behaviors comport reasonably with the core values and which do not?

Avoid overused and/or trite catch phrases that may sell for promotional purposes but are useless in measuring the "how" of individual and organizational performance. It's easy enough to post the core values on the company website and make them a pretty part of the office environment. But nailing them to the office walls doesn't make the values real. The challenge is bringing these values to life, which requires infinitely more effort than it takes to purchase frames and hooks at the local craft store.

> *Make the effort to inculcate the core values into on-going performance reviews and appraisal processes to drive regular, often tough, conversations about the behaviors (the "how") that lead to the accomplishments (the "what").*

Values should be reinforced through rewards. Compensation, promotions, public recognition, and other benefits should include and align with a clear values component. At IMA, for incentive bonus compensation every employee is rewarded based on the same mathematical formula (X % based on achievement of company-level goals; (100-X) % based on achievement of individual/departmental goals). But more importantly, the on-going performance review process requires conversations about the core values because they are built into the physical performance appraisal form. An accompanying tool is a rubric we developed that describes, for each of IMA's five core values, a set of behaviors that align with unacceptable behavior at one extreme and role model behavior at the other.

But, we can't be too analytical or mathematically precise in the area of human behavior and alignment with core values leading to genuine, lasting and vulnerable trust. And, there are no "one hit wonders" when it comes to building lasting values that are part of an organization's fiber, part of its DNA, that remains steadfast while leaders come and go. You must work on the values side relentlessly and have many fierce conversations.

Reinforcing clarity in the area of values is vital, from the moment a new employee steps in the door. Don't bother with hours spent on administrative procedures. If they are smart and are armed with the right resources, your new employees will figure all of that out. Spend time from day one communicating the importance of values, what the values mean relative to achieving the organizational mission and strategy, and consequences for appropriate and inappropriate behavior. Over time, much like the way our parents taught us, we will not need formulae to guide our behaviors—we will not only know what is right, but also what is expected and required for individual and organizational success.

Sustainable Trust

If your organization has core values, dust them off and ensure you and your leadership team make them tangible every day through actions and behaviors. If you don't have core values, or they are dated, get to work. Invest the time and effort to understand the drivers of trust and realize that creating sustainable business outcomes really does start with core values. This is the path to enriching careers, organizations and society at large.

IMA Global Core Values
Respect for the Individual

We treat each other with respect and dignity, valuing individual and cultural differences. We communicate frequently and with candor, engaging in healthy debate and listening to each other, regardless of position or level. We work hard to create an environment that respects individuals in an atmosphere of open communication, growth, and learning.

Passing for Serving Members

We enable individuals to use their capabilities to the fullest to deliver exemplary products and services to members. That enablement extends to being passionate advocates in advancing our global profession. WE care for all members and each other—building enduring relationships—and driving continuous improvement. We appropriately recognize our volunteer leaders, who are so giving of their time and expertise.

Highest Standards of Integrity and Trust

We understand and abide by the IMA Statement of Ethical Professional Practice in our everyday actions. Our personal conduct ensures that the IMA name is always worthy of trust—our members around the globe deserve nothing less. We treat each other fairly, keep our promises, make decisions objectively, take responsibility for our actions, and admit our mistakes. We maintain confidentiality as appropriate.

Innovation and Continuous Improvement

We believe innovation and a spirit of continuous improvement are engines that keep us relevant, vital and growing. Our culture embraces creativity and seeks different perspectives. We behave like owners of a "business," managing risks and identifying new opportunities in serving members and advancing the profession.

Teaming to Achieve

We encourage and reward both individual and team achievements, proactively working across organizational boundaries to always "remember the member." Our spirit of team achievement extends to advancing our profession and to being responsible and caring partners with our various communities.

Jeffrey C. Thomson

Jeffrey C. Thomson, CMA® is president and CEO of IMA®, one of the largest and most respected global associations focused exclusively on advancing the management accounting profession. IMA has more than 65,000 members in 120 countries, with about 200 professional and 100 student chapters. IMA confers the CMA (Certified Management Accountant) credential to accountants and financial professionals in business.

Section II:

Trust in Practice

In Apple We Trust?

By Cynthia Figge

In terms of company supremacy, Apple must surely rank near the top. They have maintained one of the largest market values for a public company and *Fast Company* named Apple as "The World's Most Innovative Company" in 2012. What could be better? At the end of 2012 in a December 6th Business Week article. Apple's CEO, Tim Cook, said he would continue the company's focus on creating great products to enrich people's lives ("higher cause for the product") under his leadership. He also noted that Apple would become more transparent to both make a difference and have others follow its leadership. For a company where secrecy has been sacred, was this a signal that transparency is being adopted as a business driver—perhaps ultimately an issue of customer loyalty and trust? Or was the external mounting pressure from Apple stakeholders great enough to change the company's course? Or both?

Cook said, "My own personal philosophy on giving is best stated in a [John F.] Kennedy quote, "To whom much is given, much is expected." I have always believed this. Always. I think that Apple and Apple's employees have done enormous good and can do even more…"

"Our transparency in supplier responsibility is an example of recognizing that the more transparent we are, the bigger difference we would make. We want to be as innovative with supply responsibility as we are with our products. That's a high bar. The more transparent we are, the more it's in the public space. The more it's in the public space, the more other companies will decide to do something similar. And the more everybody does it, the better everything gets…"

"It's a recognition that we need to be super secretive in one part about our products and our road maps. But there are other areas where we will be completely transparent so we can make the biggest difference. That's kind of the way we look at it."

Completely transparent? In late January 2013 Apple released its seventh Supplier Responsibility Report. It covers excessive work hours, underage labor, and environmental impacts of the manufacturing process. Over 1.5 million workers make Apple products, and the company claims to track more than 1 million workers weekly and publish the data monthly on its website. Further, the company said last year that 1.3 million workers and managers received Apple-designed training about workers' rights, health and safety, and Apple's own Supplier Code of Conduct. Apple claimed, "We're going deeper into the supply chain than any other company we know of, and we're reporting at a level of detail that is unparalleled in our industry."

Why this unparalleled level of detail? Behind closed doors with a group of IT executives (not including Apple) I participated in a debate about this specific issue. Beyond the question about supply chain transparency and how much to reveal was a larger question—is treating people fairly and justly a corporate social responsibility (CSR) and the kind of special issue that activists and socially responsible investors care about? Are we beginning to see CSR as a business driver, and will over time consumers, employees, investors and supply chain partners base their trust and loyalty in a company not solely on whether they produce great products, but also whether they address real needs, are compassionate, and sustainable?

If we are moving in the direction that business must also address real needs and be compassionate and sustainable, how do we know how companies are doing in CSR? How can we determine who to give our time, trust and money to in exchange for products and services? Where should we place our brand and company loyalty? My firm, CSRHub, has built a tool to measure how companies are doing concerning employees, environment, community and governance. CSRHub provides access to corporate social responsibility and sustainability ratings and information on over 7,000 companies from 135 industries in 91 countries. CSRHub rates twelve indicators of employee, environment, community and governance performance and flags many special issues. We aggregate and normalize over 23 million data points coming from 200 sources, including eight ESG (environment, social, governance) analyst firms, well-known indexes, publications, "best of" or "worst of" lists, NGOs, crowd sources and government agencies.

These ratings are updated monthly. The following chart shows selected ratings from CSRHub on Apple, Amazon, Dell, Google, HP, Intel and Microsoft, close competitors and peers who are all working on their transparency, supply chain, community development, diversity and labor issues. The overall score is based on the average CSRHub user profile weights for the twelve subcategory scores.

Company name	Overall	Human Rights & Supply chain	Diversity & Labor Rights	Environment Policy & Reporting	Leadership Ethics	Transparency & Reporting	Community Dev & Philantropy
Intel Corporation	64	54	64	64	64	59	60
Hewlett-Packard Co.	63	59	63	62	65	57	53
Dell, Inc.	63	59	61	66	64	60	56
Microsoft Corp	61	54	62	61	63	53	56
Apple Inc.	55	51	52	57	55	50	39
Google, Inc.	54	56	63	50	52	49	60
Amazon.com, Inc.	45	36	49	40	48	45	33

Apple ranks 6th in this group of companies in human rights and supply chain, 6th in community development and philanthropy (only surpassing the laggard Amazon), 6th in diversity and labor rights, 5th in leadership ethics and 5th in transparency and reporting. Clearly Apple is not yet perceived as pulling peers forward in these important measures of corporate responsibility. Apple's score in community development and philanthropy, 39 on a scale of 0 to 100, is well below the CSRHub average score of 45. According to "To whom much is given, much is expected"; Tim Cook and Apple have a way to go.

However, progress is a journey, and is measured in part by intention and forward movement. Consider Nike (Number 1 on *Fast Company's* Most Innovative list 2013). In their 15 years of CSR reporting, they have set a high bar in their industry for supplier responsibility and transparency. They score 62 in human rights and supply chain, and 61 in community development and philanthropy. They've come a long way since being accused of using sweatshops, although the pressure for increased transparency continues. CEO Mark Parker says, "Over the past 15 years, we have moved from an approach of simply reacting to criticisms to pursuing sustainability as an integral driver of our long-term growth." Their website says, "Its' not just about getting better at what we do—addressing impacts throughout our supply chain—it's about striving for the best, creating value for the business and innovating for a better world."

I believe companies that are building a culture of transparency and sustainability will likely perform better in the long term than those that do not. So how do successful companies build this culture?

First, a company must overcome its reluctance and resistance to openly communicating with NGOs, employees, communities, and stakeholders. At CSRHub we have found a correlation between more data, more transparency and better-perceived performance. This may not be intuitive to the legal team or risk managers, but cleaning and air drying (a/k/a airing) "dirty laundry" is critical to building understanding. This understanding may open the door to grace, while a company begins to take the challenging and difficult steps to build long-term sustainability and trust.

Second, develop metrics that enable your company to track your progress, and benchmark your progress against peers and competitors. In a Harvard Business Review article by David Lubin and Daniel Esty titled "The Sustainability Imperative" the authors say, "Developing metrics that allow companies to measure benefits and understand costs is essential to adapting and refining their strategy, as well as communicating results." Companies need an external measure of their sustainability progress —and they need benchmarks that compare them to their competitors, so they know how much further they need to go. The team at CSRHub has spent five years developing a measurement instrument that provides this type of broad and uniform metric.

Third, go public with a CSR report and reveal your policies and practices. Whether they like it or not, companies that don't create a CSR report are still rated. Rating agencies use what they can find, even if it's not always high quality information. Some ratings are based on model-driven estimates and projections. Going public strengthens transparency, and gives good-performing companies credit where it is due for the improvements they have made. In the CSRHub database of 7,000 companies, we estimate only 20% of US companies and 36% worldwide have issued a CSR report. The percentage of those using a higher-quality standard such as the Global Reporting Initiative is even lower.

Fourth, proactively report to leading ratings agencies such as CDP (Carbon Disclosure Project). In 2011, CDP noted that Apple and nine other companies with large market caps didn't respond to the group's annual survey. Greenpeace attacked Apple in a study of cloud-computing companies, "Three of the largest IT companies building their business around the cloud—Amazon, Apple and Microsoft—are all rapidly expanding without adequate regard to the source of electricity, and rely heavily on dirty energy to power their clouds." (Apple responded soon thereafter with an announcement that it was approved to build a 20-megawatt solar power facility across the street from its data center in Maiden, North Carolina. This could be an example of the virtuous circle of pressure at work.) The reporting of *New York Times* author James Glanz and others have exposed and increased pressure for improvement and change.

Fifth, keep evolving your products and services toward solving the emerging global need for sustainability. Consumer preferences are being driven by a market force I call sustainability natives. Sustainability natives have an innate understanding of the ecological and social issues facing the planet. They do not debate whether these challenges exist or are an imperative for their generation. They instead take for granted the need to creatively solve sustainability's challenges of efficiency (reduced material and energy throughput and reduced waste), and sufficiency (what does society need to truly create a sustainable economic equilibrium for 7 to 10 billion people). Their expectation that business takes a lead in tackling these issues is a given. Sustainability natives expect more from the corporate world around them. According to Cone Communications, "83% of Americans want MORE of the products, services and retailers they use to support causes." And in their day to day job, 88% of sustainability natives will choose employers based on their CSR and 86% would consider leaving their job if CSR no longer held up (according to PriceWaterhouseCoopers). Born into a certain assumption about the imperative of sustainability, this generation bridges the professional and personal and marries their values and their dollars spent.

At a brainstorming workshop with college students on business solutions to societal problems, the following question was raised: are companies truly becoming sustainable if the highest rated companies on CSRHub are in the low 70s (out of 100)? Surely the best cannot be only a C+. Even more concerning to the students was the question of sufficiency—do we even need the unsustainable products and services that we are trying to make more sustainable? Isn't this an exercise straight from the Emperor's New Clothes?

Far beyond dreaded greenwashing, this harkens to a deeper point: can capital-ism be sustainable if its driving force is consumption? Aren't the two necessar-ily at odds? After all, even if we lightweight a 12 ounce soda can and recycle it after consumption, we still have a product that combines water—a precious resource—with an average of 10 packets of sugar to create a drink with no nutri-tional value. And how many pairs of shoes or multiple iPods do we really need? Questions from sustainability natives about what we really *need* to consume may rattle the sustainability field—and it should. Their call is to challenge the consumption-centric economic model at its very core.

Sixth, develop a compassionate organization. When business people know the difference between the fundamental right to do something and the right thing to do, and then do the right thing, a business is becoming more compassionate. Deep attention and concern for fair and equitable practices for employees, contractors and workers in the supply chain puts a company on the path to becoming a compas-sionate organization. Responding to the clear signals about the earth's resources and energy use and aligning business practices with these constraints, is a way to develop a compassionate and sustainable organization. Finally, attracting people who are genuinely diverse and bring multiple skills of creativity, emotional and social ability and engaging them in co-creating a sustainable company develops a more compassionate organization. See the TED prize Charter for Compassion for steps to creating a compassionate organization.

These six steps are key to building trust. For trust ultimately is a business driver and enabler of transformation and positive change.

Cynthia Figge

Cynthia Figge is a forerunner and thought leader in the corporate sustainability movement. She is COO and Cofounder of CSRHub, the world's largest database that aggregates and organizes data and knowledge on the social, environmental, and governance performance of 7,000 companies to provide sustainability ratings to the marketplace. In 1996 she co-founded EKOS International, one of the first consultancies integrating sustainability and corporate strategy. Prior to founding EKOS, she was an officer of LIN Broadcasting / McCaw Cellular, and led new businesses and services with Weyerhaeuser, New York Daily News; and with New Ventures. Cynthia is Board Director of the Compassionate Action Network International. Cynthia received her bachelor's degree in Economics and an MBA from the Harvard Business School. She lives in the Seattle area.

Four Lock Box

By John Gerzema

The long-term payoff for Kenya could be seen in the rising health and education levels of the farm children who will soon be young adults. With its urban population growing at nearly five percent per year, Kenya will need more jobs in commerce and industry, and these positions require workers with sufficient schooling. However, many of today's adults in Kenya also need immediate access to work and incomes, and cannot devote years to study. For this segment of the population, one of the world's oldest aid groups—Catholic Relief Services—promotes a saving and lending scheme that serves people who are so poor that they cannot qualify even for the kind of microfinance loans popular in many parts of the world.

"More than credit, these people are in need of a safe place to keep their money," explained Guy Vanmeenen, whom we met at an office in the Westlands neighborhood of Nairobi. It is home to many aid organizations and the businesses that serve them. Belgian born, Guy is tall and slender, with dirty blond hair. His commitment to antipoverty work emerged during a backpacking trip through South America in 1989, where he was shocked by the conditions he saw in very poor communities. In Kenya, he works with people who have no access to financial institutions, but as Vanmeenen found, their communities enjoy a tradition of savings clubs. Sometimes as large as two-dozen people, these community organizations meet weekly, collect very small payments from members, and then distribute the sum to individuals who each get a turn in the role of recipient.

Although the clubs allow members to benefit from a periodic infusion of cash, no interest was paid on the savings, and certain obvious weaknesses were inherent in the informal system. First, if attendance varied, then the receipts and disbursements could vary in an unfair way. Second, the scheme could fall apart before every member got his or her turn to be paid. Third, it was inflexible and made no provision for emergencies or community interests.

Soft spoken but also passionate about his work, Guy obviously admired the thrift and resourcefulness of the people he served. "People do save, even if they save by buying and caring for chickens," he said. He also believed that he could help the very poor take additional steps toward financial security. In villages and city neighborhoods, he helped formalize the savings clubs by equipping them with ledgers, lockboxes, and a lending plan. The lockboxes, which secure both contributions and records, were each equipped with four locks and could be opened only with keys held by four separate members of the club.

As safe as a bank, the box system reinforced trust that already existed among neighbors. The lending plan encouraged members to consider requests for loans and to set interest rates charged to borrowers. Accustomed to paying double-digit rates, sometimes on a daily basis, the cash box groups typically set rates that would reach as much as thirty percent per year. Most loans are repaid in a matter of days or weeks, so individual borrowers are able to clear their accounts by repaying principal and just a small additional amount. However, the groups see an average twenty-seven percent return on their savings per year. For most small savers, these earnings represent the first gains they have ever seen from investment.

Besides the lending, most of Guy's groups also operate social benefit projects, which might fund some improvements for a community, and they offer emergency aid for participants whose families are struck by illness or some other crisis. Aid allocations are determined by group members, who are likely to be wives and mothers. Seventy percent of the savings group enrollees are female. "Women have more social skill and are more accustomed to coming together to solve problems," added Guy.

Remarkably, in seven years of operation, the savings club members have poured $8 million—often a nickel or dime at a time—into the lockboxes. Guy's next step involved savers in training programs that equipped them to help establish new groups. Certified by Catholic Relief Services, but operating as entrepreneurs, these consultants collect fees for helping people form and operate new groups. Because the trained consultants are paid by every group they serve, they have a stake in spreading the practice. In a self-perpetuating cycle of empowerment, poor people who are "microsavers" become microentrepreneurs.

Guy's ultimate goal is a financial system that is run by and for the most impoverished people in the world and that requires no outside funding or direction. "We're moving from a subsidized approach to a market approach," said Guy. "We have seven hundred private service providers, and they have recruited ninety apprentices." Fears that the private consultants might neglect the poorest people in their communities have been calmed by studies showing that they continued to serve the original, targeted groups. Soon the system could function so well on its own that Guy and the Catholic Relief Services bureaucracy will not been needed. He's okay with this outcome.

"It's about empowerment," he told us. "People now say, 'We don't have to depend on handouts.'" In fact, some of the savings clubs have decided to share their wealth with neighbors. In villages, they supply aid to widows and orphans on a case-by-case basis. "When the project ends," said Guy, "we will leave behind the capacity for people to do it themselves.

In Kenya, and across the eighteen countries we traveled to for our new book, *The Athena Doctrine* — trust is now paramount. In our data, which reflects nations as diverse as China, Mexico and France, trust has declined by fifty percent since the crisis. People now trust one in four companies on average, making its scarcity in the marketplace an object of value. In data across thirteen nations, seventy-six percent of people disagree that 'my country cares about its citizens more than they used to', while three-quarters disagree that 'the world is becoming more fair'. In today's marketplace, consumers respond to companies who care about them and the larger world. When asked about the most important thing a company can stand for, 'kindness and empathy' shot up by 400% since the crisis.

Trust in its most ideal form is something tangible and experiential. It exists in a social contract as basic as a four-lock box. In the last decade, six of the ten fastest-growing economies in the world were in Africa, and international financial institutions expect that a rising middle class will make the continent the next great market for business. The developments that inspire this confidence have prompted hundreds of American corporations and their competitors from around the world to make investments in Africa. Overtures made by Chinese enterprises have caught the attention of American officials, who don't want the United States to be overshadowed anywhere in the world. Not long after our visit, Secretary of State Hillary Clinton arrived in Nairobi with dozens of businesspeople in tow, including executives from Walmart, Boeing, and FedEx. The delegation was making a tour of the region, intent on showing that the United States appreciated it potential. Clinton, noting the essential role of democracy in the country's development, pledged support for 2013 elections.

During Clinton's African tour, a South African analyst named Chris Lanberg told the *New York Times* of an "unprecedented interest in Africa. Every single important country whether China, France, Britain, India, Brazil, Turkey, you name it, they are all queuing up."[27] As the world gets in line to serve industry and consumers, Kenya and its neighbors may prove that they deserve the nickname bestowed on them by the editors of the *Economist,* who have dubbed Africa "the Hopeful Continent."

John Gerzema

John Gerzema is a social strategist who uses data to help companies adapt to new consumer interests and demands. He is chairman of WPP Group's BAV Consulting and his book; The Athena Doctrine examines the rise of feminine traits and values, with Pulitzer-Prize winner Michael D'Antonio. jgerzema@bavconsulting @johngerzema www.athenadoctrine.com

Trust: The Great Economic Game-Changer

How trust can mean the difference between life and death in business
By Robert Porter Lynch

Survival is not a Given

Success in any business venture, large or small, is not assured. Even the combination of a great strategy and a great product will not guarantee success. Nor will a company's size insure against failure. Startups and venerable giants alike can be struck down by a seemingly invisible disease: distrust.

Banks, airlines, and auto companies are just a few of the industries torn asunder by the distrust disease. Dishonest business practices ripped apart the banking and investment industry worldwide, causing trillions of dollars of economic damage. Every year large airlines file for bankruptcy and the common denominator is nearly always labor strife—a long history of labor-management distrust which causes highly inefficient delivery of services. Sports leagues like the National Hockey League and the National Basketball Association have been stricken by strikes that nearly threatened their very existence.

What's more, the disease of distrust tends to spread like an uncontrolled virus, soon becoming a plague that feeds on fear and greed.

U.S. Auto Industry Succumbs to the Distrust Disease

One industry that's dear to everyone is the auto industry—the world's most visible and best-studied business sector. In 2009, General Motors and Chrysler both filed for bankruptcy and Ford came darned close. Being "too big to fail," every taxpayer in the United States, through the action of the President, became an investor in GM and Chrysler through a bailout program (as taxpayers also did with the banks that failed).

What is not well known is that in the five year period leading up to the auto crisis, the "Big Three" U.S. automakers collectively had lost over $100 billion in the prior five years running up to the 2008 financial meltdown. The financial cataclysm did not cause their failure; it just put them over the precipice.

How could such large companies, staffed by highly educated management professionals, make such horrific mistakes? What really happened? What can we learn from this debacle?

How Distrust Became Deadly in Detroit

Twenty five years ago, the Japanese auto manufacturers played a very minor role in manufacturing automobiles in the United States. But Toyota's vaunted "Lean" production model ("Kaizen" meaning continuous improvement) threatened Detroit's Big Three—Ford, GM, and Chrysler.

As the Japanese manufacturers—Toyota, Honda, and then Nissan—began building cars in the U.S., they tapped into the same supplier base used by the Big Three.

Today, most cars are assembled from components provided by outside suppliers. Typically 70-80% of an auto (such as seats, wheels, radios, and tires) is produced by suppliers, and the remaining (such as engines and transmissions) are made by the manufacturer, who then completes all the assembly.

The Japanese manufacturers on North American soil took a strategy with their supply chain to build trust: high levels of cooperation, respect, mutual sharing of ideas, continuous innovation, and a willingness to share in the cost savings those new ideas would bring. For example, if a supplier could redesign a group of parts to make them into only one part, thereby shortening assembly time, reducing complexity of inventory, and lowering potential warranty costs, the supplier would be rewarded by a 50/50 share in the savings.

Senior VP of Procurement, Dave Nelson spoke of the insights Honda had about human behavior. He said the Golden Rule prevailed—treat people with dignity and respect, don't beat up on suppliers like lowly vendors, and never play the blame game when something goes wrong. I asked Nelson about innovation with his suppliers, and his remarks were quite insightful:

> *"When we receive a suggestion from our suppliers, we split the savings 50/50. However, if a supplier is not making their profit numbers, we give them a larger percentage of the savings (in the short term), sometimes up to 100%. It helps them out."*[1]

Having earlier spoken with GM suppliers who indicated that their relationships with GM were unprofitable, I asked Nelson about costs over the course of model run. He mapped the cost structure on a pad of paper using a target costing approach. (See Figure 1) He smiled and as he said that a product that cost $1.00 to manufacture had been reduced to $.58 by the end of the model run, which put over a billion dollars a year on the Honda's bottom line.

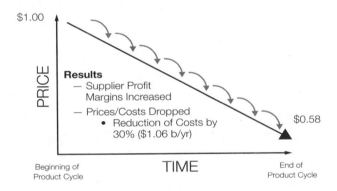

Figure 1: Cost Reductions by Honda Suppliers

Not totally convinced that this was in the best interests of suppliers, I asked Nelson about supplier profitability over the product life cycle. He assured me everyone gained by this approach. Pressing farther, I challenged him. Honda was committed to ensuring the sustainability of their supply base.

---

1   Interview, October 21, 1997 Pinehurst, NC

"We regularly monitor the financial condition of our suppliers. I can assure you they are more profitable at the end of the product life cycle than at the beginning."

The Japanese manufacturers saw their suppliers as critical partners in the whole chain of value creation. Similarly they saw their employees in the same way; along with their newly emerging dealer-distributor-service network that interacted with the customer. Each member in the value-creation process was treated honorably as a cherished partner. Toyota, for example, was not easy on their partners; they expected top quality and continuous improvement. But if a problem arose with a supplier, Toyota's presumption was: "we" have a problem, "we" must determine the cause, and "we" must mutually solve. [2]

During the 1990s, Toyota and Honda gained ground fast, eating away at the Big Three's once monumental market-share. By building trust with their suppliers and treating them fairly, each grabbed a larger chunk of market share with higher quality, all the while keeping themselves and their suppliers profitable. [3]

In stark contrast, Detroit's Big Three bludgeoned their key suppliers, using adversarial, short sighted relationships with their key suppliers, to the detriment of all. Constant margin squeezing decimated the supply base. GM and Ford saved money in the short run, but at the at the expense of consumer value who received poor quality cars; and the suppliers were financially weakened—a flawed strategy.

My personal experience in the automobile industry illustrates the difference in mind-sets dramatically. Working with a wide variety of auto supply companies in the 1990s was very revealing. Most auto suppliers provided parts for General Motors, Ford, Chrysler. Some were qualified as outsourcers for Honda or Toyota. For those that supplied both US and Japanese auto manufacturers, I would ask about their experiences. The worst buyer was, unquestionably GM, followed closely by Ford. Both were notorious for nickel and diming their suppliers, bullying behavior, and illegally canceling contracts or violating proprietary material of their suppliers.

---

2   GM, on the other hand was loathe to accept any responsibility for supplier difficulties, and would first place blame on suppliers, who may have been victims of poor planning or communications.
3   Another test of the power of Honda's quality control is represented by used car prices. A Cadillac, at the ten year point in its life will have lost a far greater % of its original value than a Honda. Typically the Honda depreciates at about half the rate of a Cadillac.

At one workshop on supplier alliances I conducted in Detroit for CEOs of auto suppliers, I asked what kind of cars they drove themselves? Universally all the CEOs said their personal cars were Japanese. I asked "why?" They all agreed: "Because we know what goes into them!" One CEO meekly raised his hand and said "We have a token GM car which we only drive to meetings with GM for fear of retaliation."

The lack of cooperation was extremely costly

GM's Procurement Czar in the 1990s, Ignatio Lopez' notorious negotiations techniques ran roughshod over every supplier in GM's supply base; he used ignominious and illegal tactics to pressure every supplier into price cutting that left them either abandoning GM or selling to GM below their costs of production. He'd tear up legitimate contracts in the face of the supplier or illegally take supplier's proprietary drawings and give them to Chinese vendors for bids. One ploy that irritated every supplier was to demand an immediate price cut of 20% or lose their contract. Suppliers were faced with producing at a loss, or shutting down large production lines, resulting in even bigger losses. Quality slipped, production lines often didn't have the parts ready for assembly, and GM's warranty costs consistently outpaced their profits.

Vendors weren't the only group to receive GM's wrath; its labor relations fared no better. At one GM plant in California there was a backlog of over 5,000 grievances, the result of a long-standing war between labor and management. Workers were boozed up or drugged up on the job. The absenteeism was often so high (exceeding 30%) that the production line couldn't be started, which meant production halted. Workers regularly sabotaged cars on the assembly line, putting ball bearings or Coke bottles in the doors and frames so they would rattle around and annoy unsuspecting buyers.

Rancor and distrust was so thick you see, smell, and taste it. Self-esteem was destroyed, and adolescent revolt became everyday adult action.

Ford, not to be outdone, unilaterally changed contracts, reprogramming their computers to reduce the amount of any invoice by 5%. Adding insult to injury, Ford then obtained totally unrealistic bids from unqualified suppliers, which were used to pressure legitimate suppliers to succumb to unfavorable price reductions in order to keep their contracts.

Every part was examined to squeeze out more costs.

Severing Trust with Customers

Here's a tragic example of price squeezing: The Explorer was one of Ford's most profitable vehicles, yielding $3-5,000 to the bottom line every time one was sold.

However, customers complained of the Explorer's harsh ride. Rather than spend money reengineering the suspension's spring-tension levels to make the ride a little softer, Ford let pressure out of the tires. Firestone, the tire manufacturer shot back that the lower tire pressures were below design specifications and would result in blowouts. Firestone recommended the addition of another nylon belt around the tire to enable it to run effectively at the lower pressures, reducing the failure rate by a factor of five.

Ford vetoed the idea—it was too costly. The addition of a nylon belt would add another 90 cents to each tire's cost, eating away at Ford's profit margins.

The tires failed horribly. Ford was forced to replace all 13 million tires on its vehicles, at a total cost of about $3 billion. The recall and associated suits cost Firestone more than $570 million. But worse, more than 100 people died in crashes caused by failures of tires on Ford Explorers; law suits were filed around the world.

"The whole thing just screamed greed," said La Rita Morales, part of a jury in California that earlier this year awarded an Explorer driver $23.4 million in damages. *"I didn't believe in my heart that a company like Ford would put out a product with question marks over it."*[4]

The debacle cost Ford billions of dollars in lost sales and law suits. All for a 90 cent belt. The tire manufacturers blamed Ford, and Ford blamed the tires. The lawyers blamed everyone. Law suits dragged on for years.

Distrust Costs US Automakers their Economic Prosperity

Warning signals were everywhere during the years leading up to the 2008 meltdown and the impending "too big to fail" bankruptcies. The disease of

---

4   Internal Ford Documents about Explorer Rollovers By Peter Whoriskey, Washington Post Staff Writer, May 8, 2010

distrust in Detroit had become virile. An annual automotive benchmark study in 2004[5] sent emergency signals unequivocally:

- U.S automakers' relations with their suppliers suggest more trouble if they don't change the way they deal with their U.S. suppliers …[who] are shifting their loyalties—and resources (capital and R&D expenditures, service and support)—to their Japanese customers at the expense of the domestic Big Three.

- Supplier trust of Ford and GM has never been lower; conversely, trust for their Japanese counterparts has never been higher. Suppliers are increasing product quality at a greater rate for the Japanese.

- US automakers have little regard for their suppliers, they communicate very poorly and they generally treat suppliers as adversaries rather than trusted partners. In all the other industries studied such as aerospace, electronics, and computers, no one treats their suppliers as poorly as the US automakers do.

- US automakers continue hammering their suppliers for price reductions and multi-million dollar cash givebacks and suppliers are responding by giving them less support.

- This shift in loyalty is not driven by cost reduction pressures on suppliers, but rather on how the US automakers work with their suppliers across a wide range of business practices.

- The greater the trust between buyer and supplier, the more suppliers are willing share and invest in new technology, and provide higher quality goods and higher levels of service, which lead to greater competitive advantage and market share.

The author of this study, John Henke, presented this observation:

> *"What is apparent is that the Japanese manufacturers are applying continuous improvement practices to their supplier working relations just as they have done to their manufacturing processes, and as a result they continue to win the cost-quality-technology race."*

---

5   Planning Perspectives, Inc Report, Aug 2, 2004. Responses from 223 Tier 1 suppliers including 36 of the Top 50 and was based on 852 buying situations. Participating suppliers' combined sales represent 48% of the OEM's annual purchase of components

By 2008, things had gone from bad to worse for the Detroit Big Three, who had combined losses of over $100 billion for the prior five year period, while at the same time driving 500 suppliers a year out of business. Their flawed strategy of distrustful relationships took its toll not only on their businesses, but on the surrounding community.

Today, the effects on the City of Detroit's economy are horrible. The municipality is losing population at the highest rate in the U.S.; housing values are at the bottom. Detroit Mayor Kilpatrick, taking his cues from his Big Three counterparts, extorted money from city contractors, was convicted, and sentenced to jail. In 2009 the median home sale in Detroit was a sickly $6,000. By 2013 the City of Detroit was $14 billion in debt—bankrupt—a "ward of the state."

Harsh Conclusions

It's important for every business leader in America to understand that:

Distrust destroyed Detroit by enabling innovation to flow away to other regions where partners focused human energy on innovation, not warfare.

This is the real message of trust and hope for our commercial future. Trust is not just good ethics; trust is about building the relationships that charge the human spirit with the collaborative energy to tackle new problems together; to build bold new futures synergistically; to join forces across the boundaries of supply chains to innovate; to safely know that the one will not be trapped by foolish win-lose gamesmanship; and to challenge the status quo with the assurance new ideas are welcome.

Trust's Hidden Advantage: Innovation

Lest one be lured into a false sense of hope brought about by the good feelings of trust, believing trust alone will assure business success, there is really much more. Trust, while highly desirable, is not the end or the goal; it's just the beginning of a larger process.

Toyota, Honda, and Nissan, unlike their U.S. rivals, understood that trust was the foundation of *collaborative innovation*—the hidden source of competitive advantage. By removing fear, doubt, suspicion, and manipulation from the business relationships, a much more powerful program of joint problem solving, removal of non-valued work (such a redundancy), reduction of waste, and acceleration of work flow could flourish. High trust is not the goal; it opens the pathways to real value creation, which then manifests in competitive advantage and profitability.

Trust enables everything to move faster, more effortlessly, and with less conflict. Mistrust causes everything to be more complicated, slower, and far more fragmented. Because virtually all innovation is a *collaborative* effort; and there can be no collaboration without trust.

Fortunately for the U.S. auto industry, the 2008 debacles shook the foundations of ill-conceived beliefs. New leadership has made some improvements to their supplier relationships, but so far nothing earth shattering that would make a compelling case for taking advantage of trust as an economic game changer.

How to Channel Trust into Collaborative Innovation

Exactly how important is trust?

Our studies show, time and again, high trust organizations have at least a 25% competitive advantage over their low trust counterparts. Embedding a system of trust into your alliance yields enormous rewards for all stakeholders. Trust unleashes latent human energy and enables it to be aligned on a common purpose. Leaders who want to support collaborative and trigger innovation should keep the "FARTHEST" principles in mind:

Fairness in all your dealings to be sure that everyone gets a fair shake. Successful innovation leaders are perceived as being even handed, good listeners, and balanced in their approach.

Accountable for your actions. When you make a mistake, admit it and move on. Accountability is the external manifestation of internal Integrity. Leaders without integrity are quickly dismissed as hypocrites.

Respect for others, especially those with differences in skillsets and points of view is critical. Without respect for others, trust cannot be built. Giving respect is the first step in gaining respect.

Truth is an absolutely essential component of building the type of trust that triggers innovation. Remember, your emotions or perceptions are seldom real truths. Stick to the facts—things that are measurable or concrete. And remember, a critical comment has about five times the impact as a positive comment. So balance your truths carefully.

Honorable purpose must be the foundation of all your actions. If people

perceive your purpose for innovating as strictly for selfish purposes, without
a component impacting the 'greater good,' you will not be perceived as
trustworthy.

Excellence in standards. Innovation is propelled by the idea of always getting
better, improving continually, reaching for the highest level of performance.
If anyone sloughs off, they must realign to the highest measures, otherwise
others will be resentful or fall off in their performance.

Safety & security are essential to all human beings. This includes ensuring
that there is "No such thing as Failure, Only Learning." Be careful not to
punish what might look like a failed attempt at creative solutions; encourage learning from failure. And always avoid the Blame Game. Fear does
not produce innovation. You will know when people feel safe—they will be
laughing. Creativity is not all grinding labor; it's having fun and laughing a
lot, spontaneously creating in the moment—that's magical. Research shows
that laughter releases endorphins that trigger creativity.

Transparency & openness enable everyone to see intentions, share data, and
exchange ideas in a culture that supports challenging of ideas and develops
new insights.

What's more is that the real advantage of trust is that it is the deepest yearning
of all humans; we were born with it, and it's our birthright to retain it. Many
leadership situations require influencing without authority, which can only happen when those we wish to influence trust us. Trust produces highly effective
people, high performance teams, useful ideas and innovations, and people who
want to come to work because it is a co-creative experience.

Robert Porter Lynch

*Robert Porter Lynch has spent the last twenty-five years formulating the best-practice
design architecture of organizational synergy—how exceptional leaders energize
collaboration to produce sustainable innovation in alliances. He has written several
groundbreaking books on strategic alliances, serves as Adjunct Professor at the Universities of Alberta and British Columbia, and is founding Chairman Emeritus of the
Association of Strategic Alliance Professionals. Lynch's book:* Trusted to Lead *is
scheduled for publication in 2013.*

You Can't Take 164 Years of Trust for Granted

By Deb Mills-Scofield

Menasha Packaging Corp (MPC), a 164 year old, 6th generation family business, has grown from making wooden pails in 1849 to a design-oriented packaging company that today delights customers, employees and their communities with over $1 billion in revenue. How? By leveraging their culture of entrepreneurship, collaboration, and autonomy based on trust and faith in each other.

In Menasha's history, there have been times of great trust and times of wavering trust. The early 1990s were a time of tension between many corporations and their unions. During that time, MPC, a strong believer in collaboration, started a formal team-based manufacturing program in their plants between management and plant workers, including union representatives. The output was increased innovation from the employees on the floor that improved productivity and the outcome was increased collaboration and trust. While this may be common sense to many of us today, it was not the "norm" 20+ years ago.

Fast forward about 10 years and MPC was not doing very well. As a niche player in a highly commoditized market ("Brown Box"), they didn't have the economies of scale and scope to compete with the big players. Just prior to Mike Waite (an 'out-law' as he is married to the youngest daughter of what was then the current generation) becoming president in 2003, MPC had a formal ceremony burying the old mission statement and announcing a new one. Performance was deteriorating; there was diminished trust in leadership. Employees didn't have any sense of the company's future direction, other than it was probably bad and that any commitments could be up in the air. The company was put up for sale.

Early in Mike's new role, he gave air cover to an experiment by two leaders on an entirely new business model. It was at this time Mike engaged my services to develop a new, 'bet your career' strategic plan. The leadership team believed culture was key to success; turning the company around meant they wouldn't be sold; not being sold and being successful would restore trust and faith, renew autonomy and entrepreneurship resulting in more success, which would further strengthen the culture—a virtuous cycle. The strategy focused on People, Products and Processes with aggressive top and bottom line goals emphasizing the non-traditional new business model. The "AND/BOTH" (not "Either/Or") strategy allowed MPC to achieve customer AND employee-advantage with increased customer value AND decreased costs (not price).

Because employees' skepticism about leadership remained high, they were included in the creation of the plan. A rigorous strategic communication program was created, including a letter from the leadership team to all employees. It included leadership's commitment to the plan and MPC's core values and gave employees the right to hold the leadership team accountable without repercussions. Mike visited all the plants to share the commitment letter and explain why and how employees were critical to success. HR aligned everyone's goals from Mike down to the plant floor. This helped employees understand their part in the plan—how they contributed and could have impact. It provided transparency of the Why, What, How and interdependencies between all roles and responsibilities. It confirmed commitment to the plan.

The best demonstration of commitment is always through action. Mike made himself vulnerable, key to gaining trust, by openly saying, "I don't know" when he didn't and asking employees for their input and ideas on how to discover the answer. He invested time and money in employee training and education. He invested in equipment to make money not just cut costs. Even now, employees who feel they need new equipment or capabilities create and present their own business case, including the ROI, to their management. If the case is compelling, it gets funded. Mike's willingness to spend money to make money has increased employees' passion to try new things.

New communication and recognition/rewards programs were put in place, and still remain. Frequent transparent communications, including recognitions, awards, customer testimonials, product awards etc., still stress leadership's stead-fast commitment. Even achievements of employee's families' are recognized, in-cluding scholarships from the Menasha Corporation Foundation. Profit sharing plans were changed to give a more meaningful (higher) amount to employees. And, Mike still hand writes notes to employees for special occasions and events, which to many means more than money.

The results? Within 18 months of the plan's creation, almost every employee knew the strategic plan and why he or she mattered. Once employees realized the leadership team was committed, more self-organizing teams arose, employee retention increased, key customer wins increased, costs decreased, and profits increased. Employees saw that the direction was really working both in terms of the leadership's continued communication and commitment and most definitely in the results.

A powerful example of trust is MPC's self-organized teams (SOT), a component of the strategic plan. These SOTs developed and expanded more broadly than expected. Part of the reason for this may lie in the investment of time and money in Lean training. The focus on Lean, not Six-Sigma, put power in the hands of the people doing the actual work and accelerated the innovative culture. As Lean thinking started to permeate MPC, innovative thinking was a no-brainer—part of the continuum of looking at things differently and focusing on effectiveness instead of just efficiency.

Some of these SOTs have worked with MPC's customers on new products and ser-vices that significantly increased customer success. In fact, MPC has brought entirely new products, capabilities and opportunities to the marketplace. One of my favorite examples originated with a major account manager in one location who knew MPC could be doing much more for their customers. He asked 20 non-management em-ployees, from production, print, design, customer service and sales to come together to create something that would increase value to the customer **and** either decrease or at least keep MPC's cost the same. Everyone came. They didn't check with their management, but they did check with peers to align schedules. The result of this first, now ongoing, team meeting was a highly successful product. The team used various designs, finishes, and 3D animation to develop the idea and then allocated resources for prototyping and testing with customers. Management only became involved once the results of prototyping were successful and a new piece of equipment was required. The team created the business case, management signed off and this 'process' is now a template in MPC.

The success of these self-organized teams spread to other areas within MPC—such as production, procurement, operations, quality, customer service, finance, IT, HR, etc. For instance, the strategic plan identified the need for better project management. Mike asked a few employees to figure it out and come back with a solution. These people, from different plants, were not 'freed up' to do this—although it was part of their 'day job'. They were not relieved of any work. It didn't matter; the team's passion for solving the project management challenge was strong. They created a discovery process and used a 'divide and conquer' method instead of appointing a leader. They looked at what had worked in other areas of MPC, focusing on Bright Spots (Positive Deviance). They created and presented a detailed solution to the leadership team, including specific people to staff new, reallocated positions and technical tools. The result? It's been a huge success, providing people with internal growth opportunities and significant value to customers. Clearly, SOTs require and reinforce trust, both within and among the teams and with management, who worked hard to remove obstacles and get out of their employee's way.

The MPC culture extends to the communities in which it lives. Mike views himself as a steward of the company and its communities not just because he's part of the family, but also because he grew up in the community. MPC's success directly affects the quality of schools, healthcare and sports teams. Employees see each other outside MPC's walls in the grocery stores, on the football and soccer fields, at school concerts, and at the gas station. This raises the level of accountability, according to Mike and his leadership team. MPC employees are active on school boards, in food pantries, soup kitchens and local shelters. One plant's motto is "Never Walk by a Free Sample." Employees collect sample-sized health and beauty supplies from hotels, salons and doctors' offices to donate to local shelters. Employees, and MPC at the corporate level, support various fund raising groups related to diseases affecting MPC families, and packages are always being sent to our troops.

One of my favorite examples of a community-based SOT is from the Muscatine, Iowa plant. Muscatine has an annual Great River Days cardboard boat race. Last year, a team from the local plant took time during lunch and after work to design and test prototypes, settling on a 30' long and 11' tall Pirate Ship and a canoe-like boat. They even used their Lean training to design and build the boats! The team commented that this took them way out of their comfort zone. And, on it's maiden (and only) voyage, it carried 4 employees for 10 minutes without leaking!

The benefits of trust are evident within MPC—both tangibly and intangibly. The tangible results are continual, consistent increases since 2005 in market share, revenues, profits and ROI, even during the recession. Sales and profits continue to increase significantly as a result of capitalizing on earlier investments, facility alignments and two acquisitions. Even MPC's Retail and CPG market sales increased in the down market. All years, including the 'recession years', ended with a strong cash position and exceptional current receivables. While the bigger integrated firms had dismissed MPC in the past, they became a formidable competitor. Instead of just taking market share, they created new share with new solutions in new markets, what some call "Blue Ocean." Many customers view MPC as a vital part of the merchandising process. Key retailers require CPGs to use MPC's products and services in their stores and CPGs can measure how MPC's products help both their top and bottom lines.

The intangibles are more powerful. When you walk through MPC's plants, you can feel the energy; employees on the floor smile and say "hi," people are laughing and working together and feel free to ask for help. Employees do not fear new ideas or failure. Innovation pipelines are visible. MPC continues to invest in training, education and equipment so their employees can try new ways to work, easier ways to make "stuff" and new ways to put things together. The attrition rate is low and MPC attracts talent around the country to work at this "cool" company in the Fox Valley of Wisconsin. The board has more confidence in the leadership team, which results in a willingness to invest and take risk. The legacy and story of MPC, a private family-held business, is strong with the emphasis on doing things better and making things better—things that affect customers as well as the communities where their employees live.

When you ask Mike what his goal is, he says, "I want to make sure our people get to live their dreams at home." It's that simple, and it works.

Deb Mills-Scofield

Deb Mills-Scofield helps companies create and implement highly actionable, adaptable, measurable, and profitable living innovative strategic plans. She is also a Partner at Glengary LLC, a nearly-stage Venture Capital firm in Cleveland. Deb is a co-creator of Alex Osterwalder's book, Business Model Generation *as well as contributor to several other books and is currently working on her own. She blogs at* Harvard Business Review, *her own site, and is recognized as one of the top 40 bloggers on innovation. Deb graduated from Brown University in three years, helping create the Cognitive Science concentration and went to AT&T Bell Labs where she received one of AT&T/Lucent's top revenue generating patents. She is active at Brown University, mentoring and advising in several formal and ad hoc programs and guest lecturing. Deb is a Visiting Scholar in Brown's joint E-MBA program with IE in Spain and on the Advisory Counsel for Brown's School of Engineering. As part of her "all business is social" philosophy, she asks her clients to match and donate 10% of her fee to improve lives in their community.*

Section III:

Trustworthy Leadership

The ABCDs of Leading with Trust

By Randy Conley

Trust or Consequences

The world is in desperate need of a new kind of leadership. The type of leadership we've seen during the last several decades has produced record low levels of trust and engagement in the workforce. Clearly what we've been doing isn't working. We need a leadership philosophy grounded in the knowledge and belief that the most successful leaders and organizations are those that place an emphasis on leading with trust.

There is an epidemic of workers who are uninterested in their work, disengaged from their jobs, and distrustful of the leaders and organizations for whom they work. According to a recent survey from Deloitte, only 20% of people say they are truly passionate about their work, and Gallup surveys show the vast majority of workers are disengaged, with an estimated 23 million "actively disengaged," resulting in a loss of more than $300 billion annually to the U.S. economy (Deloitte, 2010).

The statistics on trust in leaders and organizations is just as bleak. According to the "Trust Matters: New Links to Employee Retention and Well-Being" report, 50% of employees who distrust their senior leaders are seriously considering leaving their organization, compared to only 14% of those who DO trust their leaders (Kenexa High Performance Institute Worktrends Report, 2011). Deloitte's 2010 Ethics and Workplace Survey reports that 48% of employed Americans who plan to look for a new job as the economy improves are doing so because of a lack of trust in their employer and a lack of transparent communication from senior leadership (46%) (Deloitte, 2010).

Distrust in the workplace has negative health and well-being implications for employees as well. Employees who distrust their leaders are seven times more likely to report they are mentally and physically unwell, according to the Trust Matters report. And 62% percent of employees who lack trust in their leaders report unreasonable levels of stress compared to just 13% of those who do trust their leaders.

Trust Improves the Bottom Line

Progressive organizations are increasingly taking intentional steps to build high-trust cultures because it helps improve the bottom line. A Vice President at one of North America's laigest home improvement retailers shared his experience of seeing how trust directly impacts the performance of their stores. During his 22-year career, he observed, and company engagement surveys have confirmed his observations, that when a high level of trust and engagement exists in teams or stores, people costs around accidents, turnover, inventory shrink, and sick hours are less, and customer satisfaction, sales, and profits are higher. Conversely, in stores or teams that have a lack of trust, the engagement, revenue, and profit results are lower and the people costs are up.

That corporate leader's experience is mirrored in several studies and reports that show the benefits of trust in the workplace. Research by the Great Places to Work Institute, publisher of the Fortune 100 Best Companies to Work For list, has shown that between 1997 and 2011, high trust companies outperformed the Russell 3000 and S&P 500, posting annualized returns of 10.32% versus 4.02% and 3.71%, respectively. Additionally, those best companies provide 4 times the returns than market average for comparative low-trust companies and typically experience a 50% lower turnover rate.

A Common Language of Trust

A critical step for leaders and organizations to take to realize the benefits of high levels of trust is to establish a common definition and framework of how to build trust. Most people think trust "just happens" in relationships. That's a misconception. Trust is built through the intentional use of specific behaviors that, when repeated over time, create the condition of trust. Oddly enough, most leaders don't think about trust until it's broken. No one likes to think of him or herself as untrustworthy so we take it for granted that other people trust us. To further complicate matters, trust is based on *perceptions,* so each of us has a different idea of what trust looks like. Organizations need a common framework and language that defines trust and allows people to discuss trust-related issues.

Research has shown that trust is comprised of four basic elements. To represent those four elements, or the "language" of trust, The Ken Blanchard Companies® created the ABCD Trust Model—Able, Believable, Connected, and Dependable. For leaders to be successful in developing high-trust relationships and cultures, they need to focus on using behaviors that align with the ABCDs of trust.

Leaders build trust when they are:

Able—Being *Able* is about *demonstrating competence.* One-way leaders demonstrate their competence is by having the expertise needed to do their jobs. Expertise comes from possessing the right skills, education, or credentials that establish credibility with others. Leaders also demonstrate their competence through achieving results. Consistently meeting goals and having a track record of success builds trust with others and inspires confidence in the leader's ability. Able leaders are also skilled at facilitating work getting done in the organization. They develop credible project plans, systems, and processes that help team members accomplish their goals.

Believable—A *Believable* leader *acts with integrity.* Dealing with people in an honest fashion by keeping promises, not lying or stretching the truth, and not gossiping are ways to demonstrate integrity. Believable leaders also have a clear set of values that have been articulated to their direct reports and they behave consistently with those values—they walk the talk. Finally, treating people fairly and equitably are key components to being a believable leader. Being fair doesn't necessarily mean treating people the same in all circumstances, but it does mean that people are treated appropriately and justly based on their own unique situation.

Connected—*Connected* leaders show *care and concern* for people, which builds trust and helps to create an engaging work environment. Research by The Ken Blanchard Companies® has identified "connectedness with leader" and "connectedness with colleague" as 2 of the 12 key factors involved in creating employee work passion, and trust is a necessary ingredient in those relationships. Leaders create a sense of connectedness by openly sharing information about themselves and the organization and trusting employees to use that information responsibly. Leaders also build trust by having a "people first" mentality and building rapport with those they lead. Taking an interest in people as individuals and not just as nameless workers shows that leaders value and respect their team members. Recognition is a vital component of being a connected leader, and praising and rewarding the contributions of people and their work builds trust and goodwill.

Dependable—Being *Dependable* and *maintaining reliability* is the fourth element of trust. One of the quickest ways to erode trust is by not following through on commitments. Conversely, leaders who do what they say they're going to do earn a reputation as being consistent and trustworthy. Maintaining reliability requires leaders to be organized in such a way that they are able to follow through on commitments, be on time for appointments and meetings, and get back to people in a timely fashion. Dependable leaders also hold themselves and others accountable for following through on commitments and taking responsibility for the outcomes of their work.

By using the ABCD Trust Model, leaders can focus on the behaviors that build trust, and by sharing this model with those they lead, create a common framework and language for discussing issues of trust in the workplace.

Rebuilding Damaged Trust

Despite their best intentions, there will be times when leaders break trust with those they lead. A 2010 Maritz Research survey reported that only 11% of respondents strongly agreed that their managers showed consistency between their words and actions. Although trust can take a long time to build and just a moment to destroy, there is hope for recovery if the parties involved are willing to put in the time and effort necessary to restore a healthy level of trust to the relationship. Leaders can follow this five-step process to rebuild broken trust:

1. **Acknowledge**—As we've learned from the success of the 12-step recovery programs, the first thing that has to be done is acknowledge that a problem exists. Depending on its severity, a breach of trust can have difficult and emotional consequences that many leaders would rather avoid. Yet to begin the rebuilding process, leaders must acknowledge that the situation exists and needs to be addressed.

2. **Admit**—The second step is that leaders have to admit their part in causing the breach of trust. They need to take responsibility for their actions and for whatever harm was caused. This is a crucial step in the process that leaders shouldn't overlook. Refusing to admit mistakes reflects negatively on the "believability" of a leader and can let a mistake in judgment turn into an indictment of character.

3. **Apologize**—The next step in repairing damaged trust is for leaders to apologize for their role in the situation. A good apology incorporates steps one and two (acknowledging the mistake and admitting your involvement) and also expresses regret for the harm caused and assurances that the offense won't be repeated. The apology also needs to be motivated by sincerity and remorse, not contrived or forced. Finally, avoid making excuses, shifting blame, or using qualifying statements that detract from the apology.

4. **Assess**—The fourth step is to assess which element(s) of the ABCD Trust Model were violated and create an action plan to improve in those areas. In their assessment, it's important for leaders to narrow down the specific behaviors that caused the breach of trust. Repairing a breach of trust can seem like a daunting task, yet if leaders identify the specific behaviors that were at the root of the issue, they can create a manageable and realistic plan to move forward.

5. **Agree**—The final step in the rebuilding process is for the leader and the offended party to agree on what is going to be done differently moving forward to help rebuild trust. This step is an ongoing process of evaluating the consistency of the leader's behavior and its alignment with the agreed-upon action plan.

Leading with Trust

Trust is a precious, highly valuable commodity and should be treated as such. All successful relationships are based on a foundation of trust, and when high levels of trust are present, productivity, efficiency, innovation, and profitability flourish. When trust is absent, people avoid risk, decisions are questioned, bureaucracy increases, and productivity and profitability diminish.

Leading with trust is the defining leadership competency of the 21st century. Learning and practicing the ABCDs of trust will allow leaders to build and maintain high levels of trust with all stakeholders and unleash the power and potential of their organizations.

Randy Conley

Randy is the Trust Practice Leader for The Ken Blanchard Companies®. He works with clients around the globe helping them design and deliver training and consulting solutions that build trust in the workplace. He has been named a Top 100 Thought Leader in Trustworthy Business Behavior by Trust Across America. Randy holds a Masters Degree in Executive Leadership from the University of San Diego and enjoys spending time with his family, bike riding, and playing golf. You can follow Randy on Twitter @RandyConley where he shares thoughts on leadership and trust

References

Deloitte. (2010). 2010 Ethics & Workplace Survey.

Great Place to Work. (2013, January 30). *What are the benefits?* Retrieved January 30, 2013, from Great Place to Work: http://www.greatplacetowork.com/our-approach/what-are-the-benefits-great-workplaces

Kenexa High Performance Institute Worktrends Report. (2011). *Trust Matters: New Links to Employee Retention and Well-Being.*

Maritz Research. (2013, January 30). *Maritz Poll: Managing in an Era of Mistrust: Maritz Poll Reveals Employees Lack Trust in their Workplace.* Retrieved January 30, 2013, from Maritz: http://www.maritz.com/Maritz-Poll/2010/Maritz-Poll-Reveals-Employees-Lack-Trust-in-their-Workplace.aspx

Zigarmi, D., Houson, D., Witt, D., & Diehl, J. (2013, January 30). *Employee Work Passion: Volume 3. Retrieved* January 30, 2013, from The Ken Blanchard Companies: http://www.kenblanchard.com/Business_Leadership/Effective_Leadership_White_Papers/Employee_Work_Passion_Volume_3/

Leading Out in Extending Trust

By Stephen M.R. Covey and Greg Link

> *Trust men and they will be true to you;*
> *treat them greatly, and they will show themselves great.*
>
> — *Ralph Waldo Emerson*

In our work, we often ask leaders and executives around the world to reflect on their lives or careers and to identify a time when someone took a chance on them, extended trust to them, or maybe believed in them even more than they believed in themselves. Whenever we do this, without exception, the feeling in the room changes. People become deeply touched and inspired as they recall their experiences and acknowledge with gratitude the impact those experiences have had on their lives. And they become even more inspired when we invite them to share and they take in each other's experiences.

We encourage you to take a minute now and do the same thing. Think of someone who extended trust to you. Who was it? What was the situation? What difference has it made in your life?

Leaders in all walks of life lead out in extending trust to others. In doing so, they build the capacity and confidence of those who are trusted. They unleash human potential and multiply performance. They inspire reciprocal trust in both directions—back to those who extended it and forward to others who could benefit from it.

Leaders Go First

In order to increase influence and grow trust in a team, an organization, a community, a family, or a relationship, someone has to take the first step. That's what leaders do. They go first. They lead out in extending trust. In fact, the first job of a leader is to inspire trust, and the second is to extend it. This is true in a formal leadership role, such as CEO, manager, team leader, or parent, or in an informal role of influence, such as work associate, marriage partner, or friend.

In the exercise we described earlier, after asking leaders to reflect on their experience when someone extended trust to them, we then ask, "When have you led out in extending trust to someone else?" This often brings people up short as they realize that they have missed opportunities—sometimes many opportunities—to extend trust and initiate an upward cycle of trust. You might want to think about your own experience. Have there been times you extended trust to others and really made a difference in their lives? Have there been times you didn't but now perhaps wish you had?

Bottom line, if you're not extending trust, you're not leading. You might be managing or administering, but you're not *leading*. "You manage things; you lead people." And real leadership requires trust. As renowned leadership authority Warren Bennis put it, "Leadership without mutual trust is a contradiction in terms."

When managers don't extend trust, people often tend to perpetuate vicious, collusive downward cycles of distrust and suspicion. As a result, they become trapped in a world where people don't trust each other— where management doesn't trust employees and employees don't trust management; where suppliers don't trust partners and partners don't trust suppliers; where companies don't trust customers and customers don't trust companies; where marriage partners don't trust each other; and where parents don't trust their children and children don't trust their parents.

But when managers take the lead in extending trust—in a relationship, on a team, in an organization, or in a community—negative, collusive cycles of distrust and suspicion can be broken, and a game-changing shift in possibilities can occur.

Of course there is risk in extending trust. That's why it takes courage. But there is also risk in *not* extending trust. In fact, there is often *greater* risk in not trusting. As a society, we have become very good at measuring the risks and costs of extending too much trust, but we're not good at all at measuring the risks and costs of not trusting enough.

So how do we navigate through the decision-making process and determine whether or not to extend trust, and—if so—how much and under what conditions?

There are two factors you will find most helpful in deciding to extend trust wisely: 1) your *propensity to trust* and 2) your *analysis* of the situation, the risk, and the credibility of the people involved. It's the combination of the two that creates good judgment. Creating the highest synergy between these two factors is more of an art than a science. It takes assuming positive intent in others—unless there's good reason to do otherwise. It takes determining when verification will enable trust—or when it will get in the way. It takes discernment and sometimes the willingness to take a leap of trust, possibly even when "logic" may direct otherwise.

Clearly, deciding to extend trust does not result in a simplistic, "one-size-fits-all" solution for every person or every situation. What's smart for one person may not be smart for another. What's smart in one situation may not be smart in another. Still, successful leaders and organizations have a definitive propensity to trust and lead out in extending trust to others.

For example, Zane's Cycles is one of the largest bike shops in the United States. Zane's allows customers to go out the door for test drives on their bikes without asking for any identification or collateral. When customers offer to leave their driver's licenses, they are politely refused. The message Zane's communicates to its customers is: "Just have a great ride. We trust you." As its founder, Chris Zane, put it, "Why start out that relationship by questioning their integrity? We choose to believe our customers." The company's high-trust message also communicates clearly to its employees that Zane's is in the business of building customer relationships, not merely selling products. The result is $13 million in annual sales, with a 23 percent average annual growth rate since opening in 1981, and a loss to theft of only five of the 5,000 bikes sold each year.

When leaders lead out in wisely extending trust, their actions have a ripple effect that cascades throughout the team, organization, community, or family and begins to transform behavior in the entire culture. Sometimes the acts of leaders extending trust become legendary. For example, when CEO Gordon Bethune burned the Continental Airlines policy and procedure manuals in the parking lot and told his employees they would be trusted to use their own judgment, that act became the symbol of Continental's new culture of trust.

One reason some managers don't extend trust is fear of losing control. They think they will have greater control in a culture that depends on rules, policies, and regulations to cover every contingency. In actuality, the relationship between trust and control is inverse: the greater the level of trust, the greater the level of control. The French sociologist Émile Durkheim put it this way: "When mores [cultural values] are sufficient, laws are unnecessary; when mores are insufficient, laws are unenforceable." In a low-trust culture, it's literally impossible to put enough rules and regulations in place to control people's every action. In a low-trust relationship, the legal agreement can't be long enough to cover every possibility. We submit that the best way to increase control is to create a high-trust culture. And for a high-trust culture to exist, managers must lead out by extending trust to others.

Leading out and extending trust creates a culture of immense momentum, possibility, and power. The increased freedom of expression, the autonomy, the enhanced trust, and the greater speed at which things can be accomplished make an enormous, tangible, measurable difference in performance. This is one reason extending trust is smart. It's not built on the assumption that what we need is more rules, more regulations, and more referees; it's built on the evidence that extending trust and creating a high-trust culture (in which top performance is expected) bring significantly greater dividends for stakeholders on every level.

For us, a poster child for leading out in extending trust is Warren Buffett of Berkshire Hathaway. The most remarkable thing about Buffett's approach is that his headquarters staff managing Berkshire's 77 separate operating companies and more than 257,000 employees is a mere 21 people—unheard of by any measure. Stanford Business School's David F. Larcker and Brian Tayan call it "the lowest ratio of corporate overhead to investor capital among all major corporations" in the world.

When we asked Grady Rosier, the CEO who runs McLane, a $33 billion Berkshire Hathaway business, how Buffett is able to create trust so quickly, he replied, "You have to understand the core business philosophy at Berkshire Hathaway—

the trust. Warren's ability to acquire quality companies is built around the trust. Warren leaves them in charge of their businesses, and they're happy about that, and nobody wants to let Warren down. And that's the way it just cascades down the organization as to 'this is what the expectation is and this is what we're going to do.'"

How does Buffett handle a span of control that includes more than 77 direct reports? He operates on the premise of what he and his business partner Charlie Munger call "deserved trust"—they assume that their people deserve trust unless they prove otherwise. It's not blind trust. It's Smart Trust. It includes a discerning selection of people, clear expectations, and high standards of accountability. People respond to it, they thrive on it; they're inspired by it. Munger captures this beautifully:

> *Everybody likes being appreciated and treated fairly, and dominant personalities who are capable of running a business like being trusted. That's how we operate Berkshire—a seamless web of deserved trust. We get rid of the craziness, of people checking to make sure it's done right. When you get a seamless web of deserved trust, you get enormous efficiencies. Berkshire Hathaway is always trying to create a seamless web of deserved trust. Every once in a while, it doesn't work, not because someone's evil but because somebody drifts to inappropriate behavior and then rationalizes it ... How can Berkshire Hathaway work with only [21] people at headquarters? Nobody can operate this way. But we do ... It's what we all want. Who in the hell would not want to be in a family without a seamless web of deserved trust? We try for the same thing in business. It's not rocket science; it's elementary. Why more people don't do it, I don't know. Perhaps because it's elementary.*

One person's or one company's act of extending trust often inspires those on the receiving end to reach out and extend trust to others. Often those experiences become part of a "genealogy of trust." Somewhere along the line, a parent, teacher, manager, or leader extended trust to that first individual and inspired him or her with a desire to make a similar difference in the life of someone else. Over time, each act of extending trust becomes part of a legacy of trust that increases prosperity, energy, and joy in families, relationships, organizations, communities, and even countries ... for generations.

The question to ask ourselves is this: "What kind of legacy am I passing down to future generations—to my family, my personal associates, my community, my organization, my nation? Is it a legacy of trust that will create increasing prosperity, energy, and joy?" This is what creating a "renaissance of trust" is all about. It's about the snowballing effect of extending trust one act, one person, one team, and one organization at a time.

Where might you begin to enhance your legacy of trust? Is there a business colleague for whom, or a situation in which extending trust might change a vicious downward cycle into a virtuous upward cycle? Is there an opportunity for you to lead out in extending trust in your team or organization?

Wherever you start, your decision to lead out by extending trust to others will be a game-changer. You may not see results immediately. And you will certainly never see the full impact as those you trust, in turn, reach out and extend trust to others . . . who then extend trust to others…and so on, over time. But you will have the deep satisfaction of knowing that you are investing in something magnificently bigger than yourself—something that can truly affect every relationship in every team, every organization, every family, and every community throughout the world.

Stephen M. R. Covey and Greg Link

Stephen M. R. Covey and Greg Link are cofounders of FranklinCovey's Global Speed of Trust Practice, which teaches trust in more than 100 countries worldwide. Stephen is the New York Times *and #1* Wall Street Journal *bestselling author of* The Speed of Trust: The One Thing That Changes Everything. *Stephen and Greg are coauthors of the bestseller* Smart Trust: Creating, Prosperity, Energy, and Joy in a Low-Trust World. *They are sought-after speakers and advisors on trust, ethics, leadership, and high performance and have worked with business, government, and educational entities throughout the world.*

Leading *from* the Heart: Build Your Business by Attaining Trust

By Lolly Daskal

Thought leaders sometimes talk about TRUST as an essential component to any successful company. It goes way beyond that. Trust is the heart and soul of an organization.

Lasting success in business, like life, is dependent on forging meaningful relationships. The most important element of an effective relationship is not leadership, standards or ideas. It's trust.

Trust is the foundation of any successful and secure relationship. We can't develop relationships or have worthwhile interactions, transactions or communications if trust does not exist. Trust is not something you're born with. It's something you develop, a core quality you have to keep practicing.

For business leaders, that means letting go of their assumptions and engaging with colleagues and customers with an open heart, an open will and an open mind.

Let me illustrate this with an example from my career as a leadership coach and consultant. A year ago I was invited to consult with a prominent business experiencing significant organizational challenges. The president of the company admitted, "My organization doesn't trust me and I have no connection with my employees." I asked him if he trusted his colleagues. He replied he didn't. "How do you expect your employees to trust you," I asked, "if you're perceived as not trusting them? They're picking up on that and they will remain distant from you."

Employees didn't trust him because he didn't trust them, nor was he willing to change. He expected the change to come from his employees. I told him we shouldn't do business together, as his mindset didn't resonate with me. A week later I received a call. He had re-thought his attitude and said, "I'm all yours. What would it take for me to gain trust in this organization?" He committed to communicating more, connecting more and more openly demonstrating his capabilities. He recognized that trust is the principal element of leadership and that it is contingent upon how the leader acts. Employees expressed increased job satisfaction and loyalty to the corporation, as seen through an internal company feedback survey, and as a result of being able to trust him.

Trust tends to only become an issue in business during the aftermath of a corporate catastrophe or a scandal. Business has acquired a reputation for having little use for trust. 'Watch your back' and 'Look out for number one' are commonplace strategies amidst the corporate greed and wrongdoing. Some see trust as an antiquated concept, belonging to a simpler time when a handshake was as good as a contract. In today's global 'Get it in writing' world, trust seems at odds with Darwinian hard-edged deal making.

In fact, trust is not merely a "soft skill" or a social nicety. Research shows building trust is as important to successful and sustainable organizations as customer service or teamwork. A study by Watson Wyatt found that the rate of return to shareholders was almost three times higher at companies with high levels of trust than at those with low levels.

As the business leader in the example cited earlier discovered, trust in senior executives' leadership capabilities sets the tone for the entire organization. Untrustworthiness might ensure a CEO's short-term survival but, in an age where anyone can electronically communicate perceptions to a worldwide audience, behavioral disconnect will be exposed in the long-term. Customers listen to more than words. When workers are unhappy and uncomfortable, they say things about their company they don't even realize they're saying. By contrast, if employees know their leader is capable and dependable, they delight in discussing his values and virtues.

Failing to build trust can have devastating effects on the character of a corporation. Large organizations save millions of dollars by cultivating a climate of trust. Without trust, morale suffers as disengaged workers question decisions and focus their energies on political turf wars, squandering their productive and creative potential. Production costs increase through high turnover, missed opportunities and an inefficient and inexperienced workforce. Legal and HR issues drain resources from mission-focused work and financial losses arising from a loss of trust may even jeopardize an organization's future.

Building trustworthy organizations means building trustworthy leadership. How do senior executives achieve this?

Through leading from the heart. Only then can leaders create the foundation for securing meaningful relationships powered by trust. The elements of trustworthiness are found in the Four C's: Competence, Connection, Credibility and Consistency.

Competence:

In any endeavor, trust is earned when you show you know what you're doing. An insecure leader may attempt to prove his or her competence through bragging and bluster or trumpeting personal credentials. However, true competence is expressed quietly. It lies in demonstrating knowledge and the inner confidence and assurance the leader brings to problems and complex situations.

Competence is developed through experience and requires work. Time must consistently be spent maintaining a knowledge base and learning about new and emerging ideas. Possess the security to know you do not have all the answers all of the time, and be willing to defer to employees with extensive experience or skills in a particular area. Competence extends to the attitude you exude. Build trust by personifying a model for the workplace behavior that fosters productivity through punctuality and accountability. Reward the effort employees put into their own development. Keep hiring and promoting based on ability, achievement, growth and commitment.

Connection:

Connection is at the heart of trust. When you are connected, you care about others and you communicate with them. It goes beyond just knowing the names of your employees. Deep connections mean giving them a chance to speak and respectfully listening to their thoughts. You help them build confidence by encouraging them and giving them the room to solve problems for themselves. Reward risk-taking even when it doesn't work out.

Connected leaders understand the value of communicating—not merely day-to-day information or expectations, but also their long-term vision and plans. Connected leaders are publicly and privately generous with recognition and give credit to their employees while challenging them to new levels of attainment. They are understanding in their response to problems and slow to place blame. They maintain confidentiality and don't play favorites; when a conflict or problem occurs, they deal with it fairly. Leaders whose trust is based on connection among employees at every level of their organization, create the strongest kind of teams—those whose members naturally understand and support each other.

Credibility:

Credibility is built on a foundation of integrity. It is an expression of the values you hold for yourself and your organization. It's impossible to fake. We're always hearing news stories about a prominent person whose private behavior was deeply at odds with his or her publicly professed values. Leaders with genuine credibility don't need to spend much time expounding their values, because their actions do this for them. They are honest about their own limitations and setbacks. They view their failures as opportunities for learning.

Credible leaders hold themselves and everyone within their organization to the highest standard of ethical behavior. Standards are clear and unchanging. No cutting corners, no minor cover-ups, no fudging numbers. Mistakes are handled not with punishment, shaming, or by placing blame, but rather by confronting the consequences of the error and making it right through implementing the systemic changes required to prevent it from happening again. Above all, credible leaders build trust by honoring their commitments, especially those they make to their employees and the people they serve. To borrow an old-fashioned phrase, they are as good as their word.

Consistency:

Consistency- the final attribute of trust-building- fuses the disparate elements of the three C's discussed above. It requires the same hard work as competence, the same commitment to others as connection, and the same self-awareness as credibility. Consistency brings these traits together, adding ownership and accountability.

Consistent leaders are constantly evaluating themselves, measuring their accomplishments against their goals, their words against their actions and their capacity against the needs of the day. They have the gift, in the words of Robert Burns, "to see ourselves as others see us." Leaders build consistency among their employees by inspiring a culture of accountability, ownership and openness through their actions and by expecting others to do the same.

Competence, connection, credibility, and consistency are contingent upon each other. The four C's are interconnected and their existence at an organization creates a virtuous cycle that creates trust. None of these four elements of trust—competence, connection, credibility, and consistency—can be developed by hiring a consultant, running through a checklist, delegating, or through insincere effort. Building trust requires a willingness to see how those choices not only affect us personally and those around us, but extend to our entire business.

Trust is a risk we willingly take to move away from emptiness and fear in order to lead from the heart. Leading from the heart is about going inward and allowing our best parts to emerge. It's also about reaching outward to the best parts of others. It's about internalizing your values so strongly that they govern everything you do.

When we lead from the heart, we build trust as the foundation of every relationship—with our employees and colleagues, with our family and friends and with the people we do business with. **Without trust we will never be able to capitalize on the uniqueness and diversity of people through inclusion, particularly in this global environment.** True inclusion requires an agile leadership style and a willingness to adapt behavior which can occur only from an authentic, deeply embedded mindset of trusting through open mind, open heart and open will.

Trust is a form of giving and it can be established and grown only from our best selves. Building trust begins with our values, with the way we create relationships with others. It begins, in short, when we lead from the heart.

Lolly Daskal

Lolly Daskal is a leadership coach, consultant and writer dedicated to helping cultivate the right values, vision and culture for individuals and organizations. She is the founder of Lead from Within, a global consultancy whose clients range from heads of state and CEOs of large multinational companies to budding entrepreneurs. Lolly's coaching, consulting and speaking uses a heart-based leadership approach designed to help people to achieve their full potential to make a difference in the world. The Huffington Post called Lolly, "One of the Most Inspiring Women in the World." You can visit Lolly's website at www.lollydaskal.com or follow her on Twitter at @LollyDaskal. Her weekly global Lead from Within tweetchat, in which Lolly discusses emerging and important leadership topics, engages with a Twitter community of over 3.5 million people.

Leading with Trust: Learning from Mistakes

By Amy Lyman

Becoming a trustworthy leader is a lifelong journey that starts with possessing or developing the qualities of honesty, caring, persistence and consistency in relationships. These are essential qualities to have if leader/follower relationships are to be based in trust. Trustworthy leaders also possess visionary thinking and communication skills that they use to inspire people to move forward, following the leader's direction.

Leading a group of people forward is different from having people go with you because of compliance. Compliance happens when people just do their job, are uninspired by the mission, are motivated simply by the paycheck, or are so worn out by politicking that compliance becomes their best choice. Compliance is not what employees aspire to, yet what they may fall into.

People follow trustworthy leaders out of commitment. When leaders help employees to see how their own work contributes to the mission of the organization they are able to more fully commit to that work. When leaders convey their overall vision to employees, a high trust, highly committed organization can be created.

This distinction between compliance and commitment is useful for understanding how some people become great leaders while others run growing, yet uninspiring, companies. In my experience researching great leaders and the qualities that distinguish them from average leaders I've seen that the ability to inspire commitment rather than compliance is a key differentiator.

A leader's ability to connect people with a powerful mission and vision, and to embody the mission and vision in action, motivates people to commit. Actions that are based in the qualities of trustworthiness link people's commitment to the organization with their trust in the leader.

Creating Commitment

Most people are trustworthy. We trust our friends because over time we've learned that they are worthy of our trust. We're confident that the promises they've made to us will be kept. This same analogy applies to leaders we choose to follow. We look for evidence over time that we can trust and commit to following them.

In the workplace, one method for determining the trustworthiness of a leader can be found in her approach to learning from mistakes. The best way to learn from mistakes is by acknowledging the mistake, examining what happened, evaluating options, and then trying again. When this occurs a follower can see the leader's learning process, and can also see if that same learning process is supported for others. If employees make mistakes are they also encouraged to acknowledge, examine, evaluate and try again?

An organization in which learning from mistakes in a constructive way is the norm, will be an organization where people openly share ideas and listen to critiques for the betterment of the whole. A leader who shares stories with employees, colleagues and other leaders about how he has learned from his mistakes as well as the mistakes of others, will, through his honest dialogue, begin creating relationships based on commitment rather than compliance.

These sorts of stories provide a mechanism for assessing the consistency of a leader's actions and words. Do the stories—that talk about constructive learning from honest mistakes—match the actions that occur within the organization? If so this can heighten an employee's personal commitment to the organization as a place where one's own growth and development is of interest to leaders. It will also encourage employees to persist in their efforts to be successful.

Learning at the Best

In my own research on what makes for trustworthy leaders I often hear leaders at Best Companies to Work For speak of their debt to mentors or former colleagues who helped them learn from mistakes by reviewing situations in which things hadn't gone well. The best teachers of this 'review' learning were people who recognized their own mistakes, analyzed what happened, considered alternatives to avoid the same dilemma again, and then told the story. Telling the story was key, as this helped the mentor learn from the event each time she told the story, and helped the young leader-to-be to learn as well.

Other teachers—of tremendous value yet where the lesson was more difficult— were people who taught about what 'not to do' rather than by providing positive examples. These teachers were described as people who moved forward in their actions paying little heed to the damage they caused. Thankfully many people who are currently great leaders learned from the experiences they had with this second group of teachers and followed their own commitment to 'do things differently' when they had the chance.

I'd like to share two stories to illustrate ways that trustworthy leaders learned from their own mistakes or the mistakes of others. These stories show how each leader used the experience to help others learn and how this has resulted in people's ability to follow—willingly and with commitment.

Scripps Health

Chris Van Gorder, CEO of Scripps Health, began his career as a police officer, yet left due to an on-the-job injury. His work in health care started with his first position as an emergency room clerk and then as a security guard (not at Scripps), working night shifts to support himself as he attended school. As he told the story to me, it was one night when he was doing his security rounds in the quiet halls of the hospital, that he had an encounter that would later significantly influence his own actions as a leader.

He happened to notice that the hospital administrator was walking down the hall toward him, perhaps returning from a meeting. Chris was thinking that this could be a significant opportunity-to meet the administrator-given the unlikely possibility that he, a night security guard, would run into him again.

He recognized the administrator by his photo, on the wall of the hospital, placed in a position of honor. "I was about as low on the totem pole as you can be in my position," Van Gorder remembered, "and here's the hospital administrator, walking down in the basement in the middle of the night. And I went, 'Wow—I am going to get a shot at meeting this guy.'

"And I will never forget what happened. He walked by me as if I didn't even exist."

As Chris told me this story, 25 years after it had happened, the emotion of that moment was palpable. Its impact on Chris' leadership philosophy was profound. As he says, "Everyone has their role and their purpose in life, and sometimes, in fact most times, the people who are out in the field doing good work are far more important than I will ever be in my position as CEO. I always try to treat people well so that they know how much I respect their hard work."

The 'mistake' that Van Gorder experienced in that moment in the hallway is unfortunately something that many people experience on a daily basis—passive lack of recognition from a leader. Why would anyone choose to follow that leader? A person may still do their job well, support colleagues, provide good service, and have a personal goal of doing a good job. Yet committing to the leader is not going to come out high on the list of results from an encounter like this.

The true cost of this type of encounter is paid when a leader asks for more from employees, wants to take on a new challenge, or tries to rally people to tackle difficult issues within the organization. Without trust—and the respect that comes with it—people will not be committed to follow the leader.

Learning from this type of an incident though is a very positive outcome. Van Gorder has done that, and many people have benefited. The lessons from this 'meeting that didn't happen' form some of the building blocks of Van Gorder's personal leadership style and are used to teach others about the importance of acknowledging people, conveying respect and being trustworthy.

EILEEN FISHER

At EILEEN FISHER (EF) learning from mistakes is taken so seriously that it is included in the Leadership Principle "Tell the Truth". People are asked to 'tell the truth' in part by being open about mistakes and recognizing that in the midst of a mistake a new solution can be found.

Leaders have placed a clear mark on this practice by directing people to learn from what they may struggle with by openly sharing their mistakes with others. People are invited to comment on each other's work with kindness, and they are also asked to comment on their own work when the mistake is personal. Everyone is included—leaders and front line employees—in the notion that mistakes happen, and all can learn from them.

Leadership principles exist in many organizations but they are not always so clearly written as those at EF. What do they do at EF to help people put the Leadership Principles into practice, teaching people to be comfortable with the idea that making mistakes is a learning experience? As often happens in organizations with trustworthy leaders, the learning and sharing start at the top.

Eileen Fisher herself tells stories about the mistakes she made early in her life as an entrepreneur, emphasizing the reality that everyone makes mistakes, and everyone can learn from what goes wrong. She sees mistakes as the greatest learning opportunity people have, connecting the idea of mistakes to one of possibilities, rather than to fear or shame. She uses her own mistakes to illustrate her point of view and to be a role model to help others learn how to share.

In the early days of the business, Eileen worked with only one fabric. One season while the spring deliveries were being shipped out, she began receiving phone calls from buyers saying the garments were bigger than the samples they'd seen, and the fabric felt different. The returns came flooding in. This problem put her in danger of losing the business, as she couldn't manage the returns financially by herself.

Friends advised her to sue yet Eileen felt a win-win option would be better. She met with the factory owner, showed him the product compared to the samples, and they worked out a deal that made it possible for Eileen to produce her next delivery. They shared the expense of the mistake so neither was left in the lurch. In addition Eileen learned that it was too risky to work in only one fabric. This discovery led her to diversify into other fabrics and her business literally exploded with growth.

Another mistake happened many years later, when the company was larger. Eileen decided to split the collection into two separate lines, EF and EF New York, creating a casual line with lower prices and an elegant line geared towards work and formal wear. It was a struggle to convince department stores to put the EF New York collection in the area of their stores that women shopped in for work clothes. Splitting the line caused department stores to split the collection and the change had a cannibalizing effect. The end customer chose to shop one or the other collection, and sales dropped.

Eileen realized that this change, though well intended, actually contradicted her original design concept. Analyzing the steps that lead to this mistake got leaders to look back to the roots of the company and build up from what was EF's strength rather than trying to fill the needs of both sectors of the stores.

Have either of these stories, and Eileen Fisher's own ability to learn from her mistakes, influenced other leaders within the organization? In 2011 when EF's Business Planning leader had two new employees starting around the same time, she held a special team meeting for them to focus on the big picture of the team and company, and to cover the company values. She began the meeting by talking about the company's approach to making mistakes, explaining that everyone is at EF to learn and that "it is important to make mistakes since that's how we learn." She shared her own stories of mistakes made, and to inject some fun into the situation, she bought huge pink erasers for each team member, on which she wrote "For Really Big Mistakes!"

The stories of mistakes made, lessons learned and the success that followed, along with the humor of the pink erasers, has deepened the process of learning from mistakes that has helped EILEEN FISHER to be so successful.

The story from Scripps Health CEO Chris Van Gorder illustrates the powerful impact that a brief encounter can have on our lives and of our ability to learn from the mistakes of others long past the time of the incident. It is also a powerful reminder to leaders that any encounter can be an opportunity to build up, or tear down, trust.

Leaders who learn from their mistakes and share their stories will develop committed rather than compliant followers. When they ask for more from people they will have a green light rather than dragging feet. Leading with trust works.

Amy Lyman

Amy Lyman is author of The Trustworthy Leader *(Jossey-Bass ©2012) and co-founder of Great Place to Work® Institute. During her tenure at the Institute she developed the company's consulting services in the United States, and oversaw the finance, legal and operational activities of the entire organization. She served as President for many years, and as Chair of the Board of Directors until 2008. She currently studies the qualities that distinguish great companies from good companies, focusing on the role of the trustworthy leader. She has written numerous articles and is a featured speaker at management workshops and conferences. Amy received her Ph.D. from the University of Pennsylvania and her B.S. from the University of California, Davis. She began her consulting work while a research fellow at the Wharton Center for Applied Research. Read more: http://www.trustworthyleader.org/eng/About.html*

Ethical Leader as Ethics Coach

By Chris MacDonald, Ph.D.

Trust is crucial for any organization. But whether organizations are trusted by key stakeholders, and whether there is trust within an organization, must depend in large part on questions of ethical leadership. Ethics is the foundation of trust. This makes ethical leadership a crucial ingredient for building trustworthy organizations.

The term "ethical leadership" has two quite different but related meanings. First, we can think of ethical leadership as having to do with the ethics *of* leadership— that is, with questions of honesty and integrity as they apply to people in leadership positions. Second, we can think of ethical leadership as being about how it is that leaders, more or less regardless of their own values and virtues, can help lead people to make ethical decisions. And while the first way of thinking about ethical leadership is clearly important, the second way is perhaps even more so.

But really, both these understandings of ethical leadership are important, because an ethical leader inevitably has a dual role. He or she must first, of course, act ethically in carrying out the duties associated with leadership. Because of the importance of the decisions typically made by leaders, making those decisions ethically is disproportionately important. But a second responsibility is the responsibility to lead others in the making of good decisions. That is, it is one of the responsibilities of ethical leadership for the leader to do what he or she can to help others with the ethical choices and challenges they face. It's worth noting that the vast majority of decisions in any organization, even a highly hierarchical one, are not in fact made at the top. Leaders set policy and make strategic decisions, but those decisions are carried out by an army of people lower down in the hierarchy who must inevitably make innumerable decisions of their own along the way to implementation. Thus the ethical leader can arguably do more good by helping others make ethical decisions than he or she can by making ethical decisions directly.

In other words, an ethical leader has a crucial role to play in acting as a sort of 'ethics coach' within the organization. It is that role that I want to explore here.

To begin to see what it might mean for a leader to act as an ethics coach, let's begin by looking at the factors that go into ethical behaviour. We can think of ethical behaviour as having three essential elements.

First, ethical behaviour requires sensitivity to the ethical dimension of our decisions. And of course, issues and decisions with an ethical dimension abound in organizational life. Any decision that affects human interests, that makes someone better or worse off, or that can either promote or impinge upon someone's rights, must be seen as a decision with an ethical component. And what decision doesn't have one of those features? But too often we are blinded to the ethical dimension of our work. In some cases, we think of our decisions as purely technical ones. In other case, we may be so focused on our missions that the ethical issues that should be obvious to us are lost in the shuffle.

Second, ethical behaviour requires that we have the insight to figure out the right thing to do, even when that is unclear. Of course, in most cases the right thing to do is pretty clear. We all know that it is generally wrong to lie, to manipulate people, to hurt people, and to take what's not ours. But life in organizations can be more complicated than that. For one thing, in the world of business we need to grapple with special questions related to the ethics of competition. It is good for consumers when businesses compete fiercely, but there must be reasonable limits on the competitive tactics that get used. Just what those limits are can be unclear. And the complexity of organizational life and relationships itself raises challenges: even those of us who were raised to be persons of integrity can find ourselves at a loss for what to do when special issues like Conflict of Interest arise.

Third, ethical behaviour means not just knowing the right thing to do, but actually doing it, as often as possible, even when competitive pressures and feelings of obligation to one's organization make doing the right thing hard. In such cases, doing the right thing means having the willpower to do it, the determination to avoid excuses, and sometimes the guts to stand up in the face of pressure from peers and superiors.

To these three fundamentals of ethics, we can add a fourth element when the person in question has a leadership role. An ethical leader needs not just to recognize, to know, and to do, but also the ability to help others to make ethical decisions, as well as a dedication to building that capacity within the organization.

So what can ethical leaders do to help others make ethical decisions? What form does ethical coaching take? Answering this requires looking back at the three essential elements of ethics discussed above.

First, consider ethical sensitivity. An ethical leader can contribute, here, not just by leading by example, although that is certainly important. The ethical leader also needs to act as coach by actively reminding others of the ethical dimension of the work they do. The ethical leader needs to be the one who is willing to put ethics on the table, rather than to sweep it under the rug.

Next, let's look at knowing what to do. Here, the ethical leader as ethics coach has many roles to play. Providing structured ethics training may be one part of the puzzle. So might engaging employees in writing or revising the organization's code of ethics. But another element is making oneself available to talk not just about organizational objectives—sales targets and deadlines and so on—but about the moral complexity of the work you do. And in this capacity, the ethics coach must be committed to the idea that there is no such thing as a silly question. In addition, the ethics coach must approach the task with humility. Being an ethics coach doesn't mean being an ethics expert, or continually telling other people what to do in an authoritarian way. It means a willingness to engage in dialogue. An ethics coach should not make decision for others, but instead help them to make their own decisions, and to learn to make better decisions over time.

Finally, what how can the ethics coach help others to actually *do* the right thing? The most crucial element, it seems to me, is for the ethical leader, in the role of ethics coach, to be willing to help others past the obvious hurdles. In conversation, the ethics coach must be ready for instance to help others see past the obvious attractions of self-serving rationalizations. The ethics coach must, for example, be ready to explain why "I had no choice" is seldom a viable excuse, and to outline the limits of the claim that "everybody does it." Likewise, the ethics coach must be ready to offer suggestions for how to raise thorny ethical considerations with third parties.

The ethics coach should be a source of strategies and conversational tactics to help others put ethics on the table when doing so is hard.

It goes without saying that fulfilling the role of ethics coach is not easy. Many who think of themselves as good leaders, and as persons of integrity, still may find it challenging to put themselves into the role of ethical leader, as I've discussed it here. Being good at seeing the right thing to do, and at doing it, does not automatically mean that you'll be good at helping others to see and do the right thing. Being an ethics coach, in other words, is arguably a separate capacity, one that must be developed just like any other capacity.

Here are five concrete steps you can take in order to begin to assume your role as ethics coach. Note that this isn't about "becoming" an ethics coach—that's not a final designation that you can achieve once and for all. It's a role that you choose to take on, and work to fulfill.

1. Learn the basic vocabulary of ethics; educate yourself on the terminology that experts in the field have found useful in making key distinctions and expressing important values. You can't coach others on ethics if you don't know how to talk about the topic.

2. Learn what you can about the known barriers to effective ethical conversations about ethics. Many people find it hard to talk about ethics. Find out why, and do what you can to start breaking down those barriers.

3. Think about what you do—and what you can do—to make your workplace a place where employees are empowered to make ethical decisions. Is your organization one where ethics is on the table? Do employees feel trusted to make decisions and to take a range of ethical factors into consideration?

4. Reflect frequently not just on the substance of the choices you make, but also on the underlying values and principles and how you would explain them to others. Even when the right thing seems obvious to you, it might not seem obvious to others. Could you, if asked, explain to others why you made a particular decision, and why they should make the same decision in a similar situation?

5. Practice talking about ethics. It doesn't come naturally to everyone. That means doing more than reading up on the topic. If you only talk about it when there's a crisis, you won't sound genuine. You cannot build this crucial coaching capacity by saving it for special occasions.

Chris MacDonald

Chris MacDonald, Ph.D., is Director of the Jim Pattison Ethical Leadership Education and Research Program at the Ted Rogers School of Management at Ryerson University (in Toronto, Canada). A philosopher by training, he has published widely in business ethics, bioethics, professional ethics and philosophical ethical theory. He is co-author of a best-selling textbook called The Power of Critical Thinking. *He's been called one of the "Top 100 Thought Leaders in Trustworthy Business Behavior" and has been declared one of the "100 Most Influential People in Business Ethics," four years in a row. For nearly 7 years, he has been the author of* The Business Ethics Blog *(www.BusinessEthicsBlog.com), the world's #1 blog on that topic.*

The Four C's of Trust

By John Spence

For nearly twenty years, I have been traveling worldwide teaching and coaching the ideas, concepts and philosophies around the notion of trust. The very foundation of being an effective and successful leader is built upon a strong bedrock of trust. As a student of leadership, I have studied the work of many experts including Kouzes, Posner, Bennis, Goldsmith, Greenleaf and others who, like me, understand that without genuine trust from your followers, one can never be a true leader. Building trust, however, can be a complex and challenging endeavor. Luckily, I have spent my entire career trying to make complex things easy to understand, so I'd like to share with you my personal philosophy of leadership and what I call the "Four C's of Trust."

Let me begin with a matrix that will help you understand the Four C's of Trust.

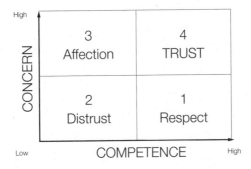

Figure One

The two axes of the above diagram are COMPETENCE and CONCERN. Quadrant one represents leaders with very high competence and very low concern. These leaders are good at what they do but have little concern for their followers. Many would view this leadership style as the old Theory X of command-and-control, "Do as I say, not as I do." I use the word RESPECT to describe leaders in this quadrant. Their followers respect their competence, they respect their experience, they respect their expertise— but they do not trust them because they know that the leader is self-interested. Perhaps ten or twenty years ago, this leadership style might have produced some level of effective results, but today's worker will reject this treatment. Actually, today's young workers demand respect from their leader first, before they decide if the leader has "earned" their respect. This is a major turnaround from how things used to be when I entered the workforce in 1989, where it was basically if your boss said "jump," you said "how high, sir?" Today, if the leader cannot demonstrate high competence and show true respect for his or her followers, it will not be long before he has no followers.

In quadrant two, we have a leader with low competence and low concern—how exciting! I use the word DISTRUST to describe this person who does not possess any leadership qualities and truthfully, you don't even want them on your team. If this individual does not quickly show an aptitude for learning and empathy, as well as respect and some level of collaboration, it is likely time to make him "available to industry," i.e., unemployed.

Quadrant three is a leader with high concern, but low competence. This is someone who is very nice, but is also completely incompetent, and to which I have assigned the term AFFECTION. Everyone loves this person who has been around forever, and everyone cleans up his mess, does his work, fixes his reports and smoothes over the customer problems he has caused. This person is fun to be around and you'd like to have him over for a barbecue. However, he cannot be trusted as your leader because he does not have the skills, expertise and/or discipline to effectively deliver the required results. He is a great person—not a great leader.

In quadrant four, we finally arrive at the characteristics of a true leader- someone who demonstrates both high competence and high concern. This is the person who effectively builds and sustains TRUST. He has high IQ and high EQ; he is rigorous in his thinking and demand for excellence, but never ruthless with his employees; he consistently works hard on self-improvement and stretches himself, while also showing empathy, connection and concern.

Great salespeople must also exhibit the traits of good leaders. The salesperson who forgets about quota, the numbers and trying to sell products and services—and instead displays towering competence, a genuine concern for the customer and an intense desire to help them—will see many, many more sales.

In order to build a high level of trust with your team, you MUST practice the Four C's:

CONSISTENTLY COMMUNICATE that you are COMPETENT and you CARE.

In other words- in everything you do, in every action you take, in every word you say, you must clearly communicate to all of your followers:

"I'm good at what I do—and I do it because I care about you."

How long does it take to build a level of trust this way? Sometimes it takes years. How long does it take to lose all of the trust you have created? Nanoseconds. This is why effective leadership is so incredibly challenging. As soon as you take on the mantle of "leader," you live under a microscope twenty-four hours a day, seven days a week, 365 days a year. Your team sees everything you do or don't do, and they hear everything you say or don't say. It is likely your employees sit around their dinner table in the evening talking to their families about—you! If you are highly competent and show true concern for them, they talk to their families about how much they love their job, how wonderful their boss is, how exciting their work is. But if you fail to consistently communicate that you are competent and you care, they will go home and tell their friends and families that they hate the person they work for, can't stand the company and find their work totally boring and un-engaging.

While I might be stretching a bit with my example above, here is some real data to back up my very broad strokes: several recent studies show that 88 percent of people who leave an organization do not leave their job, they do not leave the pay, they do not leave the hours, they do not leave the workload—they leave because they dislike their immediate supervisor; they can't stand their leader![1] Think of the wasted money, the wasted talent and the lost opportunities that bad leadership can inflict upon an organization. To put some real numbers on it, a research report I just looked at said that as much as 50 percent of lost productivity in any organization is due to poor leadership. [2]

Conversely, great leadership can have a massive positive economic impact on a business. It is well known that the number one factor for creating highly engaged, loyal and satisfied customers is highly engaged, loyal and satisfied employees. It is also important to note that many studies indicate that super high-performing employees, who could basically work anywhere they wanted to, stay at their company and their job mostly because they love the person they work for and the work they do. Recent research by Trust Across America and other well-respected organizations demonstrate beyond a doubt, that trustworthy organizations deliver significantly higher revenues and shareholder returns. The results are compelling that high-trust leaders build high-profit organizations.

Living under a microscope with your followers watching your every move is not fun or easy. Yet, it is exactly why I love the challenge of being a leader because it forces me to be a better person than I might be if left to my own devices. When my team is under pressure and they look to me for leadership, I don't get to do what I feel like doing, what my emotions are driving, what I think I can get away with, no, I have to do what I believe an "ideal leader" would do. Not the leader I am today, but the leader I hope to become. If I can discipline myself to act that way more and more often, eventually I will become the sort of leader I aspire to be.

A few weeks ago, I was lecturing to a large group of business students from the Entrepreneurship School at the University of Florida, when one of them asked me to define leadership. In the hundreds and hundreds of lectures I have given, I've never been asked that question in quite that way. After I gave little thought, I responded quite comfortably with, *"The definition of a leader is someone who is a living role model of what they hope their followers will one day become."*

---

1   Branham, Leigh, *The 7 Hidden Reasons Employees Leave: How to Recognize the Subtle Signs and Act Before It's Too Late*, Amacom, 2005

2   Zenger, Jack and Folkman, Joseph, "How Extraordinary Leaders Double Profits", 2010

John Spence

"Making the very complex...awesomely simple" is no mere catch phrase, it is truly *John Spence's mission in life. At the age of 26, John was named CEO of an international Rockefeller foundation, overseeing projects in twenty countries and reporting directly to the Chairman of the Board, Winthrop P. Rockefeller III. John has presented workshops, speeches and executive coaching to more than 300 organizations worldwide including; Microsoft, IBM, GE, Abbott, Merrill Lynch, Qualcomm and dozens of private companies, associations and not-for-profits. John is the author of* Excellence by Design: Leadership, The six key characteristics of outstanding leaders *and* Awesomely Simple, *Essential business strategies for turning ideas into action and has been a guest lecturer at more than ninety colleges and universities across the United States including Cornell, Rutgers, Brown, Stanford, the Wharton School of Business at the University of Pennsylvania and is an instructor in the Entrepreneurial Masters Program at MIT.*

Stewards Build Trust

By Bob and Gregg Vanourek

Business, leadership, and life are all about relationships, and relationships are built on trust.

In business, lack of trust leads to disengagement by employees. Stephen M. R. Covey, author of *The Speed of Trust* and *Smart Trust*, recently told webinar participants that the average organization has only two engaged workers for every one disengaged. By contrast, world-class organizations have over nine engaged employees for every one disengaged. High-trust groups enjoy two to five times the productivity of low-trust groups.[1]

In his corporate turnaround experience, Bob witnessed firsthand how lack of trust can have exorbitant costs, from vendors who demanded cash in advance to employees sitting cross-armed in the all-hands meetings where Bob introduced himself as the new CEO. Their body language spoke volumes about the absence of trust.

When Bob and colleagues took over Recognition Equipment (a $250 million New York Stock Exchange company that produced optical character recognition hardware and software) in the midst of an ethical scandal, they quickly discovered the firm was far behind on the development of a new currency-counting machine for the Federal Reserve. They called the customer, opened their books and engineering notes, and invited the Fed to audit their aggressive recovery plan. Instead, the Fed defaulted Recognition and awarded the contract to a foreign firm at more than twice the original price. Trust had been broken.

---

1 Robert Whipple, "Meaning of Trust," The Trust Ambassador blog, January 6, 2013, http://thetrustambassador.com/2013/01/06/meaning-of-trust/

Gregg saw the costs of the lack of trust in a high-growth, online, education startup when a critical vendor could not keep up with the rapidly scaling order complexity and volume. Instead of sitting down together to address the root causes, the conversations rapidly turned to finger pointing, butt covering, and threats of litigation. Years later, the battles continued, at great cost to both companies.

Trust is complex. Many behaviors can undermine trust. Below is a partial list of "trust busters":

1. Abusive behavior
2. Accountability lacking
3. Appreciation lacking
4. Arbitrary use of power
5. Blaming
6. Commitments not met
7. Communication poor or secretive
8. Compensation plans encourage inappropriate behavior
9. Controls/processes lacking or excessive
10. Corner cutting to get results
11. Disloyalty
12. Disrespectful behavior
13. Empowerment lacking
14. Favoritism
15. Goals impossible to achieve, constantly changing, or conflicting
16. Improper personal relationships
17. Micromanagement
18. Responsibility without authority
19. Shared values lacking, or not explicit
20. Tolerating toxic behavior

Given these potential trustbusters, it seems establishing a trustworthy organization is next to impossible. Some people will cheat, take advantage of others, abuse their power, and worse.

Yet, our experience and research on organizations all over the world tells us leaders can establish trustworthy organizations. These organizations are on the noble quest to be excellent, ethical, and enduring (what we call the triple crown):

Excellent: achieving exceptional results and impact

Ethical: doing the right thing, even when it's costly or hard

Enduring: standing the test of time and operating sustainably

All three of these components of triple crown leadership instill trust. Organizations on the triple crown quest recruit and promote people with integrity, emotional intelligence, and fit with the desired culture of character, trust, and high performance.

Organizations with a healthy culture—think of Southwest Airlines, Patagonia, and DreamWorks—create a self-reinforcing, positive cycle of trust-building with their stakeholders. Employees identify more with the enterprise, bringing more of their talents and efforts to the table, positively affecting productivity, staff retention, profitability, and relationships with customers and suppliers.

Zappos.com, the online retailer, has as its mission to "live and deliver wow" customer service. Its CEO, Tony Hsieh, empowers his employees with all his authority to deliver "wow." One customer forgot to pack her Zappos-bought shoes on a trip to Las Vegas, coincidentally the home base of Zappos. Unfortunately, Zappos was out of stock when she called for a replacement. The telephone clerk found where she was staying, left the office without asking permission, walked the Vegas malls until he found her shoes, had them gift-wrapped, and personally delivered them. No charge. That's how Zappos grew to $1 billion in sales in just ten years before being acquired by Amazon.

Customers trust Zappos; vendors trust Zappos; employees trust each other; and Amazon trusts Zappos.

Leaders of trustworthy organizations realize you can't change human nature, but you can influence human behavior. They align people for peak performance. They develop and unleash what we call leadership "stewards" to protect and nurture a culture of character in the company.

Stewards Build Trust

Stewards step out of their functional roles to speak up when behaviors threaten the desired corporate culture. Stewards speak up, even as a voice of one, even when they have no positional authority. They work on the organization, not just in it, to ensure the shared values forming the culture are not just empty pronouncements posted on the web site.

Such stewardship builds trust and helps protect the culture, even when leaders take detrimental actions. People trust they can speak up to challenge behaviors of anyone in the organization, even the CEO. Such trust liberates people to commit, innovate, and lead.

Trustworthy organizations *self-regulate*, providing the active checks and balances the enterprise needs to be its best. Self-regulation is peer review at its best, going beyond rules and regulations, beyond reliance on one's individual judgment (which can easily rationalize trust-destroying behavior). Employees in trustworthy organizations may or may not have formal authority, but they do have an irrevocable license to act by the organization's shared values and culture of character.

In trustworthy organizations, stewardship pervades the organization. Such stewardship is transformative, entailing a host of new responsibilities for the board, the CEO, managers, and people without formal authority. We outline those responsibilities below.

1) Trust Responsibilities for the Board. Boards cannot discharge their fiduciary duties without attention to the organization's shared values, culture of character, and levels of trust. Having a good "tone at the top" is not enough. Boards must set a tone that travels "from" the top all the way down and around.

At Tyco, John Krol (Outside Lead Director) and Ed Breen (CEO) replaced the entire board in the wake of epic scandals to regain credibility. "The fall of Tyco," Krol told us, "was brought about by lack of governance and board responsibility." Investors could not trust the old board to do what was necessary to turn Tyco around.

Krol and Breen involved the new board in reviewing and approving the new values, board principles, and company code of conduct. Krol told us, "It starts with the board."

Board members become stewards by:

- Personally modeling behavior consistent with the culture of character.
- Including criteria for character, cultural fit, and trustworthiness in officer selection and appraisals.

- Ensuring the existence of confidential channels for employees to raise ethics and trust concerns.
- Requiring ethics and culture training for everyone, including the board.
- Ensuring that compensation plans do not have unreasonable goals or outlandish rewards.

The job of building trust is too important for the board to neglect or delegate.

2) Trust Responsibilities for the CEO. Trust-building CEOs go beyond the narrow mandate of just getting results. They become the prime stewards of the organization, working with the board and management team to build the organization's culture of character, trust, and performance. CEOs must have the confidence and grace to foster trust, knowing when to give power away and when to retain it.

CEOs become stewards by:

- Personally being trustworthy and extending trust to others.
- Hiring and promoting trustworthy officers.
- Developing processes to monitor trustworthy behavior, such as ethics refreshers, incident reports, and vendor programs.
- Leading the board and senior management on the development and dissemination of shared purpose, values, and vision.
- Verifying that the confidential channels for employees to raise ethics and trust concerns are robust.
- Getting rid of toxic employees, even if they are star performers.
- Ensuring compensation plans contain reasonable goals and rewards.
- Keeping their ego under control.

3) Trust Responsibilities for Managers. Managers should also be trust stewards. Most employees get their leadership signals from their immediate supervisors, not the CEO or the board. Managers must transcend the boundaries of their job descriptions and embrace the organizational values, amplifying the efforts of the board and CEO.

The head of marketing should take responsibility, not just for pricing and promotions, but also for building a trustworthy organization. The head of information technology must build firewalls around the character-based culture as well as the data networks.

Chip Baird, CEO of North Castle Partners, a highly successful private equity firm, told us, "We have a culture in which people are constantly calling others on any breakdowns in our values or operating principles. If you don't have a culture where people are able to call each other, including me, on a breakdown, you quickly devolve to hypocritical values on the wall."

In Bob's early months at Recognition Equipment, it was time for the first earnings release under the new management. Bob drafted the press release with a positive spin on the numbers. Tom, the general counsel, objected in a meeting, "We can't say that." His concern was about perception, not a legal issue: "I don't care if I'm a voice of one in this room," he declared. "We're in an ethical mess. We have to be squeaky clean."

Tom served as a steward, actively stepping outside his position to influence his boss, knowing that reestablishing trust with investors was essential. Bob toned down the press release.

Managers become trust stewards by:

- Personally being trustworthy and extending trust to others.
- Giving staff members a license to act in accordance with the shared values.
- Participating in ethics training and mandating it for their staff.
- Coaching employees on trustworthy behavior.
- Publicly celebrating ethical practices from employees and vendors.
- Speaking up and objecting when they have concerns about proposed actions.
- Blowing the whistle outside the chain of command when things have gone too far.

4) Trust Responsibilities for Employees without Authority. Anyone can lead, regardless of whether they have formal authority. No matter their title, people can influence others through their behavior. People without authority become stewards when they go beyond their area of expertise to advance the trust in the organization and protect the culture of character.

Bob once had an exceptional administrative assistant who was a leader among her peers and worked assiduously to help the company in its turnaround. One day, Bob drove to a nearby city and back for a meeting. He noted the mileage and gave her the gas receipts. After a while, she came into his office and said, "I can't submit this." She reminded him that he received a monthly car allowance covering trips like that. "How will it look if you submit this expense?" she asked. "It's just not right."

Without her courage to speak up, an oversight by the CEO could have broken the trust needed in the turnaround. She was a steward, who made Bob a better one too.

Employees without authority become stewards and build trust by:

- Modeling exemplary behavior, reinforcing the culture of character through actions and communications.
- Recognizing they have an automatic license to act in accordance with the shared values—and using it.
- Speaking up when someone violates the values.
- Blowing the whistle on ethical breaches when things have gone too far.

In summary, trustworthy organizations outperform low-trust organizations. Since people are human and make mistakes, leaders must proactively work to build trust in their companies. Trust-building organizations self-regulate by developing and unleashing stewards who, in turn, build and monitor a culture of character, trust, and high performance.

Stewards build trust, and trust changes everything.

Bob and Gregg Vanourek

Bob and Gregg Vanourek are co-authors of Triple Crown Leadership: Building Excellent, Ethical, and Enduring Organizations *(published by McGraw-Hill and a 2012 USA Best Book Awards finalist). Bob is the former CEO of two New York Stock Exchange companies. Gregg teaches at the Stockholm School of Entrepreneurship. They are father and son.*

Section IV:

Building Trustworthy Teams

Practicing Trustworthy Behaviors

By William Benner

In today's world and unfortunately for the foreseeable future, trust has suffered greatly and does not appear to be improving by most measurable business standards or personal assessments.

Reduced confidence and declining expectations in government, business, leadership, management, work teams, co-workers, and even friends and family appear the norm nearly everywhere one looks.

Ask anyone to name five (5) people they trust implicitly — without any reservation or concern about their potential betrayal or the possibility of diminished care and positive intent—and see what you get in response. Many people are hard pressed to identify just one or two, much less five individuals they trust with total conviction. This is truly a sad commentary that affects not only business results, but as importantly, our basic humanity.

"To trust" or "not to trust" seems to be "the" prevailing question as we assess and strive to achieve supportive, meaningful, and effective human interactions. Our willingness to be truly vulnerable by extending trust to another individual "with or without" prior experience has become seemingly more difficult and suspect on our part.

Even those we deeply love and cherish may question our "best and truest of intentions" if their fears, unexpressed expectations and personal needs are not satisfied or reassured in a positive and reinforcing manner through our behaviors and actions. Maybe the whole notion of remembering to be careful when trusting others is part of our "learned DNA."

While this conditioning of distrust may be with us for all time, it does not necessarily have to overwhelm or diminish the perceived and actual goodness of our intentions, especially if we ask ourselves: 1) what trustworthy behaviors do I practice on a regular basis, and 2) how are my behaviors perceived by others with whom I interact and presumably trust as well? Having conversations of trust are difficult and not necessarily welcome because we may not fully trust ourselves. Realistically, how can we expect others to be trustworthy in their interactions with us if we don't first examine and adjust our own potentially untrustworthy behaviors?

There are many internal and external factors that can affect the ability of individuals and team members to trust one another and accomplish personal goals and team objectives:

- Highly competitive, rapidly changing and uncertain business environment
- Inability and/or unwillingness to address performance issues as a team
- Poor communication skills and inability to listen for understanding
- Lack of clarity about the team's shared mission and direction
- Lack of confidence in the team leader and/or team members
- Failure to remedy problems that surface on the team
- Unclear expectations for business outcomes
- Lack of collaboration by team members
- Minimal or no personal accountability
- Low levels of personal engagement
- Inability to resolve conflicts
- Low tolerance for risk
- Lack of respect

These types of conditions, when left unchecked, can eventually create a state of "cordial hypocrisy" in which team members are courteous and cordial on the surface, but insincere when supporting one another in the company of others. Even if trust was initially attained, restoration of trust on the team then becomes almost impossible to achieve.

Fortunately, however, we can overcome this condition of distrust and team malaise by continuously practicing behaviors and taking actions that:

- Ensure Personal and Team Accountability
- Apologize for Missed Commitments
- Appreciate One Another
- Clarify Team Goals and Direction
- Clarify Individual Roles and Responsibilities
- Collaborate with the Intent to Improve and Excel
- Recognize Others for their Contributions
- Communicate Openly
- Empower Self and Others
- Create Face Time and Quality Conversations
- Practice Honesty and Transparency
- Build, Maintain, and Restore Trust
- Provide and Enhance Regular Performance Feedback
- Promote Reliability and Keep Promises
- Respect Diverse Viewpoints
- Confirm Faith in One Another
- Demonstrate Willingness to Listen and Change

While trust is at epidemically low levels in our business environment, all is not lost. Challenges can be turned into opportunities to improve and excel, if we practice these trustworthy behaviors on a regular and consistent basis.

To help advance our overall understanding of the dynamics of trust, we have examined the results of team effectiveness surveys, specifically the Triscendance Trust Assessment of Leadership Teams. Based on these survey results from 2008-2011, common themes regarding team trust have been identified, including the highest and lowest scoring trust survey statements and those trustworthy behaviors deemed important by team members and leaders. The data covers a diverse group of organizations from the academic, pharmaceutical, engineering, bio-medical research, specialty chemicals, insurance, and local government sectors.

The highest (positive) and lowest (negative) scoring survey statements are shown below and the highest scoring results suggest that: 1) teams rally well and pull together when faced with crises, 2) team members and team leaders typically demonstrate integrity and sincerity with one another, and 3) team members are perceived as having the necessary skills and expertise (i.e., competence) to accomplish the team's objectives.

Conversely, the lowest scoring statements indicate: 1) difficulty in raising issues of individual trust and performance with team members, 2) concern that not all information is shared in team conversations, and 3) team members do not typically have conversations with one another when they have concerns about one another.

Highest (Positive) Scoring Trust Survey Statements

1. Team members demonstrate integrity
2. The team leader demonstrates integrity
3. Team members can be counted on during crises
4. Team members have the required level of expertise to accomplish the team's objectives

Lowest (Negative) Scoring Trust Survey Statements

1. Team members raise issue of trust with one another directly
2. Team members raise performance issues with one another
3. On our team nothing is withheld from our conversations
4. Team members have conversations about concerns they have with each other

From these survey results, we have identified thirty characteristics **practiced by trustworthy teams** and group them into the **four basic categories** listed below. Think about which of these characteristics describes the team(s) in your business and organization:

Caring about what's important as a team

1. Clear vision and direction for the team
2. A shared purpose and team goals
3. Clear roles and responsibilities
4. Shared expectations of the team leader by the team members
5. Shared expectations of the team members by the team leader
6. Ensure the competence of team members and the team leader
7. Understand and embrace change

Behaving as a team

1. Promote team member and team leader engagement
2. Provide performance feedback and take appropriate actions
3. Open and expand dialogue and communication
4. Support and appreciate one another
5. Encourage creativity and innovation
6. Recognize and utilize individual strengths and capabilities
7. Hold one another accountable without wavering
8. Collaborate with the team members and team leader
9. Celebrate successes and failures
10. Ensure all ideas are heard and not summarily dismissed
11. Listen with the desire to understand different points of view
12. Take calculated risks without fear of retribution

Building individual and team relationships

1. Be truly reliable and sincere with one another
2. Enable individual and team empowerment
3. Strengthen personal relationships
4. Show respect for team members and the leader
5. Practice integrity and honesty always
6. Trust one another to do the right thing
7. Learn to trust and extend trust to one another

Addressing problems and concerns

1. Confront one another directly and professionally
2. Eliminate fear and unnecessary oversight
3. Apologize for mistakes and missed commitments
4. Eliminate cordial hypocrisy

As you review and assess these trustworthy team and business practices, thinking about the following questions should be useful:

- Which of these characteristics do my team members, team leader, and I practice on a regular basis?
- Which of these characteristics are typically missing in my personal and the team's daily interactions?

- How would I rate myself, my team members, and the team leader on each of these trustworthy characteristics on a scale of 1-5 (1- Almost Never, 2-Sometimes, 3-Generally, 4-Often, 5-Almost Always)
- Which of these characteristics carry the highest priority for action by the team, and why?
- How will I open this conversation with my team?

"We live in an era where trust is the currency of the age" according to Dov Seidman Founder and CEO of LRN, a company that helps businesses develop ethical corporate cultures and inspire principled performance; and author of *HOW: Why HOW We Do Anything Means Everything…in Business (and in Life)*. Put simply, trust is everything.

In the book *Mistakes Were Made (But Not By Me): Why We Justify Foolish Beliefs, Bad Decisions, and Hurtful Acts*, authors Carol Tavris and Elliot Aronson additionally note that: "in the final analysis, the test of a nation's character and an individual's integrity, does not depend on being error free. It depends on what we do after making the error."

So what new and/or enhanced behaviors will you commit to practice on a regular basis to engender trust with your team members and in your personal relationships? And how well do you trust yourself to follow through on those commitments? If we challenge ourselves in this manner, we have the potential to build more effective teams, establish deeper personal relationships, generate positive business outcomes, and create a more trustworthy and healthy world.

William Benner

William Benner is President, WW Consulting, Inc. and a former executive, leadership advisor, and consultant with the Federal Reserve System, Office of the Director of National Intelligence, and Booz Allen Hamilton. Bill's company provides executive coaching, organizational and leadership team trust, leadership development, employee engagement, and human capital consulting services for business, Federal agency, local government, and nonprofit clients. He holds BA and MPA degrees from the University of Virginia and has recently published the chapter "Leadership Behaviors that Promote Individual and Organizational Success" in the book "Leadership: Helping Others to Succeed" (2012). He is also a Founding Partner of Triscendance LLC and has been selected by Trust Across America as one of the "Top 100 Thought Leaders of Trustworthy Business Behaviors for 2013." Website: http://www.wwconsult.us

Building the Trust Muscle: In Our Companies, In our Teams, In Ourselves

By Mary C. Gentile, PhD

Trust is an essential element in the smooth and efficient functioning of the economy on the broad scale; of individual companies in the marketplace; and of interpersonal and organizational relationships at the micro level. Agreed?

When trust in the broader markets is threatened or compromised by widespread abuses, regulation is stepped up, often in haste, almost always adding to business costs—even when necessary—and sometimes with unintended negative consequences, akin to tossing out some babies along with the bath water.

When trust is violated by an individual business, in a world of social media and global communication at the touch of a keystroke, word spreads rapidly to competitors, suppliers and customers leading to public relations challenges, at best.

And given the reality that all businesses are at heart "social," when individual managers breach the relationship of trust with their reports, their peers and their bosses, repair and restoration of a healthy working bond and company culture is slow, difficult and not necessarily possible at all without a major leadership transition.

For all these reasons, the statement above—that trust is an essential element in smooth and efficient business functioning—is one of those "business truisms", a starting assumption in management discourse. And yet, precisely because it is taken-for-granted, trust is often over-discussed and under-practiced.

No one publicly debates the necessity for trust in business transactions, to allow for efficient arms-length business transactions and to reduce the cost of regulatory compliance, monitoring and penalties. However, actual behaviors are often slow to change. Too often, when scandals hit or when bubbles burst, we rush to the bully pulpit, proclaiming the necessity to clean up our acts; to place transparency and integrity at the heart of our business dealings; to treat employees and consumers with the respect that comes from honest communication and practices that are consistent with the business mission and values statements.

But without actual rehearsal for trustworthy business behavior, trust is a lot easier to espouse than to enact.

We all wait to be tested, hoping it might never come to that. And we like to think we will be up to the challenge if it occurs, and even make the assumption we will be. After all, research suggests that we tend to claim greater ethics than our actions demonstrate. But secretly we say "whew" when it's someone else's transgressions that are caught and made public, and then condemn them all the louder—proclaiming the need for "moral courage" and commitment—while our own self-image remains safe, at least for now.

However, what we really need is not simply resolve or moral courage, but moral *competence*. Instead of grand statements of ethical commitment, or perhaps in addition to them, we need the mundane, everyday-ness of rehearsal for action. Instead of leaders who simply exhort their employees to behave honorably and then promote this commitment to investors and consumers, we need leaders who invest their own time, their personal energy and their organization's resources in building laboratory conditions for pre-scripting and rehearsing trustworthy behaviors in the real world context of a particular industry and region.

So what do these laboratory conditions look like? A few years ago, with venture funding from The Aspen Institute and Yale School of Management, we set out to develop a new approach to values-driven leadership development. This work resulted in an innovative new pedagogy and curriculum for management education and for corporate leadership programming, now based and supported at Babson College and called "Giving Voice To Values" (www.GivingVoice-ToValues.org). The GVV approach has been piloted in hundreds of management education and business settings on all seven continents and continues to expand rapidly. (Most of it is available in a free, open-source format on-line.)

At its heart, this approach to building and supporting trustworthy behavior in our organizations and in ourselves is simply about asking a new and different question when it comes to ethics. In any given situation, instead of asking first and exclusively, "what is the right thing to do?"—an important question to be sure –, "Giving Voice To Values" is about asking "once we know what we believe is right, how do we get it done?"

This simple shift in question unleashes a whole new world of energy, motivation, creativity and innovative thinking among business leaders and their teams. Rather than framing ethics and trust in business as all about "constraints on action," this shift positions trustworthy business behavior as an example of a "can do" mentality. Energetic and motivated business practitioners are not typically drawn to constraints; they see themselves as the kind of people who can overcome odds, compete effectively, build successful enterprises and "win" in the marketplace. So let's frame the challenge of values-driven business behavior as one of finding ways to actually do the thing that, although publicly espoused, is too often privately, candidly seen as nearly impossible to achieve.

We do this in several ways. First, we gather and share *positive examples* of times when individuals and organizations have actually found effective ways to voice and act on their values-driven positions, as opposed to focusing primarily on the cautionary tales. We gather actual stories of managers and leaders at all levels in their organizations who found creative ways to reframe the typical ethical challenges of their industry, their function or their regional context. The stories are often disguised but they are always based on real experiences: the Indian entrepreneur who turned around a failing and corruption-ridden enterprise to make it both economically and ethically successful; the CFO who found a way to push back on pressures to "manage earnings" in the context of a publicly held firm; the junior accountant in a non-profit who used respectful questions as a way to push to close a loophole that promoted distorted tax reporting of corporate contributions; and so on.

Second, we provide opportunities for individual practitioners to reflect upon their own individual style and preferences around communications, risk, personal purpose and interpersonal interaction, so they can *play to their own strengths* when it comes to finding ways to voice and enact values-driven behaviors in the workplace. The idea is not to ask someone who sees him or herself as aggressive and hard charging to be more conservative or cautious, nor is it to ask the fearful or risk-averse employee to be more morally courageous. Those exhortations are doomed to failure because they ask people to be other than who they are, or believe themselves to be.

Instead, we ask people to recognize the positive strengths in their own style, whatever that may be, and to frame their values conflicts such that they play to those strengths. The introvert may use the well-placed question, or the carefully orchestrated side-conversation to make sure that important issues are part of a decision-making discussion. On the other hand, the practiced debater may more directly challenge a decision, and the risk-taker might frame the situation as "taking a risk in the service of something that really matters to me." The idea is that everyone is capable of being part of the values-driven conversation; they just may use a different dialect, a different set of tools, to participate in it.

Third, we focus upon creating opportunities for actual *"rehearsal for action"* when it comes to trustworthy business behavior. Very often the most visible, most costly challenges to the public trust in business are fairly predictable: deceptive marketing practices; falsified earnings reporting; failure in safety compliance; lack of consistency in employee relations; and so on. So if they are so predictable, why don't we actually practice the different arguments or literal "scripts" we might use when confronted with such challenges? The kinds of information we might gather to make our values-driven case? The exemplar stories of ethical success and/or of the costs of deception that we can use to stir the troops? Research suggests that habits can be formed through this practice, so instead of framing our values and ethics conversations within our firms as occasions to communicate the rules and the regulations or to preach, let's frame them as opportunities for creative problem-solving and group generation of effective strategies and tactics for dealing with the challenges we know will arise.

Finally, we create occasions for *peer coaching*, so that the process of generating and voicing values-driven positions is a less lonely one. One of the twelve Starting Assumptions of "Giving Voice To Values" is that "we are not alone." Each of us is not the only one who would like to act on our values. It is just that we often won't know who else feels the same way until we go a bit public with our concerns. Creating opportunities for peer coaching allows more of us to come out of the ethical closet.

None of the strategies outlined briefly here are new or rocket science, and they all have research and/or experience behind them. And all these strategies can be easily folded into existing leadership development programs, regular team meetings, mentoring and performance development conversations, and so on.

The innovation is to apply them to the subject of Trust and Values. Too often, when it comes to ethical challenges, we throw all that we know about effective communications, persuasion, negotiation and even power and influence out the window, assuming instead that ethics are simply a matter of moral courage and standing up for values. Of course, such courage can be a good and necessary thing, but it is also a pretty high bar to set for all of us on a daily basis. The idea behind the "Giving Voice To Values" emphasis upon pre-scripting, rehearsal and playing to our own individual strengths, is that building the "moral muscle" and the moral competence and the moral *habit* to enact our values will mean we do not need the same seemingly Herculean levels of moral courage quite so often.

Mary C. Gentile

Mary C. Gentile, Ph.D. is Director of Giving Voice to Values *[www.GivingVoice ToValues.org], launched with The Aspen Institute and Yale School of Management, now based at and funded by Babson College. This pioneering curriculum for values-driven leadership has over 435 pilot sites globally and has been featured in* New York Times, Financial Times, Harvard Business Review, Stanford Social Innovation Review, McKinsey Quarterly, *etc. Gentile, Senior Research Scholar at Babson College and educational consultant, was previously faculty and administrator at Harvard Business School for ten years. She holds a B.A. from The College of William and Mary and Ph.D. from State University of New York-Buffalo. Gentile's publications include:* Giving Voice to Values: How To Speak Your Mind When You Know What's Right *(Yale University Press, Summer 2010, www.MaryGentile.com;)* Can Ethics Be Taught? Perspectives, Challenges, and Approaches at Harvard Business School *(with Thomas Piper & Sharon Parks);* Differences That Work: Organizational Excellence through Diversity; Managerial Excellence Through Diversity: Text and Cases, *as well as cases and articles in* Academy of Management Learning and Education, Harvard Business Review, Risk Management, CFO, BizEd, Strategy+Business, *etc. Gentile was Content Expert for the award-winning CD-ROM,* Managing Across Differences

You Can't Take Trust for Granted

By James M. Kouzes and Barry Z. Posner

The first order of business for Jill Cleveland on becoming finance manager at Apple was "to learn to trust my employees. After being responsible only for me for so long," she told us, "it was very difficult to have to relinquish control. But I understood that in order for my employees, and thus myself, to be successful, I needed to develop a cohesive and collaborative team, beginning with trust as the framework." If you are going to be an effective leader then you, too, must create a structure for trust in your organization. Without it you can't lead.

The truth is that trust rules. Trust rules relationships. Trust rules your influence. Trust rules your team's cohesiveness. Trust rules innovativeness. Trust rules brand image. Trust rules financial stability. Trust rules performance. Trust rules just about everything you do.

But sometimes trust is tested. Ours certainly was a short while back.

In one of the frequent leadership workshops we conduct we involve participants in an activity called the "trust fall." You may have done this yourself, but in case you haven't, imagine the following scenario.

Your work group is at an off-site meeting, participating in some team-building exercises, one of which is the trust fall. Team members stand in two rows of six people each, about two feet apart, and face one another. At the head of the rows is a stepladder. Each team member is invited, one at a time, to step onto the top of the four-foot ladder, turn to face away from the group, cross both arms, remain straight and stiff, and then fall over backwards. The team's common goal is to catch each person by everyone putting up their arms at exactly the same time, making a safe cradle for falling colleagues.

The first person climbs the ladder, and on cue falls backward. Every member of the team reaches out and catches the person. They lower her safely to the ground. The faller heaves a sigh of relief and thanks everyone for doing their jobs. The second person now goes up to the top of the ladder. On cue, he falls over backward and is caught. And this continues for everyone in the group, with the team adjusting as needed each time depending upon the demands of the situation. (Is the faller heavy or light? Is the faller tall or short?)

As a result of repeated successes at performing the trust fall successfully, people feel pretty good about themselves and their ability to work together. They see firsthand how trust works, what it means to put their trust in others, and what it means to know that someone else trusts them. Teammates get to experience how trust connects each person to all the others, and how, by working reliably together, they can do something that none can do alone.

Both of us have seen and participated in this team-building exercise hundreds of times over the years. On one occasion recently, the group had a few extra minutes before needing to start the next activity, so they asked Barry if he'd be willing to be the faller. Here's what proceeded to happen as Barry tells the story:

Since I'd done this many times before I suggested a new variation. I said to the group, "How about if I lay down on the ground, looking up as someone else is falling, and take a photograph of the team catching him as he descends? Now remember, you have to catch this person; if you don't, he will fall right on top of me!" The group laughed nervously. Then I added, "Having observed you do this for one another, I trust you can do this again."

The team got itself organized to do what it had just done successfully ten times in a row without failure. But this time around a few members of the team weren't paying attention to the task at hand, and they didn't put their arms up in unison with the others. The group members who did put their arms up couldn't bear the faller's weight. He tumbled through their arms and landed right on top of me. The faller wasn't injured—after all he had something soft to fall on! —But I got the wind knocked out of me.

The various group members helped me get back on my feet. They exclaimed: "Sorry." "Are you all right?" "Are you sure you are all right?" "Does anything hurt?" "I guess we really screwed up, right?" "We didn't pay enough attention." "We were too cocky." "Suppose you'll never do this again, will you!"

I took a few moments to catch my breath. I thought about how to respond to all of these various concerns and comments, but especially the last one, "Suppose you'll never do this again, will you?" which is code for "You trusted us and now look what happened."

What's the lesson? There's a sucker born every minute, and this time it was I? After a few minutes of catching my breath and considering the options, I thought I saw two key rules emerge from this experience (although I'm not recommending this particular piece of experiential learning for anyone):

Rule #1: You have to keep working on trust and never take it for granted. Of course, this is true for all relationships.

Rule #2: Sometimes trust breaks down. So, see Rule #1.

You Have to Keep Working on Trust

Every single relationship is built on trust. It's foundational. It's fundamental. And foundations and fundamentals need constant attention.

Building trust is a process that begins when someone is willing to risk being the first to open up, being the first to show vulnerability, and being the first to let go of control—and then reciprocating these actions. And in the leader-constituent relationship, leaders go first. If you want the high levels of performance that come with trust and collaboration, you have to be the first to demonstrate your trust in others before asking them to trust you.

Dawn Lindblom, executive director for the Red Cross in Eastern Washington, learned the importance of being the first to trust when she had her initial encounter with Gail McGovern, who had just been appointed as the President and CEO of Red Cross nationally. Dawn wanted to know whether she could trust Gail McGovern. Gail was touring the nation and introducing herself to the organization's regional leaders, and this trust question was put to her point-blank in one of those meeting: "Can we trust you?" Gail's response was: "I can't answer that for you but let me tell you that I trust each and every one of you.'" Dawn told us that it made all the difference in the world to her knowing that Gail was going first, that Gail would earn their trust by taking the first step and trusting them, their commitment, and competence.

Taking the lead on trust means going first in disclosing your values and beliefs. It means going first to be open about your failures and your weaknesses. It means going first in sharing your concern for the wellbeing of others. It means going first in listening carefully to others. It means going first in accepting someone else's advice rather than taking your own. It means going first in sharing knowledge and information with others. It means going first in building your and others' capabilities to deliver on promises. It means going first in talking about performance standards, customer expectations, and about *why* what you do matters.

Going first is a scary proposition. Trust denotes the willingness to be vulnerable to others even when doing so may risk real harm. (Like people falling on top of you!) You're taking a chance. You're betting that others will keep you safe, that they'll take good care of the information you communicate, the resources you allocate, and the feelings you share. You're taking the risk that the other party won't take advantage of you. You're relying on them to have the skills to do what's right. You're counting on them to do their part. You're exposed to the consequences of others' actions, not just to your own. Your influence is stake, your money may be at risk, and your career may be on the line. And, especially in the beginning, there's absolutely no guarantee that if you trust first, the other party will reciprocate.

But, the payoff of going first in trusting others is huge. Trust is contagious. When you trust others, they are much more likely to trust you. When you create a climate of trust, you create an environment that allows people to freely contribute and innovate. You nurture an open exchange of ideas and a truthful discussion of issues. You motivate people to go beyond compliance and inspire them to reach for the best in themselves. And, you nurture the belief that people can rely on you to do what's in everyone's best interests.

And should you choose not to trust, understand that distrust is equally contagious. If you exhibit distrust, others will hesitate to place their trust in you and in their colleagues. You'll be left with doing more and more work yourself, constantly checking up on other people's work, spending time micromanaging. You're left with getting less than the best from your team. Not surprising is the inability to trust is one of the top impediments to career advancement is the inability to trust others.

Sometimes Trust Breaks Down

You can never assume, however, that once trust is built that it'll take care of itself. You can never be complacent about trust. Just because people trust you and other team members today doesn't mean they'll trust you and others forever. Sometimes, despite our best efforts (and theirs), people don't do their jobs. Sometimes they let us down. Sometimes they betray us. Sometimes the social bond of trust comes unglued. What do you do?

The temptation may be to hold on tighter and micromanage. You want to play it safe. You want to hide and not expose yourself to risk. But what happens when you constantly look over other people's shoulders and check up on their work? What happens when you don't take a chance on someone? What happens when you send signals that you don't trust others? What happens is that, in return, they begin not to trust you. It's a vicious cycle. When you succumb to this temptation, you end up building barriers. You end up looking out for your own interests and not for the interests of the organization. You end up with lower levels of performance. You may think you're preserving the status quo this way, but you're not. Eventually people will leave the relationship with you—unless, of course, you're asked to leave first.

Your only option is to see rule number one. Keep working on building and sustaining trust. Keep working on the relationships, on the common understandings. Keep working on making sure you are reliable and consistent. Keep working on being clear when you communicate your intentions. Keep working on aligning your actions with your words. Keep working on treating your promises seriously. Keep working on being candid and open.

What happened that day when the team let one of their members drop through their arms happened precisely because everyone took trust for granted! They assumed that everyone was doing what they were capable of doing and would continue to do so. But for that one moment they didn't.

The neat thing is that because the team learned from that particular moment that taking trust for granted could have some negative consequences, you should have seen their performance for the rest of the day! They continually checked in with and looked out for one another. And because they fully appreciated how their leader didn't give up on them and didn't lose faith in them even when they goofed up, they worked more diligently and productivity than anyone might have imagined.

About the Authors

Jim Kouzes and Barry Posner are coauthors of the award-winning and best-selling book, The Leadership Challenge, *and over thirty other books and workbooks on leadership. Jim is the Dean's Executive Fellow of Leadership and Barry is the Acolti Chaired Professor of Leadership, Leavey School of Business, Santa Clara University.*

Creating Thriving Organizations— The Bedrock of Trust and Reputation

By Brian Moriarty

"Character is like a tree and reputation like a shadow. The shadow is what we think of it; the tree is the real thing."[1]

— Abraham Lincoln

Trust and reputation are more important to companies now than ever. High visibility cases of lost trust and tarnished brands might steer some leaders to believe that relationships with external stakeholders present not only the greatest opportunities for building trust, but also the greatest risks for losing it. While relationships with external stakeholders such as customers and the public are extremely important, it is critical for leaders to recognize that the human dynamics within a company are the central driver of trust and reputation capital.

Reputation is a critical factor in valuation and accessing resources for innovation and growth. John Gerzema and Edward Lebar estimate the percentage of company value attributable to intangibles has increased from just over 30 percent in the 1950s to approximately 62 percent today.[2] Interbrand's 2011 survey lists the total value of the top 100 global brands at $1.25 trillion, with Coca-Cola alone valued at $72 billion.[3]

---

1   Abraham Lincoln, *Lincoln's Own Stories*, Anthony Gross, ed. Kindle Edition, location 1125.
2   John Gerzema and Edward Lebar Prahalad, *The Brand Bubble: The Looming Crisis in Brand Value and How to Avoid It* (San Francisco:Jossey-Bass, 2008), 10-11.
3   Interbrand, Best Global Brands (whitepaper, 2011), p18. This whitepaper is available online at http://issuu.com/interbrand/docs/bestglobalbrands2011-interbrand?viewMode=presentation&mode=embed. Captured from the Internet at 3:43 on 20 May 2013.

The majority of this valuation is tied to reputation and trust—it does not appear on a balance sheet, and chief executives and directors are well aware of this. CEOs responding to an Economist Intelligence Unit Survey cited "events that undermine public trust in your products or brand" as the single most significant threat to a company's global business operations.[4] Similarly, a 2011 report from Deloitte identifies reputational risk as a "meta risk" that is "an even greater hazard to organizational survival than a financial restatement or problematical findings in a compliance report."[5]

The widespread availability of inexpensive communications channels having global reach gives brands greater influence than ever before, while simultaneously making them more vulnerable to public scrutiny. BP, for example, lost $74 billion (or 40%) of its market capitalization in the first six weeks after the Gulf of Mexico oil spill.[6] As one Director of an FTSE 100 company contributing to a report from Populus stated:

> *I think if BP's reaction had been as it is was and the problem had been 20 years ago, they would have been said to have reacted really quickly because the media wouldn't have got in that gap, but because the whole world has moved faster, it requires the company to move faster. The media has got the news almost as soon as the company's got the news.*[7]

While the balance of power between companies, interest groups, the media and the broader public continues to evolve in the larger social environment, executives must not lose sight of the fact that the people who work for the company form the foundation upon which trust and reputation are built. As reputation experts Charles Fombrun and Violina Rindova point out, "a firm's relative standing...internally with employees" is a key driver of an organization's reputation.[8]

4   Economist Intelligence Unit, *Reputation: Risk of Risks* (whitepaper, December, 2005), 52.
5   Deloitte, *A Risk Intelligent View of Reputation: An Outside-in Perspective* (whitepaper, 2011), Risk Intelligence Series no.22, 2.
6   Steven Mufson and Theresa Vargas, "BP loses 15 percent of market value as U.S. launches criminal probe of spill," *Washington Post* (June 2, 2010), p. A1,
7   Populus, *The Trust Deficit: Views from the Boardroom* (whitepaper, 2011), 4.
8   Charles Fombrun and Violina Rindova, "Who's tops and who decides? The social construction of corporate reputations," New York University, Stern School of Business, (working paper, 1996).

John Iwata, Senior Vice President of Marketing and Communications at IBM and Chairman of the Arthur W. Page Society believes that the ongoing communications revolution is accelerating the role employees play with respect to trust and reputation. He offers the following vision:

> One day soon, every employee, every retiree, every customer, every business partner, every investor and every neighbor associated with every company will be able to share an opinion about that company with everyone in the world, based on firsthand experience. The only way we can be comfortable in that world is if every employee of the company is truly grounded in what their company values and stands for.[9]

In Iwata's vision, organizational success for global firms will depend largely upon an organization's ability to build an army of advocates who believe in the core purpose of the company, embody its values, and trust in its ability to deliver on its brand promise.

Engaged employees are central to this vision. Currently, however, the insider story at many companies is not a happy one. In a Gallup study, only 29 percent of employees report being actively engaged in their work.[10] The lack of engagement is dire even among high potential employees. A report from the Corporate Executive Board indicates that 21 percent of high potential employees are disengaged at work and that 25 percent of them are in the process of seeking other employment.[11] Many of the people most likely to drive innovation and create value for their organizations are heading for the exit door.

Some evidence suggests that ineffective leadership is at least partially to blame for these troubling levels of disengagement. A Florida State University study indicates that 41 percent of employees view their boss as lazy and 26 percent say their boss has

---

9 Jon Iwata, "Toward a New Profession: Brand, Constituency and Eminence on the Global Commons," Institute for Public Relations 2009 Distinguished Lecture delivered at the Yale Club in New York (November 4, 2009).

10 Gallup, "Majority of American Workers Not Engaged in Their Jobs," (October 28, 2011). This report, available at http://www.gallup.com/poll/150383/majority-american-workers-not-engaged-jobs.aspx, was captured from the Internet on May, 21, 2013 at 10:12 AM EST). Special thanks to Bruce K. Berger whose 2011 Grunig Lecture for the PRSA, *Employee Communication: Let's Move from Knowing to Doing,* convinced me to examine the relevance of employee engagement to reputation and trust.

11 Corporate Executive Board, "Corporate Performance at Risk as Today's Rising Talent Prepares to Jump Ship" (news release, June 1, 2010). The article, available at http://ir.executiveboard.com/phoenix.zhtml?c=113226&p=irol-newsArticle&ID=1432707&highlight, was captured from the Internet on May, 21, 2013 at 10:25 AM EST).

frequent anger management issues.[12] A report from Gallup reveals that 24 percent of employees would fire their bosses if this were within their power.[13]

The disenchantment with leaders across organizations, industries and geographical regions does not mean that organizations tend to be led by highly flawed individuals; rather, it is a sign that many managers are working with a flawed concept of leadership, requiring a greater awareness of how humans are motivated.

The traditional motivational levers used by organizational leaders have been rewards and punishments, often referred to as carrots and sticks. A common example of a carrot is a bonus awarded for achieving a predetermined goal. As Daniel Pink has noted in his book, *Drive*, the problem with carrots is that they tend to narrow peoples' focus upon a singular end, which can lead to employees losing sight of larger strategic issues, underestimating risks, and forgoing ethical considerations as they pursue particular goals.[14]

In a research study of 400 financial executives conducted by Duke University's John Graham, 80 percent of those surveyed said they would forgo critical investments in things like maintenance, research and development, the purchase of new equipment, marketing initiatives and key hires in order to help their company to meet quarterly earnings projections. Half of these executives also said they would put value-creating projects on hold if halting these projects would help the company meet earnings targets.[15] This telescopic outlook upon a singular goal, often referred to as short-termism, can blind people not only to larger opportunities for creating value, but also to behaviors that destroy value.[16]

---

12 Florida State University News Release, "Researchers probe how supervisors' misdeeds affect worker health, productivity" (December 2, 2010). The article, available at http://fsu.edu/news/2010/12/02/worker.health/, was captured from the Internet on May, 21, 2013 at 11:35 AM EST).

13 Gallup Business Journal, "Many Employees Would Fire Their Boss" (October 11, 2007). The article, available at http://businessjournal.gallup.com/content/28867/many-employees-would-fire-their-boss.aspx, was captured from the Internet on May, 21, 2013 at 11:38 AM EST).

14 Daniel H. Pink, *Drive: The Surprising Truth About What Motivates Us* (New York: Penguin Books, 2009), 51.

15 John R. Graham, Campbell R. Harvey, and Shivaram Rajgopal, "The Economic Implications of Corporate Financial Reporting," *Journal of Accounting and Economics*, vol., 40 (2005): 3–73.

16 Dean Krehmeyer, Matthew Orsagh and Kurt Schacht. *Breaking the Short-Term Cycle Discussion and Recommendations on How Corporate Leaders, Asset Managers, Investors, and Analysts Can Refocus on Long-Term Value*, CFA Centre for Financial Market Integrity and Business Roundtable Institute for Corporate Ethics (whitepaper, 2006).

Sticks, or attempts to motivate people primarily via threats or punishments, are equally problematic. In *Drive*, Daniel Pink recounts a study conducted by economists Uri Gneezy and Aldo Rustichini that examined pricing levers among parents at a daycare center. As part of the study, the daycare center sent a message to parents stating that parents would be charged a $10 fee for every 15 minutes they were late to pick up their child. To Gneezy and Rustichini's surprise, fewer parents arrived on time *after* the announcement of the penalty. Pink's assessment of this counter-intuitive result is that "the fine shifted the parents' decision from a partly moral obligation (be fair to my kids' teachers) to a pure transaction (I can buy extra time) ... The punishment didn't promote good behavior; it crowded it out."[17]

The point is not that carrots and sticks are bad, but rather that we need to be mindful of how we use them—especially with respect to how they might impact the existing motivation to fulfill the mission and purpose of the organization. The message for leaders is that the traditional motivational levers used by organizations are not working very effectively.

The good news is that leaders who develop a better understanding of human motivation have opportunities to create greater value for their people, for their organizations, and for society. Recent research suggests the following four key actions that leaders can take to help their organization's people thrive:

- Focus on mission
- Challenge people
- Encourage autonomy
- Promote civility[18]

Purpose-driven organizations have an important advantage because they are able to tap into the intrinsic motivation of their people. Intrinsic motivation refers to activities or work that people find rewarding in and of itself: for example, a pharmaceutical researcher who is driven by a desire to alleviate suffering caused by a particular disease. When work is intrinsically motivating, performance and creativity thrive.

---

17 Pink, 51-53.
18 Gretchen Spreitzer and Christine Porath, "Creating Sustainable Performance," *Harvard Business Review* (January–February, 2012), 92-99.

When employees have a voice in the mission of the organization, purpose becomes part of a living conversation with people asking, "What is the unique value that this organization provides for the world?" Companies need employees to be asking this question repeatedly. As the former CEO of Aetna Dr. Jack Rowe has said, "the greatest threat to any company is a failure to differentiate."[19]

Thriving employees help companies differentiate and innovate, creating greater value for their organizations and for the world. As Harvard psychologist Dan Gilbert has demonstrated, people tend to be most happy and productive at work when they are attempting to accomplish things that stretch them. Ideal goals are in the sweet spot of being difficult, but not impossible for people to reach.[20] Identifying the right challenges for different employees and teams is a tremendous leadership challenge that puts skills like listening, communicating and coaching at a premium.

Research from Gretchen Spreitzer and Christine Porath suggests that providing employees with a certain amount of decision-making discretion or autonomy is a critical factor in creating a workplace where people thrive.[21] The ability to make decisions is connected to intrinsic motivation in that it enables people to pursue the organization's mission in a way that they help to determine. This allows people to stretch themselves and grow in ways that they find meaningful, while unleashing their creativity for the benefit of the organization.

Promoting a culture characterized by civility and respect is a key driver of a thriving workplace that is sometimes overlooked. Companies where managers berate and bully employees are environments for disengagement.

A study led by the University of New Hampshire's Paul Harvey shows that abusive behavior can lead to job dissatisfaction, not only among those abused, but also among their co-workers. This finding is important although it should surprise no one.[22]

---

19 Dr. Rowe made this statement during a meeting of the Business Roundtable Institute for Corporate Ethics and Arthur W. Page Society Panel on Public Trust in Business in New York (May 16, 2007).
20 Daniel Gilbert, "The Science Behind the Smile," *Harvard Business Review* (January–February, 2012), p. 84-90
21 Spreitzer and Porath, p. 92-99.
22 University of New Hampshire News Release, "Targets of Bully Bosses Aren't the Only Victims" (February 2, 2013).

Equally important is Tony Simons and Judi McLean Parks' finding that organizations where the senior manager is highly trusted by employees outperform peer organizations by 13 percent on average.[23] The message is clear: organizations that are failing to assess their managers' impact on workplace climate are failing to achieve their performance potential.

The capacity of global brands to build trust among stakeholders and society depends on a company's ability to build an army of advocates, starting with their own people. As Spreitzer and Porath have shown, "Happy employees ... routinely show up at work, they're less likely to quit, they go above and beyond the call of duty, and they attract people who are just as committed to the job."[24] Thriving work environments become a magnet that attracts engaged, high performing employees.

Leaders hoping to build trust in their companies should contemplate President Lincoln's tree metaphor that opens this chapter. The character and values of organizations are roots that provide stability over time. The people who form the organization are the branches that can grow in new directions that create value for stakeholders, including society. Innovative products and services are the fruits.

The tree is the real thing. The tree (the character of the organization) determines the fruit it will produce and the shape of its shadow (its reputation). The reverse is not true: despite the attention paid to it, the shadow (reputation) does not determine the shape of the tree (character).

Leadership that effectively engages human motivation develops organizations where people thrive and where value is created. This, and nothing else, is the absolute bedrock upon which lasting trust and reputation stand.

---

23 Tony Simons and Judi McLean Parks, "Empty words: The Impact of Managerial Integrity on Employee Turnover, Customer Service and Profits," (working paper, 2002). Cited in Kurt T. Dirks, "Three Fundamental Questions Regarding Trust in Leaders," in *Handbook of Trust Research*, Reinhard Bachmann and Akbar Zaheer (ed.), (Northhampton, MA: Edward Elgar, 2006), 15–28.
24 Spreitzer and Porath, 93.

Brian Moriarty

Brian Moriarty is Director of the Business Roundtable Institute for Corporate Ethics (www.corporate-ethics.org) and an Adjunct Professor at the University of Virginia's Darden School of Business where he teaches Management Communications in the full-time MBA program and Darden Executive Education. He is the editor of the forthcoming book Public Trust in Business, *a volume of leading academic research in the area of public trust, to be published by Cambridge University Press. Moriarty serves on the board of the Carson Raymond Foundation, a non-profit sports-based youth development organization named in honor of one of his former players.*

Reinforcing Candor Builds Trust and Transparency

By Bob Whipple

The decimation of trust in organizations of all types during the past decade has been alarming, yet some groups have been able to buck the trend and are actually increasing trust. The research by Trust Across America is the most comprehensive data on organizations and consultants who are leading a rebirth of trust. My own experience provides many examples of the power of trust. This is one.

I was a Division Manager for Eastman Kodak when an unusual request came in from the Olympics. Responding to this impossible challenge involved having total trust in the system and team to allow them to break every rule in the book and put out a new product in less than three days.

On a Tuesday morning in 1992, one of the product planners received a call from a gentleman in Albertville, France. The Winter Olympics was starting to wind down, and this customer from Sports Illustrated had a challenge for us. He noticed there were colored Olympic rings embedded in the ice of the figure skating venue. His idea was to climb up into the rafters and take images looking directly down on the skaters in the Woman's Singles Finals on Saturday night, using the rings in the background. He needed some special equipment in a format we did not sell. The accelerated cycle time to get a new product to market like the one he was suggesting was 9-12 months. We had to ship the product on Friday morning to be sure it would get there on time. That meant we had to get everything done in 2½ days rather than a year.

The team assigned the task of readying and delivering this product had a blast, breaking all kinds of rules in order to make the impossible deadline. In the end, the customer had what he needed, and the next issue of Sports Illustrated included an image of Kristi Yamaguchi winning the Gold Medal while she was literally flying over the Olympic rings embedded in the ice.

The Business Unit was so thrilled that they presented the Department with a framed copy of the image signed by Kristi Yamaguchi herself. When the business unit came to the factory to deliver the picture, it was an electric moment for the workers. It is truly amazing what a trusted team of workers can accomplish.

While there are many examples of great progress like the one above, the overall trend is still far from the trust levels we experienced in past decades. We must do better.

Once lost, trust is very difficult to rebuild. There is an urgent need to reeducate all leaders on how to build trust consistently to prevent further loss of it. More than any other factor, the quality of leadership governs the levels of trust seen within any organization.

A simple three-part model of how leader behaviors can help build higher trust includes three categories of behaviors.

1. Table Stakes

These are the basic building blocks of ethics and integrity that must be present for any level of trust to kindle. The term Table Stakes comes from the phenomenon in poker where individuals must ante up even to play in the game. Traits like honesty, openness, communication, consistency, and ethics simply must be present, or the leader may as well take off his suit and hit the showers. Trust is not going to kindle or survive if the Table Stakes are not there.

2. Enabling Actions

These are the components that further help build trust once the Table Stakes are present. There are thousands of items we could name in this category. Here are some examples: following up, advocacy, fairness, admitting mistakes, and many others. The more these elements are present, the greater the ability for the leader to withstand trust withdrawals.

Enabling actions need to form a pattern of behavior that people see as consistent and prudent in building trust. It is the actions of the leader that determine the level of trust achieved in any organization; words are important but inadequate.

These first two lists of behaviors are necessary but not sufficient conditions for real trust to kindle and endure. There is a central core that must also be in play for the Table Stakes and the Enabling Actions to have their intended impact. Without this core, these elements will aid in building some trust, but their potency is severely limited.

3. The Heart of Trust—Reinforcing Candor

In this analysis, reinforcing candor takes center stage, because the concept goes far beyond integrity. It is the magic that most leaders find difficult or impossible to accomplish, but if done well, make a huge difference in creating trust.

Reinforcing Candor is the ability to make people glad they brought up an observation of a leader's inconsistency. In most organizations, people are punished in some way for bringing forward a leadership problem. Where the highest levels of trust and transparency are present, the leader has the ability to set aside his ego and reinforce those who challenge an action. Doing so greatly increases trust and allows for future trust-building exchanges. Without this critical element, the Table Stakes and Enabling Actions are not sufficient. People do not feel empowered to challenge the leader and hide their true feelings, making the maintenance of trust impossible.

One hallmark of an environment where candor is reinforced is the lack of fear. Trust and fear are incompatible. If people know they will be reinforced for initiating the difficult conversations, they will not be afraid to do so. Whenever people are reinforced for their candor, trust deepens and fear is suppressed.

The critical need to reinforce candor can be explained by a phenomenon called "the ratchet effect." Like a ratchet, trust is built up by a series of actions or "clicks" that take place over time. But, if the pawl holding the ratchet from rotating backward becomes dislodged, the entire spool of trust equity can spin back to zero very quickly.

Visualizing the Ratchet Effect in Action

Many authors writing on the subject of trust, such as Stephen M.R. Covey, describe the level of trust as similar to a bank account. Between any two people there is a current "balance" of trust that is the result of all transactions that have happened to date. Every time there is any kind of interface (whether online, in a meeting, or even with body language) there is some kind of transaction occurring. Either there is a deposit (increasing trust) or a withdrawal (reducing trust). The magnitude of the transaction is determined by its nature and importance.

The level of trust between people is precisely the same as the balance in a bank account. It is an instantaneous statement of the total worth of the relationship based on all transactions up until the present. The balance can only be increased by making consistent deposits, and being very careful to limit the withdrawals.

It is easy for a leader to make small deposits in the trust account with employees. Treating people with respect and being fair are two examples. Great leaders go about their day trying to make these small deposits as often as possible, realizing they are adding to the balance every time. While making small deposits is relatively easy, making a large deposit is more difficult.

For leaders, words alone rarely make a large deposit in trust. It has to be an action, and it often requires some unusual circumstance, like giving up some personal time off during a crisis, or relinquishing a long-standing perk if others cannot have it too.

Unfortunately, on the withdrawal side, the pattern is different. With one slip of the tongue, an ill-advised email, or even the wrong facial expression in a meeting, a leader can make a huge withdrawal. Because of the ratchet effect, a small withdrawal can become big, because the pawl is no longer engaged in the ratchet. Trust can quickly spiral to zero or even to a negative balance.

This is an example of the ratchet effect in a typical conversation: "I have always trusted George. I have worked for him for fifteen years, and he has always been straight with me. I have always felt he was on my side when the chips were down, but after he said that in the meeting yesterday, I will never trust him again."

Not only has all trust been lost in a single action, but also it will take a very long time before any new deposits can be made. The trust account dropped from a healthy positive balance to a negative one in a single sentence. In many cases, the normal small trust deposits do not even register in the account balance after a mega withdrawal.

It would be incredibly powerful if we could prevent the ratchet from losing all of its previous progress. What if there was a way to reinsert the pawl back into the ratchet during a serious withdrawal so that the mechanism only slipped back one or two teeth? Reinforcing candor inserts the pawl and provides organizational magic that has unparalleled power to build trust.

All leaders make trust withdrawals because no one is perfect. In most organizations, people do not feel safe to let the leader know they have just been sapped. There is no ability to reinsert the pawl, and trust plummets. It may even go to zero or a negative level of trust before it can be corrected over a long period of time with incredible effort.

Contrast this with another scenario where the individual knows it is safe to let the leader know she has made a blunder. The individual might say something like, "I don't think you realize how people interpreted your remarks. Your decision reduced trust, and I am concerned that long term damage may result." If this employee is sincerely thanked rather than punished for their candor, then trust will grow.

Every leader is trying to do exactly the right thing all day, every day. If an employee is so bold as to question why the leader did something, the reaction in most is for the leader to become defensive and push back on the messenger; it is human nature. Taking a defensive stance becomes a withdrawal, which does not work to reinsert the pawl into the ratchet.

Reinforcing candor is not easy. Not only does it require a leader to suppress ego, it also means performing an unnatural act in terms of being human. The solution to get mileage out of reinforcing candor is for the leader to recognize the trigger point and to modify his behavior to create the desired reaction.

> *Tip: When an employee brings forth bad news or a contrary opinion, focus on doing only one thing. When the conversation is about to end, make sure this person walks away saying, "I'm glad I brought that up."*

This tip is difficult for most leaders to execute, because they have justified their action to themselves, so it is only natural to defend it to others. It takes great restraint to listen and not have a negative reaction. The good news is that the more a leader practices, the easier this technique gets. No one will ever have a 100% batting average, but if a leader can go from 10% to 70% by focusing on his behavior, he can change an entire culture of an organization in a matter of months rather than years.

Once the leader has learned to reinforce candor consistently, something magic happens. When he practices any of the "Table Stakes" or "Enabling Actions," everyone benefits. That is why reinforcing candor is at the heart of building trust. Individuals who learn to do this well will be among the elite leaders of our time.

Bob Whipple

Bob Whipple is CEO of Leadergrow Inc a company dedicated to improving leadership in organizations. He is also a professional speaker and a member of National Speakers Association. When speaking, Bob uses the brand name of "The Trust Ambassador." He has been named by Leadership Excellence Magazine one of the top 15 consultant thought leaders in the country on leadership development. He has three published books on the topic of trust and over 300 published articles on various leadership topics. Reach Bob at bwhipple@leadergrow.com

Section V:

Restoring Trust

Five Strategies to Maximize The Power of Trust

By Patricia Aburdene

In simpler times, the value of trust was considered an integral component of every financial transaction. Successful people often sealed multi-million dollar deals on the full faith and trust of a handshake. In the past decade or so, however, a series of economic calamities has severely eroded our trust in business. Since the S&L crisis, accounting scandals, internet bubble, and the great recession, the economy has sustained so many—and such fierce—fiscal blows that many question the viability of free enterprise.

Growing numbers blame an overzealous brand of shareholder capitalism that endorses profit "first-last-and always" no matter the moral, environmental, or human costs. Ironically shareholder capitalism has twice in a single decade destroyed trillions of dollars in *shareholder* wealth—first during the tech-fueled market crash of 2001-2003 and again during the Subprime Crisis from 2007 to 2009.

In the wake of such profound economic destruction, movements like Occupy Wall Street have sprung up advocating new economic approaches. However, Conscious Capitalism, which I described in *Megatrends 2010: The Rise of Conscious Capitalism* offers a just, market-based model that is now attracting a wide, and growing following.

Unlike traditional or shareholder capitalism, which generally favors investors over other parties, Conscious Capitalists honor the contributions of employees, customers, suppliers, investors, communities, and the environment, while strongly endorsing the profit motive. Yet Conscious Capitalists also deem it essential to embrace a purpose over and above earning money—and to practice positive values, such as trust and sustainability, in business.

Today, people are starting to see that restoring trust is vital to the healthy economic growth on which humanity depends for economic security, innovation, wellbeing, a clean environment, and the freedom to pursue happiness and self-expression. The question is: how does business anchor trust into daily operations? I propose five strategies, with examples and case studies to illustrate each. They are:

1. Fully Recognize the Economic Power of Trust
2. Build Trust into the Business Model
3. Cultivate Trust by Deepening the Conversation
4. Restore Consumer Trust
5. Profit from the Power of Trust

Fully Recognize the Economic Power of Trust

Personally, I hold as economic truth that the value of trust literally translates into success and prosperity. Few have articulated the economic case for trust better than one well-known U.S. economic figure. "Our market system depends critically on trust," Former Federal Reserve Chairman Alan Greenspan told the U.S. Congress July 16, 2002, during his semi-annual Monetary Policy Report. "Trust in the word of our colleagues and trust in the word of those with whom we do business."

Build Trust into the Business Model

How does one translate the power of trust into specific policy at a particular company? The following example demonstrates how one leader embedded trust into the business model.

The financial platform of eBay, the on-line sales giant, was constructed on the power of trust. Early on, founder Pierre Omidyar posted this statement on the website: "We believe people are basically good." eBay's commercial policies were guided by Omidyar's commitment to trust. eBay then utilized its online technological expertise to reinforce trust with mechanisms that empower buyers to rate a seller's track record for trust. Result? Considerably less than one percent of eBay transactions result in fraud. Without the capacity to address the issue of trust in commercial transactions between strangers, it is difficult, if not impossible, to imagine eBay growing into a multi-billion dollar publicly traded corporation.

Cultivate Trust by Deepening the Conversation

Within corporations and the teams that make them successful, fostering an environment of trust is essential to optimum performance. This is true whether the team is focused on a high tech project, new strategy, or day-to-day operations. Put differently, the breakdown of trust is a tell tale sign that failure will soon follow. But how can organizations encourage the trust that's necessary for success?

"Trust is essential," says Alain Bolea, founder and principal of Business Advisors Network (www.business-advisors.net), which supports leaders and teams to boost performance by deepening their conversations and building the trust that creates high performance. "But you can't create trust by fiat. Certain conditions must be in place in order to cultivate trust."

What then are the prerequisites of trust? The first is safety "People must feel safe about each other," says Bolea. "Without a felt-sense of safety, people will not open up, speak their truth, or take risks." Each of these three steps is essential to high performance. "When people don't open up," he explains, "their colleagues can perceive them as holding something back [such as vital information]. You're unlikely to trust someone you think is holding back."

Until you can experience safety with a team member or colleague, Bolea summarizes, the potential for trust is blocked. There's only one way of breaking through, he says: "You must create a space where people feel sufficiently safe to say what they genuinely think and feel." Business Advisors designs and creates the platform for people to do exactly that. And the benefits are exponential.

Creating a safe space generates an uplifting spiral in a group process, because each individual's experience of safety encourages others to open up. This positive dynamic naturally *supports* people to be more open without requiring or compelling them to do so, a tactic that simply does not work.

But how much time does it take to generate this positive transformation? "Not long at all," says Bolea. "We see results in two to three hours. Once trust is ignited, there's a complete shift in how people interact with each other and what they together create. It really is quite remarkable to observe."

Restore Consumer Trust

Trust consultant, Lilach Felner, with thirteen years marketing experience at a top Israeli food production firm, honed her vision of working with clients to promote trust as she monitored global trends signaling the erosion of trust across most sectors and geographic areas. While attempting to cope with the first signs of a crisis in trust, she came to recognize several key points:

1. 21st century consumers distrust almost everybody. They're turned off by manipulative gimmicks and unsubstantiated marketing claims. Theses skeptical consumers find an ally in the "Transparency Revolution": no one can hide anything anymore, thanks to the power of social media. "The rules of the game have changed," says Lilach Felner. "There are new rules for marketing and a new set of strategic and marketing tools."

2. Marketers today face a unique set of challenges, such as high levels of products substitution, intense competition, saturated markets, and the issue of differentiating a product in terms of technical characteristics. As a result, she says, "It's increasingly difficult to succeed in the face of imitation."

3. The confluence of the first two trends led Ms. Felner to conclude: "The new competitive advantage is trust. This is what the consumer desires most. Trust is what can differentiate you from your competitors. The sooner you embody trust, the better your market position."

4. As a professional marketer, Felner learned first-hand that trust cannot be engendered through a marketing campaign alone. It is cultivated instead through the sum total of an organization's daily actions, big or small, including "the way you advertise, the quality of your customer service, your word of mouth in social media, your product's quality, price and warranty, as well as the trust-worthy people you recruit," she explains. "All these components together create the customer's 'total trust experience.'" That's why the marketing team in charge of building a trust-based customer relationship has such a challenging mission today, says Felner, who adds, "They must conduct the whole organization's orchestra and teach it to play a new type of music, a trust-based symphony."

In response to these insights, Felner created the Trust-based Strategy Model to help CEOs, marketers, and managers build greater trust, especially among customers. What follows is but a brief description of her rich and complex model.

The Trust-based Model (or Trust Model for short) is comprised of a variety of trust-building tools and assessments that illuminate where a company stands now in terms of trust and where (and how) to move toward greater trustworthiness. The model unfolds over several phases:

1. Measure the Trust Climate. The Trust-based Model first aims to get an overview of the organizational trust level, resulting a "total trust score." Next, it gages how trust levels vary from one arena to another, thus, producing a more thorough, focused diagnostic picture.

2. Map the Trust Gaps. Felner's Trust Model measures many factors that determine trust levels, including customer interaction, front line personnel, product quality, after sales service, and more. Each of these "Trust Influencers," says Felner, can be "trust builders" or "trust busters." It also examines a spectrum of 10 characteristics ranging (on a scale of 1 to 5) with 1 being more traditional and 5, more trust-based behavior. For example, does a company encourage customer feedback or fail to ask for it?

3. Anchor the Trust Strategy in Time. Close the Trust Gaps by plotting the organization's current strategy and behavior. Then map where it commits to be in two year's time in terms of nine trust-based strategies. For example, how far will it evolve from a "Low caring" to a "High Caring" organization?

4. Employ Trust-based Marketing Strategies. To further enhance trustworthiness, Felner's Model applies additional Trust-based Tools. Brands often measure their market share, but one innovative Trust-based Tool measures "Share of Trust." Another examines growth objectives in terms of high or low trust levels in current and new customers—and how these different types of customers impact sales growth.

In summary, the Trust Model cultivates trust by: 1) measuring the components that strengthen trust; 2) closing "trust gaps" by embracing trust-worthy behavior; 3) committing to a timeline for trust-based strategies; and 4) activating trust-based marketing. This multi-dimensional approach is designed to create and capitalize on the competitive advantage that is only delivered through the power of trust.

Profit from the Power of Trust

Let's now revisit the financial component of trust, which plays a key role in the two areas that make or break a corporation's capacity to earn profit: cost cutting and revenue generation. No one has better defined the role of trust in cost cutting than Stephen M. R. Covey, author of the landmark work *The Speed of Trust*. Early in the book, Covey puts forth an elegant formula depicting how trust impacts the cost of doing business. Simply stated, Covey argues that: when trust increases, speed increases, too—and costs (happily) fall. But when trust decreases, speed does too, and costs (unhappily) increase.

In other words, the absence of trust costs business a lot of money.

During the business cycle, cost cutting is the dominant strategy when times are tough. After the economy picks up, however, corporate leaders face an equally challenging imperative—growing new business. Here, too, trust plays a critical role, as this story demonstrates.

As Hewlett-Packard's inkjet czar, VP Greg Merten managed 10,000 people and a multi-billion dollar business. Much of his success, he said, was due to the transformation he experienced when his son Scott 16, was killed. Before the tragedy, Merten was hard-driving executive bent on results. Scott was a "real people person." Scott's example, says Merten, "inspired me to get better at relationships."

Every month or so, Merten blocked off a full day, gathered his team together, and focused on their relationships, asking "How do we operate with each other? Are we trusting? Or distrustful and destructive?" These trust-based practices guided Merten's business unit as it expanded from one to six factories. The Dublin, Ireland site faced numerous snags until Merten lead conflicting parties through the same trust building protocols his team practiced. Getting Dublin up and running on time, says Merten, literally contributed "hundreds of millions of dollars to HP's bottom line.

In conclusion, as trust champions everywhere can attest, the benefits of trust in terms of value creation and strategic advantage are gradually coming to light. Yet conventional business people still deny the power of trust, in part because they believe that espousing trust is tantamount to repudiating financial responsibility. Nothing could be further from the truth.

When we, as trust-based leaders, practice the transcendent value of trust, we extend "good faith" to others and earn their trust through our own reliability. At the same time, because we simultaneously continue to honor sound monetary principles, we position ourselves to harvest the dual rewards of superior financial performance and personal fulfillment. This is the true power of trust in business.

Patricia Aburdene

Patricia Aburdene is one of the world's leading social forecasters, co-author of the number one New York Times *bestseller* Megatrends 2000, *and a world-renown speaker. Patricia's books and talks have transformed thousands of companies and millions of people. Her latest book* Conscious Money: Living, Creating, and Investing with Your Values for A Sustainable New Prosperity *is a finalist for the Books for A Better Life Award. Patricia's landmark* Megatrends 2010: The Rise of Conscious Capitalism *launched a business revolution.*

Patricia is a "Top 100 Thought Leader in Trustworthy Business." She serves as an Ambassador for the Conscious Capitalism Institute and an advisor to Satori Capital. Patricia was a Public Policy Fellow at Radcliffe College and holds a BA in philosophy from Newton College of the Sacred Heart (now Boston College), a MS in library science from Catholic University, and three honorary doctorates.

Trust, Emotion and Corporate Reputation

By Linda Locke

In 2008, a musician flying from Nova Scotia to Nebraska checked his prized instrument because it was difficult to carry on board. When he arrived in Omaha, he discovered that his guitar was damaged and he immediately contacted the airline. After nine months of discussion with the airline, he was told he was ineligible for compensation because he hadn't filed the proper claim within 24 hours.

In a move that has become legendary, the musician, Dave Carroll, recorded a song and video called "United Breaks Guitars" and posted it on You Tube, and finally got the attention of United Airlines- within 24 hours.

When Carroll boarded the plane and checked his guitar with United, like hundreds of thousands of travelers that day, he trusted that he and his luggage would arrive safely. He put himself in the hands of pilots, flight control agents and baggage handlers, trusting that all would act competently.

A reputation is a promise

A company's reputation is built on trust. It's the promise an organization makes to its stakeholders about its products, processes and people. The promise is then secured by the handshake of a transaction. When people trust an organization, they are more likely to exhibit supportive behavior: buying the products and services it is selling, recommending it to friends, and taking the actions it would like. When a company lives up to its reputation, customers develop warm or trusting feelings about it.

Trust is an emotion we feel. When we trust another person we feel safe and secure. We are more likely to give them the benefit of the doubt in times of stress, because ultimately we trust that there will be a positive outcome.

After multiple attempts at resolving the airline's responsibility related to his broken guitar, Dave Carroll's emotions had moved from trust to outrage.

A lack of trust in organizations is evident in the cynicism and skepticism that permeates modern society, tracked in annual surveys such as the Edelman Trust Barometer. The 2012 survey showed that low trust in business results in increased calls for regulation because of perceptions about companies' irresponsible behavior. While the survey points out that business leaders are more trusted than government officials, nearly half of the respondents said the government does not regulate business enough.

The decline in trust has a cost

Damage to a company's reputation for trustworthiness comes with a price tag.

- Bank of America was surprised at the public reaction to its announcement of a monthly fee to use a debit card, and scrapped the plan despite its revenue potential.[1]
- BP saw significant increase in its cost of doing business as a result of reaction to its management of the Deepwater Horizon spill in the Gulf of Mexico.[2]
- The Komen Foundation faced a significant decrease in contributions when its process to decide to withdraw funding from Planned Parenthood became public.[3]

All three crises have two elements in common—a significant reputational crisis event followed by a negative impact to revenue.

A reputational crisis is one in which trust in the organization is undermined. Reputation may be an organization's most valuable asset, but its inherent intangibility may make it the most difficult asset to manage. This explains why CEOs and Boards of Directors consider it a perplexing challenge that keeps them up at night.[4]

---

1   *Bank of America drops debit card fees*, by Sandra Block, USAToday, Nov. 11, 2011
2   *Reputation, Stock Price and You* by Dr. Nir Kossovsky, Apress, 2012
3   *Komen Foundation Struggles to Regain Wide Support*, by David Wallis, New York Times, Nov. 8, 2012
4   *Third Annual Board of Directors Survey 2012—Concerns About Risks Confronting Boards—* EisnerAmper, May 7, 2012; survey of 193 U.S. company directors regarding chief concerns beyond financial risks.

Key to that challenge is understanding the emotions that drive stakeholders' expectations. Leaders often mismanage trust and reputation because they fail to think and communicate in emotional terms.

Trust as an emotional construct

When faced with consumer outrage—when trust and reputation are at risk—the first instinct of many organizations is to respond with facts. But mistrust is not often assuaged by facts.

Trust is an emotional construct and a building block for civil society and commerce. Trust is the core of every transaction and interaction. Why? We depend on others. We need them to provide what we long for—love, safety and security. Likewise, we depend upon businesses that provide essential products and services. We rely on them and are disappointed when they fail to meet our expectations.

Today, consumer expectations often extend beyond price and quality to how the companies make us feel. Are we satisfied with our interactions with clerks, customer service representatives? Do they make us feel important or ignored?

We expect companies to act ethically, fairly and reliably. When we hear an executive speak or we read about corporate activities, we make judgments about them. We decide whether they meet our expectations. These expectations shape our beliefs and our actions.

The more that companies meet our expectations, the stronger our emotional bond. When our expectations are not met, we begin to withdraw our trust, either slowly or rapidly, depending on the severity of the issue.

Unfortunately, businesses often approach their activities from a purely logical perspective. Rationality rules the boardroom while emotionality rules the living room.

Let's say a company is accused of acting unethically. The business may meet every requirement for compliance with laws and regulations. In a crisis, the instinct of executives often is to respond with the facts that demonstrate the logic of their choices and actions—in this case, with a full list of compliance actions.

If they were speaking to a boardroom of fellow executives, or a panel of attorneys, that response might suffice. But if their broader audience is a nation of skeptical families and consumer advocates, a cold list of facts may only worsen the company's reputational crisis. The company may get a reputation for unethical behavior.

Instead, facts should be just the starting point.

Facts: only the first step toward trust

The facts are the starting place to build trust. An organization must meet all of the requirements to comply with the law. If the legal requirements are not met, then stakeholders have good reason to consider a company weak in the dimension of ethics.

To earn trust, a company must go beyond the requirements, beyond the simple facts of the situation, and demonstrate that it understands the concerns of its stakeholders. Compliance with the law can be interpreted as doing the minimum; today, stakeholders have expectations regarding ethics, fairness, workplace and the environment that go beyond the attributes of a specific product. The manner in which companies engage, respond and communicate can impact how they are perceived.

In times of crisis or stress, when the environment can be characterized as "high concern/low trust," people hear messages differently. Given the asymmetry of information between large organizations and their stakeholders, companies should communicate assertively that they care about their stakeholders and are dedicated to resolving the situation. But if those communications are not backed up with action, the move will backfire.

Commitment, honesty and empathy

Risk communication science suggests that to build trust, the facts of the situation are a small part of what organizations need to communicate. Trust and credibility depend upon a company demonstrating that it has the knowledge and expertise to address a problem; that it acts with honesty and openness; and that it expresses concern and care.

A company that expresses empathy, care and concern for its stakeholders demonstrates that it understands their perspectives and is more likely to maintain their goodwill in a crisis.

In a crisis situation, here is the recommended breakdown of communications content:

- Half of a company's external communications should express care and concern;
- One quarter should express the company's commitment to addressing the situation;
- And only one quarter should focus on the facts.

Consumers today express their feelings through traditional market research and customer care surveys, but also through social media.

A company that welcomes unfettered stakeholder feedback will employ a listening platform to understand what is being said about it and its competitors—and to ascertain whether its perspective on a situation aligns with the perceptions of its stakeholders.

The more sophisticated social listening tools capture the level of emotion in the public dialogue about an issue or organization—such as the emotion expressed in comments on Twitter, blogs, Facebook and web forums.

Using tools from social psychology, a listening platform should predict the emotion that will be felt by people reading about an issue or company. By understanding trust and other emotions that drive perceptions and lead to behavior change, an organization can demonstrate empathy, caring and concern that resonates with its stakeholders.

Case study: Fear undermines trust

For example, during the 2007–2008 financial meltdown in the US, a major financial services firm conducted an analysis of the emotions about the crisis in the public dialogue. By applying a social-psychological framework to the language people were using to describe and discuss the situation, the firm found that the three strongest likely emotions were: *irreversibility, unfamiliarity* and a sense among consumers that their involvement was *involuntary*.

Irreversibility. A risk perceived to be irreversible elicits greater negative emotions than one that is thought to be reversible. In this case, consumers expressed deep fears that the changes they were seeing were permanent. This fear of permanent economic difficulty was reflected in changes in consumer sentiment about spending.

Unfamiliarity. This concept involves the emotional concern over the unknown risks from an issue. Risks perceived to be unfamiliar are less readily accepted and appear greater than risks perceived to be familiar.

Involuntary. The involuntary nature of the crisis stemmed from consumers' feeling that they were unable to have any influence over the situation; that it was not a result of personal choice.

In this case, organizations that wished to demonstrate empathy, caring and concern with their stakeholders would communicate the steps that could be taken by each relevant party (government, banks, consumers) in language that most people found easy to understand. They would explain in plain language how the situation occurred, using examples from familiar situations. And, they would describe the role of the responsible parties and what they were doing to address the situation.

Case study: Blame undermines trust

More recently, a proposition was on the ballot in California to require labeling of genetically modified food. A recent analysis of the dialogue around the campaigns for and against Proposition 37 identified three primary emotions: *human involvement, dread* and *catastrophe.*

Human involvement. This is an emotional concern that derives from the feeling that the situation is being caused by human failure or action. Risks perceived to be generated by human action elicit greater negative emotion than risks perceived to be caused by nature. If someone caused the problem, that person is expected to fix it.

When consumer commentary focuses on "human-caused risk," consumers are assigning blame. They are calling organizations to account. A company that fails to understand these expectations risks looking tone deaf, which undermines its emotional bond with stakeholders, gives rise to distrust and damages its reputation

Dread and catastrophe. These are extreme emotions. When dread and catastrophe are driving the emotional tenor of the public discussion, people are likely to be experiencing fear, terror and anxiety. They perceive the potential for fatalities, injuries or illness.

In such a situation, a company must respond with both empathy and action to preserve trust, protect its reputation and contain the issue. If people fear catastrophe, but a company responds with only the bare facts of, say, its compliance program—that company would rapidly lose the trust of many of its stakeholders. Such a misstep could give rise to calls for additional regulation.

Trust payoff ... or penalty

A strong reputation that inspires trust provides a measurable payoff.

A company that is highly regarded by its stakeholders is more likely to enjoy strong brand loyalty and long-term, high-value customers. It can expect to see lower employee turnover and easier recruitment of high-caliber employees. Such a company is more likely to benefit from higher investor confidence, a more positive regulatory environment and even lower costs of capital, as its reputation paves the way for greater trust from financial partners. That's the payoff of trust and a good reputation.

Mistrust, resulting in a weak or negative reputation, exacts a measurable cost— a reputation penalty—in the form of increased customer churn and elevated customer acquisition costs. Such a company will face higher employee training costs and related service inefficiencies. It will pay the price of regulatory constraints, increased cost of capital, lower investor confidence and an increased vulnerability to competitors.

Leaders are responsible for protecting both revenue and reputation. To fulfill this dual responsibility, they must orient their organizations toward understanding the expectations of their stakeholders as a core element of strategy.

Every leader knows perceptions are reality; the wise leader uses the drivers of trust to survive and thrive in the current economy.

Linda Locke

Linda Locke is the principal of Reputare Consulting, a consultancy that focuses on reputation, risk, crisis management and strategic communications. Locke previously served as the group head and senior vice president for Reputation and Issues Management for MasterCard Worldwide. linda.locke@reputareconsulting.com

Building Trust is Tougher Than Ever: A Trust Manifesto for Leaders

By James E. Lukaszewski

The setting was pretty intense. I was about to meet with a subcommittee of the board of directors of a *Fortune 500* company whose main manufacturing facility in Massachusetts had been raided by the FBI the previous Thursday. This special subcommittee of the board had been designated to oversee the company's response to what now appeared to be the inevitable indictment of the corporation, its leaders and a number of its employees. The room reminded me, though smaller, of the U.S. Supreme Court chambers in Washington D.C. There was a huge table; there were nearly a dozen high backed, black high-comfort chairs awaiting board members who were involved in selecting advisors for the company. As they entered the room, it was an intimidating sight. Two of the members were relatively well-known national business figures, a few were prominent attorneys, and I had yet to meet the rest of the group.

The chairman of the group opened and came right to the point. He said

"We've spoken with Hill and Knowlton, Burson-Marsteller, several large Washington-based firms, Fleishman-Hillard. Not to be impolite, but to be direct, why is it that we are speaking with *you*; who are you?"

I had been prepared for this question and simply said, "Gentlemen, I believe I'm here because I've been through this before, and this is your first time. We can discuss my credentials, or we can discuss what's going to happen to you and this company in the next 20-30 months. And, by the way, we might also talk about who will be at this meeting next year, who won't be and why."

I got the job.

The real question we talked about for the next twenty minutes or so, was how a greatly admired *Fortune 500* worldwide medical products manufacturer finds itself in the midst of a federal criminal investigation with patient deaths alleged, criminal activity involving altering medical products illegally.

Within eight weeks, the company was indicted along with six employees, and the chairman. The chairman of the company had worked with the company for nearly forty years, 19 years in sales and marketing, when the board selected him to be the new chief executive officer, now nearly 19 years ago.

I helped him clean out his desk the day before he was going to surrender himself to federal authorities to be arraigned in federal court. He had resigned as chairman. He had been suspended with pay, but was relocating his offices outside of corporate headquarters to a shopping center several blocks away. He took his last ride on the corporate jet up the following morning. He surrendered himself, was strip searched, fingerprinted, photographed, put in an orange jumpsuit with "prisoner" in five-inch high bold letters across the back, and put in a holding cell with other real and potential criminals.

His indictment was the last one of the day, clearly and intentionally: the message-sending process to other chief executives was beginning. The indictment itself took just a few minutes. He was released and flew home in a commercial jet. In my opinion, he had been indicted for show. The phrase goes something like; "They [the DOJ] can indict a ham sandwich, if they like."

Ultimately, at the end of six years, the company pled guilty to several hundred felonies and suffered severe sanctions and penalties. Six employees were convicted and much later actually went to prison. The chairman himself was acquitted mid-trial for lack of evidence. (He was the ham sandwich.) But the point is, this was a major American company admittedly acting as a criminal, in this case for the sake of competition and higher profits, and since it happened on this chairman's watch, upon his acquittal, he retired.

The point of this story is to remind us that trust in leadership and trust in major iconic brands, is extraordinarily difficult to establish, can be lost in a stupid instant, and requires enormous effort, expense, and behavior change to rebuild. This is just one example of why building trust is tougher than ever and those who lead organizations need to be more vigilant, questioning, skeptical, and engaged in maintaining trust in their organization.

The Environment of Trust has Shifted

So, what's changed to make the arena of senior leadership an area of trust decline for those who occupy these spaces today?

The short answer is that the real world came crashing into the role of top executives. Where trust is absent, that vacuum is filled with apprehension, bad news, and fear. Where money and reward dominate, trustworthy, ethical behavior seems less imperative.

So far in the 21st Century, the role of top management and leadership has changed in seven remarkable ways:

1. The growing global pressure for financial performance continues to distort leadership decision-making.
2. More people and organizations are looking over a boss' or leader's shoulder than ever before providing more pressure and less cover for management mistakes and bad decisions.
3. More critics from more quarters, including an increasing chorus of non-government organizations, special interest groups, and tougher government oversight, keep leaders in the stressful target zone.
4. There is more explosive exposure in today's nanosecond new media news cycle; bad news expands at unheard of speeds.
5. Far less tolerance for allowing "underlings" to cover for leaders "too busy" to deal with the problems their organizations are creating and facing.
6. Much greater expectation for openness and accountability.
7. Much lower and declining expectations for integrity from leadership and management.

Businesses and their leadership seem to be losing trust at every level. The Ethics Resource Center in Washington D.C. has been chronicling and bi-annually reporting on the decline in organizational integrity and trust in terms of employee and leadership behaviors and organizational attempts to reverse the decline in organizational and public confidence and trust of their leadership.

Leadership Activities have Shifted as well

The biggest difference in the last generation for leaders and their daily jobs is twofold. Their work has dropped from nearly 100% operationally focused activities to about 40% operations, the remaining 60% involving distractive non-operational decision- making and participation. Today almost anything of an adverse nature lands on the boss' desk for him or her to adjudicate, ameliorate, remediate, resolve, or apologize.

This growing focus on softer, more highly emotional, non-operating issues is redefining executive careers, which are in fact getting shorter. Studies by major executive search firms now peg the expected executive life in the United States of a new top corporate official to be less than five years. Some even peg this number at less than four years.

The impact of this change in executive leadership survival rates is dramatic. More chief executives are losing their jobs every year, earlier in their careers. The average age of leaders is declining. Today's chief executive can expect to head more than one organization during their career. Compensation at the same time is skyrocketing. Today, chief executives—even the senior executives—get paid handsomely to take and keep big jobs, and again to leave big jobs, sometimes very abruptly. This is not an environment where integrity is uppermost in the minds of those in leadership positions. Senior leaders are finding when they venture into the communities of our country that their relationship with stakeholders and constituencies has changed remarkably.

- More constituents ask more questions; bad decisions and damage repair are more stressful and take longer.
- Small forces of highly aggressive and emotional individuals can stop very big ideas.
- People without credentials have enormous credibility and powerful personal platforms in social media.
- Proposers are forced to re-prove themselves every day.
- Public debate is focused more on embarrassment, humiliation and blame shifting rather than progress, future success, or solving problems.
- Anti-corporate activists are learning the bad news habits of corporations and acting more and more preemptively, and in concert with each other.

So, what's a leader who wants to remain a leader, or an aspiring individual who wants to be an ethical, trusted leader, to do?

The Manifesto for Trustworthy Leadership: Declarations, Virtues and Trust Ingredients

Becoming an ethical, trustworthy leader begins with publically declaring ethical leadership and trustworthy intentions. Declaration matters because these statements provide followers and potential followers with expectations against which to measure leadership and trustworthiness, as well as personal behaviors within their organizations. For example, here is a set of leadership/trustworthiness expectations:

1. To tell the truth at the earliest possible time [instantly].
2. To teach by example, by parable, emphasizing the right way to do things.
3. Promptly raise the tough questions and answer them thoughtfully, and carefully.
4. Live by a known and frequently discussed system of values and virtues, which followers, employees, and associates can emulate.
5. Act immediately and strongly to prevent, detect, deter, and punish unethical and prohibited behaviors.

Most of all, trustworthy leaders need to understand, explore and infuse their work with a sense of moral excellence; with virtue. This requires that trustworthy executives identify their own virtues and talk about, describe and illustrate them as a part of their daily leadership activities. For example, behaviors that reflect:

*   Decency
*   Empathy
*   Humility
*   Integrity
*   Morality
*   Sensitivity
*   Trustworthiness

On this score alone, just between mid-2011 to the middle of 2013, 24 months, we've seen the resignations of two top US Generals, one for adultery, one for gross insensitivity and stupidity; a third major US General resigned simply due to the appearance of impropriety; and almost a dozen university presidents were summarily fired (all got big bonuses) for having bloated their resumes; two Arch Bishops and perhaps a Pope resigned for transgressions, assault, malfeasance, cover-ups; an extraordinary number of business executives came under indictment or investigation for extremely serious matters.

Trustworthy leadership is about, literally, walking, talking and living trustworthiness. It is about recognizing that trust is at stake every moment of every day, in every decision and action that leaders take. But more than that, we can actually identify the ingredients of trust and therefore, actually enumerate a level of trustworthiness.

These are the more essential ingredients or the behaviors that build trust:

1. Advance information: Telling people things they need to know, before they need to know them.
2. Bringing communities, constituents and stakeholders into the decision making process at the earliest possible time.
3. Communicating face-to-face whenever possible.
4. Demonstrating that community and stakeholder ideas have impact (by changing plans or goals).
5. Using language that those directly affected can understand, relate to, so leadership performance can be assessed.

Trust is the Absence of Fear

Perhaps, the simplest definition of trust from the perspective of the trusting is the personal confidence and the absence of fear. When trust is absent, it is replaced by fear, lack of confidence, and the expectation that those in charge will do things that are adverse to the interests those who must follow. Trustable leaders are a function of their communication skills combined with the expected personal behaviors that back-up that communication. Trust creates a sense of calmness and comfort.

On the day the company I spoke of at the beginning of this essay signed its plea agreement with the federal government, the company held an all-manager meeting at its headquarters in New Jersey. The goal was to explain what happened, the company's plea agreement, the sanctions involved, and the intents and h onerous oversight the company would be subject to for at least the next four years.

When this very tough meeting ended, the new president (the third since the as began) congratulated the management group, lawyers and consultants for getting the company through this process. He walked to each of us to make a comment. When he got to me, although he shook my hand, and said rather loudly, "Lukaszewski, whenever you're around it seems a bit like Sunday school." My response was, "Well, Bill, if my company just plead guilty to nearly 400 felonies, I think a little Sunday school might be in order, don't you think?" Everybody laughed, but Bill.

My assessment is that building trust is tougher than ever, and the job gets harder and harder, every day.

How do you measure up against the Trust Manifesto for Leaders?

James E. Lukaszewski
ABC, APR, Fellow PRSA

James E. Lukaszewskiis president of The Lukaszewski Group Division of Risdall Marketing Group, New Brighton, Minnesota. His twelfth book, Lukaszewski On Crisis Communication, What Your CEO Should Know About Reputation Threats And Crisis Management *was released in March, 2013. He is well known in the American Public Relations profession for his ethical approaches to tough, touchy, sensitive problems and crises. He has been a member of the Public Relations Society of America's (PRSA) national Board of Ethics and Professional Standards (BEPS) since 1990.* Corporate Legal Times *listed Jim as," one of 16 experts to call when all hell breaks loose."*

Rebuilding Trust in the Financial Markets

By Davia Temin

Only 22 percent of Americans trust the financial system, Chicago's "Financial Trust Index" has just reported.[1] But it doesn't take an index to tell us that public trust in the financial services industry, as well as the markets themselves, is dangerously compromised. The headlines say it all:

Where Banking Crisis Raged, Trust Is Slow to Return
(*The New York Times*)

Deutsche Bank Says Generation Needed to Regain Trust
(*Bloomberg*)

The Return of the 'Rip-Off Factor' on Wall Street
(*The New York Times*)

Losing Faith in American Institutions
(*The New York Times*)

Why You Shouldn't Trust Any Libor Rate UBS Touched
(*The Wall Street Journal*)

Another Annus Horribilis for Europe's Banks
(*The Wall Street Journal*)

Why I'm Leaving Goldman Sachs
(*The New York Times*)

Big, Rich, and Wobbly: Wall Street Banks Are Still Sicker Than You Think
(*The Atlantic*)

---

1   The University of Chicago's Booth School of Business and Northwestern University's Kellogg School of Management, *Financial Trust Index*, February 6, 2013 (http://www.financialtrustindex.org/).

Though one might think that these headlines ran at the height of the financial crisis—2008 and 2009—they did not. They—and thousands more like them—are actually from 2013 and late 2012. Not much has changed in five years.

Clearly, the financial services industry has not taken the steps needed to repair public trust shattered during the crisis. In fact in many instances, banks and other financial institutions have exacerbated the pain of their customers, continuing the diminution of trust rather than staunching it.

Individuals—already devastated by losses of savings, homes, jobs, lifestyles, and dignity during the financial crisis—found banks not only illegally foreclosing on their mortgages, and "robo-signing" documents, they also saw a raft of new bank fees being levied on their every banking activity. "Death by a thousand cuts" took on new meaning as consumers puzzled over the new charges on their bank and credit card statements.

Institutional clients have been deluged by press articles claiming that their investment banks are self-dealing—putting clients' welfare second to the banks' own welfare—not only during the crisis itself, but thereafter. One disaffected Goldman Sachs banker stated, in an open letter to the public on why he was resigning, that his fellow bankers often called their clients "muppets."[2] And, the government's dive into banks' email records has supported many of these claims.

So, despite a broad stock market rally since the financial crisis officially ended, public animosity towards banks and investment banks has not abated. In fact, if anything, it has deepened. And non-banks such as Wal-Mart and Facebook—in which consumers have far greater trust—have begun to fill in the void. Is this the death knell of the financial services industry? Have we gone from "Too Big to Fail," to "Failure is Inevitable?"

What can be done? And, even if banks have the will, is it possible to rebuild trust in financial institutions today?

Of course it is—IF the will exists. America loves nothing so much as a "comeback kid." And a company, a politician, or even an entire industry CAN rebuild

---

2   Greg Smith, "Why I Am Leaving Goldman Sachs," *The New York Times*, March 14, 2012 (http://www.nytimes.com/2012/03/14/opinion/why-i-am-leaving-goldman-sachs. html?pagewanted=all&_r=0).

public trust, as long as they are willing to truly, authentically learn the lessons that are needed, and reform.

Trust is both forged and destroyed in crucible moments. And while it could be said that the financial industry has been going through a refiner's fire, it has not yet emerged from the oven, even after five years, because it has not shown it has learned the lessons needed. It has not reformed voluntarily, believably, and enduringly. So, whether it succumbs to the flames, or can emerge finer, stronger, and wiser all rests on the will of the industry itself.

Social scientists such as Harvard's Iris Bohnet[3] tell us that trust is the lubricant—or glue—of civil society and economic growth. Trust underlies consumer, business, and counterparty confidence, and allows us to interact, engage, and trade with one another even in the absence of formal contract enforcement. In fact, you could almost call trust our world's shadow currency: it enables the smooth flow of money, trade, production, and economic growth around the world.

Globally, it is positively correlated with higher per capita income and growth rates, better functioning governments,[4] increased happiness,[5] and a decrease in crime.[6]

Distrust of course, is associated with the exact opposite—economic stagnation, decreased democratic stability, lower individual income,[7] increased crime,[8] inferior student achievement,[9] and decreased health and happiness.[10]

---

3   See e.g. Iris Bohnet, "Iris Bohnet on Trust and Risk," interview by Molly Lanzarotta. *Harvard Kennedy School*, January 30, 2007 (http://www.hks.harvard.edu/news-events/publications/insight/markets/iris-bohnet). Also see Iris Bohnet et. al., "More Order with Less Law: On Contract Enforcement, Trust, and Crowding," *American Political Science Review*, no. 1 (2001).

4   See e.g. Stephen Knack, "Trust, Associational Life and Economic Performance," in *The Contribution of Human and Social Capital to Sustained Economic Growth and Well-Being: International Symposium Report*, John F. Helliwell (ed.), Quebec: Human Resources Development Canada (2011); Paul J. Zak and Stephen Knack, "Trust and Growth," *The Economic Journal*, 111 (April 2001); and Paul J. Zak "Building Trust: Public Policy, Interpersonal Trust, and Economic Development," *Supreme Court Economic Review*, 10 (Fall 2002).

5   See e.g. John Helliwell, Richard Layard and Jeffery Sachs, "World Happiness Report," *The Earth Institute at Columbia University* (2012).

6   See e.g. Richard Wike and Kathleen Holzwart, "Where Trust is High, Crime and Corruption are Low," *PEW Research Center* (April 15, 2008).

7   See e.g. Knack, "Trust, Associational Life and Economic Performance;" Zak and Knack, "Trust and Growth;" and Zak, "Building Trust."

8   See e.g. Wike and Holzwart, "Where Trust is High, Crime and Corruption are Low."

9   See e.g. Megan Tschannen-Moran, "What's Trust Got to do With It? The Role of Faculty and Principal Trust in Fostering Student Achievement" (paper presented at the UCEA Conference Proceedings for Annual Convention 2004).

10 See e.g. Helliwell, Layard and Sachs, "World Happiness Report."

Frank Navran and Fred Garcia define trust as: "The natural consequence of promises fulfilled, of predictions that come true, and of values lived. Trust is lost when promises are unfulfilled; when predictions fail to come true; and when one's behavior is contrary to one's stated values."[11]

Worse, once a person's trust is violated through deception, it is harder and takes far longer to restore.

And, when people are hurting—or continue to hurt—they cannot trust.

These are just some of the issues facing the financial services industry, as it seeks to rebuild trust. It is a complex algorithm of issues that developed over time, converged into a full-blown crisis, and that never have been completely resolved. Worse, many of the steps that we know are critical to the rebuilding of trust— taking responsibility for bad actions, apologizing, reparation, voluntary reform, and then strict compliance to a new set of standards—have not happened yet, and may never happen.

So, I believe that in order to grapple with a complex, systemic failure such as the financial services industry has experienced takes a combination of disciplines, including crisis management, psychology, social science, negotiation skills, communications, and branding and marketing.

The first lessons come from crisis management. And like every crisis I have ever worked with, or know of, it all starts with DENIAL.

Whether it's a board, senior leadership, rank and file, the public or individuals, **our first impulse when we get a whiff of danger, or when things start to go seriously south, is denial:**

> *"This cannot be happening. Or if it is happening, it isn't happening to me. Or, if it is happening to me, then it is not really that bad. Or, if it is that bad, no one will notice; or, we've squeaked by before, we can do so again; it will pass with the news cycle; we do not need to respond; we do not need to do anything differently, or even acknowledge the problem—just stay the course, just hang in there." etc.*

---

11   Helio Fred Garcia, *The Power of Communication: The Skills to Build Trust, Inspire Loyalty, and Lead Effectively* (New Jersey: Pearson Education, Inc., 2012).

These are the first internal monologues that occur during times of crisis. This is normal, but what determines the trajectory of how a crisis unfolds is how quickly we exit our state of denial, acknowledge the problem, apologize if need be, promise to fix it, and begin to take action that fulfills that promise and addresses the root causes, as well as the perception of the problem...and then communicate, and over communicate, to every constituency involved.

The longer this takes to do, the worse the crisis unfolds, and the more trust is lost.

In our 24x7 news cycle, an hour turns into a second, so action must be immediate, resonant, and emotionally "authentic," and must at least appear to be transparent. Solutions must seem to home-grown, not legislated or imposed. And, they must pass the authenticity test imposed upon them by social media.

"The loss of trust in banks is accentuated by the social media effect," said Brett King in his 2010 Huffington Post article *What Loss of Trust in Banks Really Means.* "What we've seen in effect is the perfect storm...but interestingly most bankers don't have a clue as to why this decline in trust has been so 'harsh'...The *perfect storm* was not just the Global Financial Crisis, but also shifting consumer behaviors and in particular the role of social media in forming public opinions... in April 2009 a Nielsen survey showed that social media had already become the most dominant force in creating brand perception around trust. The problem for banks is that they generally aren't participating in social media. Thus, their brands have been hijacked by customers who just aren't happy."[12]

Denial, therefore, not only gets us into crises, it also keeps us from getting out of them if it stops us from taking needed action.

The more denial puts us on a collision course with reality—the reality that is apparent to the public—the more the public feels deceived and the more trust is destroyed.

The public needs to assign blame, and it is still doing it around the world.

Additionally, social science does tell us that the worst betrayal of trust is felt when class or status lines are crossed: "lower classes" fear most receiving an inferior outcome compared to those of a higher status. Therefore, when it comes

---

12 Brett King, "What Loss of Trust in Banks Really Means...," *The Huffington Post,* May 21, 2010 (http://www.huffingtonpost.com/brett-king/what-loss-of-trust-in-ban_b_584435.html).

to Wall Street bonuses, those of "lower status" feel disproportionately angry when upper "classes" get outsized bonuses. That is why so much anger is exhibited around Wall Street bonuses—not just perceived inequities, but class-based inequities, as well.

And the financial services industry has acted, until very recently, fairly insensitively to the rest of the country's and world's pain.

So what can the financial services industry do now?

The range of possibilities has existed from the early days of the crisis up until this moment, of course, and it goes from the least to the most activist. But, it is a fairly good bet that the less active the solution, even now, the longer it will take to rebuild trust, and the more active, the faster the trust will rebuild.

Alternatives include:

1. Do nothing. Over time, if all recovers, things will limp back to normal. If there is a loss of trust, so be it; people still have to do something with their money. This seems to have been adopted by many financial institutions over the past five years.
2. Say the "right" things, but don't really change. Put together the "right" kinds of press releases and ads—tout transparency, innovation, diligence, accuracy, restructuring—but don't actually do much, or at least, do the minimum. This, too, seems familiar.
3. Or, actually tow the line, reform, recommit to clients and the public, and then perform according to plan.

At this time in our recovery, clearly options 1 and 2 have been tried, and have failed. In order to fully embrace option 3, here are my suggestions for a game plan for the financial services industry to truly rebuild trust:

1. Short-circuit denial. Stop staying silent. Take the right kind of responsibility and authentically apologize in appropriate ways, and start putting in fixes. And implement them. (Sometimes this can mean bucking the lawyers who only want one to "neither admit nor deny" culpability. It is the wise leader who knows when to follow the advice of his or her attorneys, and when to disregard it.)

2. Start to see and talk about the world from the point of view of the "other"—in this case, clients. Demonstrate in public communications that it is not "all about us," and not even all about profitability or even shareholder value. It is about the customer. Innovate financial solutions to help those in need do not just walk away from them.

3. Acknowledge the pain of the populace (empathize), be sensitive to it, and share it. Demonstrate "good will." Don't do this only when forced to.

4. Demonstrate "reciprocity." Reciprocity is defined as: "an internalized norm inducing people to respond like to like—to kindness with kindness; unkindness with unkindness, even if it is not in a person's material self-interest to do so…" Make fixes commensurate—or more than commensurate—with the pain of others, and be willing to share in others' pain, not stay exempt.

5. Reparation must hurt! There is a complex equation that the public seems to demand: it needs to exact double or triple the pain of the aggrieved from the party responsible. In other words, the public wants to see blood first, and then they can forgive. One idea would be for Wall Street to pool 5%, 10%, or 15% of every bonus granted, and use the aggregate to bail out those about to lose their homes in each of the fifty states. A lottery could be held to choose the beneficiaries, and the public would see bankers lose remuneration, in order to help those in need. Not a bad way to build some good will.

6. Start acting like the good citizen...and living the same way. One bank, Citizens Financial Group, not only created a credo of good citizenship and good banking for all of its bankers, and all of its activities, it defined all the ways it would give back to the community. Only then did it set as its tagline: Good Banking is Good Citizenship. Because it walked the walk before ever creating its advertising, it was believed, trusted, and holds one of the highest trust scores of any U.S. bank.

7. Initiate an ongoing series of two-way communications with the public— through both traditional and social media. But make these communications real, personal and important—never robotic, formulaic, or seemingly unfeeling.

8. Communicate not only to the public, writ large, but to many small groups, as well as one-on-one. Research proves that it is easier to rebuild trust with small groups than large ones.

9. Manifest real leadership—walk the talk. Show that lessons have been learned, and don't exhibit the same behavior that was problematic in the first place. Do not let the same thing happen again.

The public and the press may be willing to forgive over time; they may be willing to suspend distrust over time, and they may be willing to build trust anew, over time. But research has found that if lying recurs, if denial recurs, if totally selfish behavior recurs, that trust may well be gone forever.

And a world, or an industry, or a financial system based on perpetual distrust will surely not continue. So, this is a case for survival, of the very financial industry itself.

Davia Temin

Davia Temin is President and CEO of Temin and Company, a boutique management consultancy focused on international reputation, risk, and crisis management, marketing and media strategy, thought leadership, and high-level leadership and communication coaching. The firm helps to create, enhance and save reputations for a wide array of corporations and other institutions at the board, corporate, product and funding levels.

Ms. Temin writes a Forbes.com column called "Reputation Matters" and is a contributor to The Huffington Post *and* American Banker. *For more information, visit www.teminandcompany.com and follow her on Twitter @DaviaTemin.*

Section VI:

A New Paradigm for Organizational Trust

Brave Leadership Builds Trust in the New World

By Ben Boyd

Over the past few years the world has experienced major crises and scandals that involved many of our most well known brands and high-profile leaders.

As a result, trust in business and in government has plummeted, creating a crisis of leadership.

Three Fundamental Shifts

Three fundamental shifts brought us to this point.

The first is *unprecedented transparency*. The general public is more empowered than ever, thanks to social media and the internet. Everyone can access endless information, drive conversation and hold people accountable for what they say and do. Everyone can now hear whatever is said, regardless for whom it was intended.

A perfect example is the confidential Justice Department memo leaked to NBC News in early February 2013. The 16-page white paper, which concluded that the U.S. government could order the killing of American citizens if they are believed to be "senior operational leaders" of al-Qaida or "an associated force," ignited an onslaught of headlines, tweets, and water cooler conversations. The document was obviously not intended to be made public, but in today's world of 360-degree transparency, that is what it became. And, once it did, the Obama administration could no longer control its message around drone strikes, leaving people to question the approach and deem it "terrifying," or at the very least "questionable."

As this demonstrates, traditional influencers are often now at the scrutiny of the broader public. No one and no one entity—not organizations, not their spokespeople, not the media—can truly control information and the way it is shared.

This highlights the second shift: *the dispersion of authority.*

It used to be that communications was top down. Organizational leaders would vertically impart information on a need-to-know basis. Put simply, it was the traditional pyramid of influence, with elites at the pinnacle, the general population at the bottom, and little interaction in between. But the dissolution of trust in authority figures changed the way this worked.

Susan G. Komen for the Cure learned this lesson the hard way when it announced it would no longer provide grants to Planned Parenthood affiliates for breast screenings. The charity argued that it was not political, but rather a result of a recent policy change that prevented it from giving money to organizations under state or federal investigation. But the decision was seen by many as a political move, and Planned Parenthood supporters and others bombarded Susan G. Komen on Facebook and Twitter, expressing their outrage with the decision. The immense public outcry forced the foundation to apologize and reverse its decision within 72 hours of the initial announcement. But the damage was done.

That brings us to the third fundamental shift: *the "how mandate,"* or the idea that *how* you do what you do matters.

Today, running a profitable business lead by top-rated leadership is no longer enough for long-term trust building—it is a standard expectation. This type of operational excellence falls near the bottom of the 16 attributes proven to build trust, as measured by Edelman's 2013 Trust Barometer.

By contrast, the data shows that engagement and integrity are the most important attributes in building trust among stakeholders. In fact, the 2013 Edelman Trust Barometer shows the "how" attributes are nearly 50 percent more important than the "what" attributes.

This means that in addition to focusing on consistent financial returns, companies must listen to customer needs and feedback, treat employees well, take responsible actions to address an issue, and commit to ethical, transparent and open business practices.

Apple witnessed this first hand. Part of the company's financial success can be attributed to the management of its supply chain—efficiently keeping costs down and reducing build time: decisions that consumers could directly appreciate. But after news reports surfaced on deficient working conditions at Apple's main contract manufacturer, Foxconn, in China, many questioned the company's commitment to ethical business practices. Investigative reports, activist campaigns and general public outcry shed light on alleged health and safety violations, long hours and low wages at the factories where iPods and iPhones were made.

It was no longer enough that Apple was churning out the market's hottest products; it had to place its customers, employees and integrity ahead of profits. The company agreed to do just that. Its chief executive, Tim Cook, published a list of all of its main suppliers, brought in an external agency to monitor factory conditions and made major efforts to improve and communicate its policies.

As trust continues to diminish and scrutiny abounds, the actions organizations are now equally—not more—important as *how* they do them. The organizations that fail to recognize and adapt to these three shifts are missing opportunities to maintain and build trust among stakeholders.

The New Reality
THE NEW DYNAMIC: The diamond of influence

PYRAMID OF AUTHORITY (Vertical)

CEO
GOVERNMENTAL OFFICIALS
BOARD OF DIRECTORS
ACADEMICS
TECHNICAL EXPERTS
ELITE MEDIA
GENERAL POPULATION
EMPLOYEES
ACTION CONSUMERS
SOCIAL ACTIVISTS

PYRAMID OF COMMUNITY (Horizontal)

The traditional pyramid of influence has been rechristened the pyramid of authority. It has not disappeared, but it has been mirrored by a new, bottom-up construct identified by Edelman: *the pyramid of community.*

In this new pyramid, engaged employees, action consumers and social activists drive real-time and continual peer-to-peer dialogue, where constant, horizontal information flow happens. Simultaneously, the top-down communications from CEO to worker to shareholder continue and remain relevant, but that information flow no longer happens in isolation.

The pyramid of authority and the pyramid of community come together to create Edelman's *diamond of influence:* a new influence dynamic that maps the intersection of top-down, bottom-up and peer-to-peer communications.

As shown in the example, the upper half of the diamond can drive the dialogue on what an organization does, but that will only get them so far.

The Crisis of Leadership

Accordingly, we have witnessed a significant change in the landscape in which we operate as communicators, marketers and business people. Too many leaders have not accepted the new reality; top-down communications remains their only commitment. Their inability to recognize the necessity to alter their behaviors has exacerbated the crisis in leadership.

The 2013 Edelman Trust Barometer shows that less than one-fifth of the general public believes that business leaders and government officials will make ethical and moral decisions. On top of that, these traditional authority figures (like CEOs and prime ministers) also continue to have lesser trust and credibility than employees, academics or "persons like yourself."

In fact, "a person like yourself" is now trusted nearly twice as much as a chief executive or government official.

In other words, influence has officially been democratized.

The Path Forward

As a result, organizations must change the way in which they engage stakeholders; they must commit to *inclusive management*. This management style is not a linear process, but rather dynamic, continual and evolutionary in nature. Leaders need to do more than just pay attention; they must engage all of their stakeholders 24 hours a day, 365 days a year, in an authentic way. Only then can they succeed in such a transparent environment.

To reach this goal, leaders must embrace inclusive management by committing to four actions: vision + share, enlist, adapt and act.

Embrace the new mandate: inclusive management

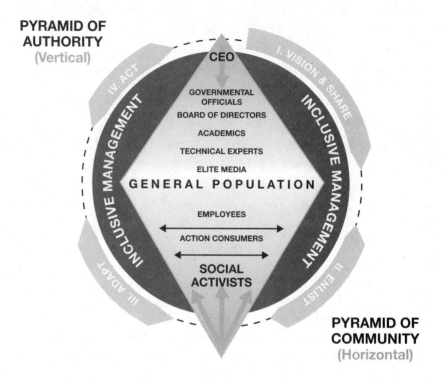

PYRAMID OF AUTHORITY (Vertical)

CEO

GOVERNMENTAL OFFICIALS

BOARD OF DIRECTORS

ACADEMICS

TECHNICAL EXPERTS

ELITE MEDIA

GENERAL POPULATION

EMPLOYEES

ACTION CONSUMERS

SOCIAL ACTIVISTS

I. VISION & SHARE

INCLUSIVE MANAGEMENT

II. ENLIST

III. ADAPT

INCLUSIVE MANAGEMENT

IV. ACT

PYRAMID OF COMMUNITY (Horizontal)

Though their influence in public engagement is dissipating, leaders still hold the authority to create a sense of purpose. It is the responsibility of a business leader to have a vision for the enterprise. But now this vision must be brought to life through robust engagement, vertically and horizontally, within the diamond. Leaders must *share* that vision through ongoing dialogue with those individuals in both halves of the diamond.

Doing so will help to close the gap between the expectations that people have for corporations, governments and other institutions in the 21st century, and actual organizational performance—which often lags.

Howard Schultz did an excellent job of sharing his vision and engaging Starbucks[1] baristas and employees to reconsider the future of the enterprise. When he returned to the coffee company in 2008, he came with a "transformational agenda"

---

1   Edelman Client

that would fix troubled stores, rekindle an emotional attachment with customers and make longer-term changes to supply chain and executive management. Schultz made sure everyone understood what was going to happen; the chain ran its biggest ad campaign ever; he engaged employees at all levels.

But vision and sharing is not enough; a true back-and-forth must take place for a vision to stick. So leaders must *enlist* everyone by asking the right questions, observing reactions and behaviors and listening to what people want, need, like or dislike. Adobe did this with its product-sharing cycle. The software company knew it had strong brand advocates and wanted to encourage this audience to provide real-time feedback on new products. So it reached out to its prerelease community, provided trial versions of new software and invited members to offer feedback on its website and Facebook.

Based on active listening, leaders must *adapt* that vision and strategy or product based on what they see and hear. In today's world everyone has input—social activists, consumers, employees and others—and this input should be considered in real and measurable ways.

When Bank of America announced its decision to impose a $5-per-month debit card fee on customers who were not carrying a minimum balance of $25,000, customers went ballistic. More than 300,000 organized a protest on Facebook, and many more went to bank branches and websites to complain. One month later Bank of America dropped its proposed debit usage fee, finally realizing that the expected revenue from the fee was not worth the reputational damage.

Finally, leaders must *act*, both responsively and responsibly. For leaders to be successful in a prism of 360-degree transparency, they need to transform feedback into genuine action. They need to innovate, build and market products and services that meet consumer expectations while still reflecting and reinforcing their own vision.

The new inclusive management model, driven around and through the diamond of influence, allows an organization's leaders to build trust and be more successful. It also grants them the permission to participate meaningfully in the evolving global conversation, and ultimately not just the license to operate, but potentially the license to lead.

In a world in which only 18 percent of the general public trusts a business leader to tell the truth, inclusive management offers a new pathway to success.

Ben Boyd

Ben Boyd, Global Chair of Edelman's Corporate Practice, enjoys a range of experience in public relations, issues communications and brand positioning, as well as corporate communications and marketing. With Edelman, Ben directs the global Corporate Practice specializing in reputation management, corporate communications and issues management. He plays a central role in the firm's work on the topic of Trust and the role of Trust in corporate positioning. Ben is recognized as a thought leader on ethics and communications as well as corporate reputation. He serves on the Communications Advisory Board for the Ethisphere Institute, which annually recognizes the World's Most Ethical Companies.

Why Trust is Our Future's Most Vital Resource

By Eric Lowitt

Trust's role in our global economy is well known. Without trust, credit would not be extended and partnerships would not form. But trust's role as *the* enabler of our ability to thrive in the future is less well explored. Think of trust between organizations as the *glue* that will pull and hold together collaborative efforts consisting of entities from the private, public, and civil sectors. No trust, no glue, no collaborations.

Few would dispute that globally we face a multitude of vexing challenges. A sample of this set of issues includes the growing divide between 'haves' and 'have not's', the erosive impact of climate change, and the emerging strain of unchecked population growth.

These challenges are bigger than the ability of any one sector (private, public, civil) to address alone. While the approach, cross-sector collaboration, is obvious, our ability to marshal such an approach is at best limited.

Historically we've looked to the public sector to provide a panacea that no longer is viable. In the U.S., the critical junction points of distress—the Civil War, the Great Depression, the financial industry driven Great Recession—essentially pitted public versus private sector interests against one another. The bitter animosity that led to the Civil War was fueled by the inhumane treatment of human beings as slaves...but for whose benefit? Mini corporations in the form of cotton farmers. One could easily argue that private sector malfeasance was the foundation of both The Great Depression and the more recent Great Recession. The point is that the private sector has been long viewed as the root of our challenges. Indeed only half of the U.S. general public trusts the private sector, according to the 2012 Edelman Trust Barometer.[2]

But civil sector trust in the public sector is much lower. The 2012 Edelman Trust Barometer also showed that global trust in government among the general public has fallen to an historic low: just 38 percent.[3] The public sector has proven to be inept; witness the U.S. government's inability to come to a binding agreement to balance our budget, the lack of a long-term plan to reign in our debt, and partisan refusal to work together for the greater good.

Can we reasonably expect that the public sector will provide global, let alone federal, leadership to address our global challenges: water, energy, food, infrastructure, healthcare, or climate change? In the U.S. there's this belief that we as citizens pay 40 percent of our income and deserve 100 percent return on investment from our government. We believe our taxes will provide blanket services to all our needs. It doesn't work this way.

Our lack of widespread trust in the private and public sectors does not provide us a 'Get Out of Jail Free' card that will make our vexing challenges disappear. The only solution is to nurture collaboration among the private, public, and civil sectors. Trust is the glue that will bind these sectors together.

The development of trust between two or more entities relies heavily upon transparency. One of the most universal signs of trust is the handshake. According to Wikipedia,

> *The handshake is thought by some to have originated as a gesture of peace by demonstrating that the hand holds no weapon.[4] Archaeological ruins and ancient texts show that handshaking was practiced in ancient Greece as far back as the 5th century BC; a depiction of two soldiers shaking hands can be found on part of a funerary steles.[5]*

---

2   See 2012 Edelman Trust Barometer, http://www.slideshare.net/EdelmanInsights/2012-edelman-trust-barometer-global-deck, accessed January 3, 2013.

3   Ibid.

4   "Dear Uncle Ezra—Questions for Tuesday, April 3, 2007". Cornell University. 3 April 2007. Question 8. Retrieved 4 September 2011. "There are many conflicting theories about the origin of the handshake. It seems that the most common one involves the evidence of the lack of a weapon in the right hand, which normally bears a weapon. It is shown to be empty by its connectedness to the opposite person's hand."

5   See Wikipedia's entry called *Handshake,* http://en.wikipedia.org/wiki/Handshake, accessed January 7, 2013.

It can be argued that the public and civil sectors' motives are clear and community minded. Government's motive is to work 'of the people, by the people, for the people', at least in the democratic societies. The civil sector, comprised of 'the people' and nonprofit organizations, seeks individual and community gain.

But the private sector's motives are viewed as far less communal: maximize shareholder value creation. A group of forward-looking companies are adopting a new view; their mandate is to maximize stakeholder value. The change itself is noteworthy; the fact that more and more companies are publicly communicating this commitment, at their expense, is evolutionary. Perhaps for the first time in the Capitalism era, we're approaching a point where the publicly communicated motives of the private, public, and civil sectors are aligned.

Transparency can serve as the currency of trust, especially the trust that is placed within those in leadership positions. The question then becomes whether leaders can be trusted to take action that can solve our most troublesome challenges. Transparency-fueled trust in leadership is like a dance: the leader must be trusted to lead for the team, not just for the self, in order for the dance to transform into a moment of beauty.

Collaboration among the private, public, and civil sector can indeed be likened to dancing; one leads and the partner follows. More and more, the private sector is taking the lead in these dances to solve vexing environmental and social challenges. After all, the perfect storm of legislation, climate change, resource shortages, and social media has placed an inordinate amount of scrutiny on the actions of corporations.

When dancing, the leader subconsciously evaluates the partner, identifying dance moves that the partner likely can and cannot do. Then the leader uses this information to facilitate the best possible dance.

The private sector is embracing the role of cross-sector collaboration facilitator. Companies such as Unilever, GE, and Grieg Shipping Group have publicly committed themselves to big goals that can only be achieved via cross-sector collaboration. Consider Unilever. In 2010 Unilever 'set itself the challenge of doubling the size of its business whilst at the same time reducing its environmental footprint.'[6] The only way for Unilever to achieve this goal is through partnerships across the private, public, and civil sectors. For example, Unilever is focused on improving the standard of living for hundreds of thousands of smallholder farmers by sharing best farming practices learned from its experience. Unilever's strategy focuses on earning and maintaining the trust of entities, such as smallholder farmers, throughout these sectors.

Many within the private sector view trust-driven collaboration as a means to achieve high performance, as opposed to a vehicle for philanthropic interests. For example, ecomagination, a GE initiative that makes environmentally conscious products, is working to strengthen the global energy system; in the process it has generated $105 billion in revenue since 2005 for GE.[7] The ecomagination initiative relies on open innovation through crowdsourcing "challenges" in which the general public is invited to submit their ideas for innovations that can secure and fortify the global energy system. Members of the general public whose ideas for innovations hold great promise receive funding from a pool of financial capital that was facilitated by GE. In this way the civil sector benefits (from having their ideas considered and a select group of people receiving funding), the public sector benefits (from the enhanced energy system), and the private sector benefits (GE earns revenue, companies that GE invests in through the ecomagination challenge receive financial and management support in order to grow). Again trust is a critical resource for GE. As an example, if the general public doesn't trust GE, then GE's flow of innovative ideas is reduced.

So trust is a critical success factor for large companies. But what about smaller businesses? Let there be no doubt: trust is just as critical. Think about what happens to the large ships that move goods around the world. What is the fate of these ships once they reach the end of their useful life? Over 80 percent are broken down by hand, not infrequently by workers with only nominal rights, on the beaches of Bangladesh and other countries. Regrettably every month sees multiple human deaths as a result.

---

6   See Unilever press release, "Unilever aims to double business, whilst reducing environmental footprint", http://www.unilever.com/mediacentre/pressreleases/2010/Unileveraimstodoublebusinesswhilstreducingenvironmentalfootprint.aspx, accessed January 8, 2013.

7   Se GE's 2011 ecomagination report, http://files.gecompany.com/ecomagination/progress/GE_ecomagination_2011AnnualReport.pdf, accessed January 3, 2013.

Grieg Shipping Group is a shipping company that is smaller than the industry's giants. But its size has not stopped the company from desiring to change the way the industry recycles its used shipping vessels. In fact Grieg Shipping Group has recently developed a profitable business, Grieg Green, which breaks ships responsibly—saving lives and reducing environmental impact in the process. Grieg Green's financial success and its ability to achieve its vision are reliant on the company's ability to nurture trust among competitors (from whom Grieg Green buys used vessels to recycle), shipyards, NGOs, and the public sector.

Cross-sector collaboration is needed to address our interconnected global challenges. Since each challenge affects the private, public, and civil sectors, it makes sense for each sector to participate in the effort to address these challenges. The need for collaboration is likely to remain pronounced in the foreseeable future. Transparency and facilitation are the fuel for cross-sector collaboration. Trust serves as the glue that will enable our healthy, vibrant, and prosperous future. This is why trust is our future's most vital resource.

Eric Lowitt

Eric Lowitt is a globally recognized expert in the fields of competitive strategy, collaboration, and sustainability. A consultant and sought after speaker, he is the author of The Future of Value, *a critically acclaimed book that connects sustainability with competitive strategy and financial performance. His most recent book,* The Collaboration Economy, *shows why and how cross-sector collaboration will spark economic growth that addresses our world's most vexing challenges. Named one of the Top 100 Thought Leaders in Trustworthy Business Behavior, Eric's work is regularly featured in top tier publications, as well as news wires, industry publications and other media outlets. He has worked for nearly two decades with Accenture, Fidelity Investments, and Deloitte Consulting, is fluent in Japanese, and earned his MBA from The Wharton School. Eric is the Founder and Managing Director of Nexus Global Advisors, a leading strategy, collaboration, and sustainability advisory firm.*

From CSR to Corporate Social Innovation

By Philip Mirvis

Three decades ago it was possible for most business leaders to do their jobs blissfully unaware of issues pertaining to societal welfare, conditions in the natural environment, human rights in nascent global supply chains, and numerous other matters. They were largely unaffected by activist NGOs and shareholder resolutions, the threat of protests and boycotts, not to mention calls for greater transparency and the dramatic increase in exposure provided by the Internet. Those days are long gone. Today the public expects much more from businesses.

Nowadays, top business leaders recognize that they have to concern themselves with serious social ills such as chronic poverty and unemployment, declining education and infrastructure in their communities, global warming and a deteriorating biosphere, worrisome demographic and consumption trends, industry-specific issues, HIV/AIDS, and more—all embodied in the heightened expectations of customers, investors, employees, regulators, and the public for accountable and responsible business behavior. Conventional CSR programs are one response. But do today's CSR programs embody the imagination, vigor, and scale to effect serious social change? Can they enable companies to earn the public's trust?

The Limitations of CSR

Trust is vital to every business. And stepping up to their social responsibilities--and delivering on them in a substantive and authentic way—can be a "trust maker" for a business. But here's the glitch: CEO's report that their companies' efforts to engage society are constrained by competing priorities, organizational complexity, and gaps in execution. In other words, companies are pushing forward on CSR--just not very far, very fast, or very effectively.

Companies can continue to move forward incrementally, dotting the "i's" and crossing the "t's", and the practices of CSR will become more or less "routinized" into business. However, this routinization process has been studied by many scholars who conclude that it is a recipe for decay. Don Sull, in his investigations of "Why Good Businesses Go Bad," attributes their decline to "active inertia." In other words, they just "keep on keeping on," insensitive to changes in the business context. And Jim Collins, in his new book *How the Mighty Fall* describes the implications as a "capitulation to irrelevance." Is this where CSR is headed?

Innovation is active, not reactive, creative, not routinized, and aimed at breakthroughs, not incremental change. This is what society needs in the teeth of tough and intractable social-and-environmental problems and it is what business needs to reestablish trust and to reinvigorate its leaders, employees, and a multitude of stakeholders. Can CSR reinvent itself through innovation?

New Directions through Innovation

There are signs that some leading businesses are reaching out beyond their fence lines, supply chains, and traditional distribution systems into the very fabric of society. As businesses venture into this new territory, they encounter a growing movement of people taking creative action under the banners of social innovation and entrepreneurship. This movement, largely taking shape outside of mainstream business, lifts up social (and ecological) innovation as a new and powerful way to address the world's ills.

What is the relevance for companies? Innovation is a key driver of business growth and essential to sharpening and sustaining competitive advantage. But as core as innovation has been to the DNA of firms, it has never been an integral part of CSR. Now, however, some leading companies are bringing social innovation into their economic, social and environmental agendas:

- Novo Nordisk, a Danish Pharmaceutical whose therapies treat diabetes, operates over 25 mobile clinics in rural areas of Africa and Asia, dispenses free medicines to people in need, and works with local hospitals to train staff and host governments to develop diabetes care infrastructure. Reaching out further, the company created and then invited competitors to join the World Diabetes Foundation and launched a "changing diabetes" campaign in conjunction with the United Nations. Meanwhile, all of its employees spend at least one day a year with someone connected to diabetes—say, a patient, caretaker, or healthcare professional—and then propose innovations in how Novo Nordisk serves its world.

- Ericsson, the Swedish maker of advanced telecom equipment, co-created with the World Meteorological Organization and Uganda Department of Meteorology a mobile weather alert application that enhances the safety of fishermen in Lake Victoria through detailed, customized weather forecasts. In turn, it jointly developed a fleet management system with DataProm, Vivo and *Telefónica* in Curitiba, Brazil to connect buses wirelessly that has increased public confidence in travel safety and reduced fuel costs and travel time.

- In late 2010, Unilever unveiled its Sustainable Living Plan that positions the company to improve the health of 1 billion people, buy 100% of its agricultural raw materials from sustainable sources, and reduce the environmental impact of everything it sells by one-half, while doubling its revenues. To achieve its aims, the company has to activate its consumers on sustainability. For instance, to reduce energy use associated with its soaps by half, consumers will have to cut their shower time by one minute. If twenty million consumers did so, the reduction in emissions would be the equivalent to taking 110,000 cars off the road! Accordingly, Unilever has announced a "Turn off the tap" campaign for the U.S.

- Intel focuses on rewarding and awarding ideas. The Intel Environmental Excellence Awards recognize employees or employee groups that have created an environmental innovation. In 2010, there were 11 winners of Excellence Awards that in total had created $136 million in estimated cost savings in addition to their environmental benefits. The company also offers Sustainability-in-Action Grants to allow employees to receive funding for an innovative sustainability idea or project. Signing on to this program in Intel India, Sonia Shrivastava designed a low-cost hardware utility that helps visually challenged people communicate and access daily information. With Intel's financial and technical support, Sonia managed a team of internal and external experts who customized a set of freeware applications and utilities on a low cost Intel® Atom™ based netbook computer and created a solution that was 85% less expensive than any other solution in the marketplace.

What these firms have done is taken a core competence of their business—its capacities to innovate—and applied it to economic, social, and environmental problems in their corporate ecosystem. In so doing, they have drawn on the talents of their employees and assets of their core business to co-create innovations with social sector and other stakeholder partners. This "next practice"—which requires developing and launching something "new"—is called corporate social innovation (CSI).

What Makes CSI Different From Traditional CSR?

Consider, in brief, these key differences between the CSR and CSI:

- Traditional CSR was born of a **philanthropic intent** by companies and is often funded by corporate foundation grants and managed by the community relation's function within firms. CSI, by comparison, stems from a **strategic intent** by companies and is funded and managed like other corporate investments.

- Traditional CSR involves contributions of **money and manpower** whereas CSI engages a company in **societal-relevant R&D** and applies the full range of **corporate assets** to the challenge at hand.

- Traditional CSR engages employees as **volunteers**—taking time "off the job" to do something worthwhile for society. While CSI may involve volunteerism, it involves strategically relevant work and **developing employees** as next generation leaders and global citizens.

- Traditional CSR has companies **contract** with NGOs or community groups to deliver social services. CSI involves a **true partnership** between companies, NGOs, and sometimes government agencies.

- Traditional CSR provides **social and eco-services** to those in need. CSI has companies and their partners (and often beneficiaries) **co-create** something new—**social and eco-innovations**—to provide a more sustainable solution to pressing needs.

- Traditional CSR has companies fund and support **social good** whereas CSI often puts them into the business, with partners, of producing **sustainable social change.**

What makes CSI different?	
Traditional CSR	**Corporate Social Innovation**
Philanthropic Intent	Strategic Intent
Money, Manpower	R&D, Corporate Assets
Employee Volunteerism	Employee Development
Contracted Service Providers	NGO/Government Partners
Social and Eco-Services	Social and Eco-Innovations
Social Good	Sustainable Social Change

Ingredients of CSI

What does it take for companies to produce social innovations? Of course, many firms have well-developed innovation protocols and innovation teams that can encompass R&D, product and marketing units, and their sales force. But these processes and personnel are oriented to innovation for traditional corporate markets and in line with commercial criteria. Social innovations, by comparison, aim to open new markets (or at least market segments) and can involve innovation in entire business models; and they introduce new players and challenges to the innovation game.

Here is a starter list of ingredients to transform CSR through CSI:

1. **Create a social vision for your company.** Dow Chemical states its purpose in this way: "Dow people include some of the world's best scientists and engineers dedicated to solving global challenges. We focus our *innovation engine* on delivering new technologies that are **good for business and good for the world.**" By 2015, the company aims for three breakthroughs that "will significantly help solve world challenges." Teams are working in the areas of water, food housing, energy and climate change, and health.

2. **Bring employees to the center of the effort.** Since 2008, IBM has sent over 1000 employees on 80 teams to 20 countries on one-month service learning assignments through its Corporate Service Corps. In Tanzania, IBM teams collaborated with KickStart, a nonprofit exploring new technologies to fight poverty in Africa, to develop modular e-training courses in marketing, sales and supply chain management for local entrepreneurs.

3. **Nurture intrapreneurship.** Jo da Silva has created an International Development consultancy within Arup—the professional service firm that designed the Sydney Opera House and Pompidou Center in Paris. Her group provides technical advice and practical solutions to reduce poverty and address social and environmental health in developing countries. Hundreds of the company's consultants have been engaged as "social intrapreneurs" to develop solutions for clients that can be spread across continents.

4. **Use the social sector for R&D and service support.** Many of the companies involved in global service projects work nonprofit partners (e.g., CDC Development Solutions, Digital Opportunity Trust, Endeavor, etc.) to identify clients in need, define projects, and handle placement logistics. NGO partners with expertise in emerging markets and placing volunteers can accelerate cross-cultural socialization and provide a "soft landing" for a company in a region where it has limited or no existing business presence.

5. **Engage a broad spectrum of interests using connective technology and social media for innovation.** Nokia runs a social innovation lab for scaling the good works of innovative NGOs; Dell sponsors a social innovation challenge for college students; and Studio Moderna leads a *Challenge:Future* competition that spans over 200 countries, 15,000 schools, and over 23,000 innovators. This is all about using social media to drive social innovation. Meanwhile, companies like Best Buy use social media to spark and shape programs such as the company's innovative reuse and recycle program for electronic equipment.

Shared Value or Something More?

Research has demonstrated that products and services based on eco- and social-innovations can produce value to society *and* to business. Michael Porter and Mark Kramer have termed this "shared value." There is no doubt that a turn to shared value opens up new avenues for value creation. At once it joins a company's interest in creating new markets at the base-of-the-pyramid with expanding its offerings for green and ethical (or socially responsible) consumers. And, it can also create real value for society.

However, shared value as such does not do very much to reconnect business to society, reduce mistrust, or address the complex issues of our time. The corporation remains at the center of this Copernican universe, and the other "planets" (Governments, NGOs, other stakeholders) merely align around its gravitational profit-maximizing pull. Meanwhile, global warming, declining school-and-student performance, a health care crisis, and just about every other environmental and social issue facing the nation (and world) are considered through the profit-making calculus, not as a matter of corporate or shared responsibility.

In my view, adding an "s," and searching for *shared values* turns companies' attentions not only to creating value for business and society, but also to engaging stakeholders—investors, employees, and consumers, community interests as well as government and nongovernmental organizations--in the defining business of business. A framework of shared values requires that corporate aspirations for profits and efficiency be considered alongside social progress and equity. This takes business out of the center of the universe and produces a solar system of interdependent and interacting sectors where cooperation is the central mode of working and mutual trust and true sustainability are our measures of success.

Philip Mirvis

Philip Mirvis is an organizational psychologist whose studies and private practice concern large-scale organizational change, characteristics of the workforce and workplace, and business leadership in society. An advisor to companies and NGOs on five continents, he has authored twelve books including The Cynical Americans *(social trends),* Building the Competitive Workforce *(human capital investments),* Joining Forces *(human dynamics of mergers).* To the Desert and Back *(business transformation case), and recently,* Beyond Good Company: Next Generation Corporate Citizenship.

Mirvis is a fellow of the Global Network on Corporate Citizenship. He is a board member of the Citizens Development Corporation, and formerly a Trustee of the Foundation for Community Encouragement and Society for Organization Learning. He teaches in executive education programs in business schools around the world.

Capitalism and High Trust: Leveraging Social Worlds as Intangible Assets

By Steven N. Pyser, J.D.

> *When people honor each other, there is a trust established that leads to*
> *synergy, interdependence, and deep respect. Both parties make decisions and*
> *choices based on what is right, what is best, what is valued most highly.*
>
> — ***Blaine Lee,*** *The Power Principle*

Achieving excellence in today's global business economy requires a winning strategy, an understanding of performance standards and a working definition of workplace trust. Business people can lay a strong foundation for success by recognizing the benefits of authentic interpersonal relationships across their organizations. These elements of communicational intelligence engender trustworthy behaviors with a multiplier effect when incubated in high trust workplaces.

Technology now drives most transactions in business and complicates formation and maintenance of trust-based relationships. However, the constraints of solutions-based, fast-paced and pressure-filled competitive business climates are problematic. A perfect storm now exists at critical interaction moments where people no longer "call" on customers in "face-to-face" mode; organizational charts connect us by dotted lines, email blasts and webcasts, making it difficult to scale and sustain trust even with the occasional personal touch.

Today, working within a 24/7 digital framework linking us with social networks, text messages, emails and voice mail applications is the norm for everyday business, leading to corresponding erosion (and the potential disappearance) of social skills. Opportunities for deception via new and powerful technology abound.

Trust-deficient situations are growing with a new push for efficiencies through computer-mediated communications. This is fertile ground for breaches of trust that increase multiple risks and potential irreparable harms to stakeholders and compromise business survival. Due to space limitations and complexity of this emerging essay topic, the reader is invited to consult the works of thought leaders cited in this writing.

The State of Capitalism

Capitalism has its critics and advocates as it guides most of the world's economies. At the intersection of capitalism and the recent devastating financial crisis stands a breakdown in societal trust. An indicia of the value and need for a global dialogue on trust can be can be found in a recent Gallup poll conducted January 2, 2013 asking, "When you think about the future of the United States—which do you agree with more: the country's best years are ahead of us (or) the country's best years are behind us?" Fifty percent of those surveyed said that America's best years are "behind us" while 47 percent said the country's best years are "ahead of us" (Street, 2013, para. 2-3), demonstrating the immense slide in trust across the nation.

The number of global business failures, as measured by the *D&B Global Insolvency Index* and other indicators, such as the *JPMorgan Global All-Industry Output Index*, serve as a stark reminder of the fragile nature of business and how it is affected by multiple externalities. To that end, *Standing on the Sun: How the Explosion of Capitalism Abroad Will Change Business Everywhere* offers sobering news of the new rules of capitalism and the shift of the United States away from the center of the global economic system and Western-style capitalism (Meyer & Kirby, 2012). The history of capitalism (both the empires it created and their fates) is documented beginning with the *laizzez-faire* capitalism of the mercantile 18th century, the Great Depression, high inflation and the "Thatcher-Reagan revolution," which collapsed with the Lehman Brothers bankruptcy of 2008. Other than increased regulation, the measure of the public trust influence of the global economic crisis or scandals and reform remains uncalculated.

Crisis of Business Trust and Leadership

We don't arrive at work with a GPS for navigating today's dynamic competitive environment. It is difficult to quantify what is expected day-by-day without a road map for guiding work behaviors. Long-term success of an organization comes from individuals' sense of job and personal security built by trust—leading to self-assurance, confidence and productivity. Trust is a dynamic force in business that cannot be defined in simple terms. It is felt and measured differently by those people and organizations affected by its reach. CoveyLink (2013) defines trust:

> *It is both character (who you are) and competence (your strengths and the results you produce). Trust is the enabling power of leadership influence. It is not soft, slow, risky, or easy. It is a measurable, definable component of all leadership success. It can be both taught and learned ... The proof of the value of trust in business is compelling: "Organizations with high trust outperform organizations with low trust by nearly three times". (citing Watson Wyatt 2002).*

The *2013 Edelman Trust Barometer*, a worldwide online research survey performed in October/November 2012 revealed:

> *"... a crisis in business and government leadership, with respondents reporting low trust in leaders' ethics and morality. In fact, less than one in five say they believe business (18 percent) or governmental leaders (13 percent) will tell the truth when confronted with a difficult issue to discuss" (Telliano, 2013, para. 2).*

Similarly, The Business Roundtable Institute for Corporate Ethics (2012) concluded, "[p]ublic distrust in business is negatively affecting companies across industries and shows that, although trust in business is in crisis, leaders can take concrete actions to build trust."

Given these current studies, the severity of the 2008 crisis and ensuing economic instability, it is not surprising to see multinational corporations paying attention to the research of Trust Across America™ (2013) unraveling the nuances of trustworthy business behavior.

Solutions for Business Trust Crisis

The findings of Zadrozny (2006) in *Leveraging the Power of Intangible Assets* offer practical advice for building business trust: "(t)he terms intangible assets or intangibles refer to any nonphysical assets that can produce economic benefits. This covers broad concepts such as intellectual capital, knowledge assets, human capital and organization as well as more specific attributes like quality of corporate governance and customer loyalty" (p. 91). New forms of employee engagement and motivation are intangibles that need to be implemented with emphasis promoting high trust work arrangements with more autonomy and control, and with corresponding accountability and responsibilities.

Not all business executives, managers, or employees have embraced the power of trust or understand its inherent benefits. For contrarians not yet convinced of the application and need for metrics of trust in the workplace, current news provides a catalogue of examples where trust was not an integral element of the global economy or a specific corporate strategy. We should always be moving to create high trust environments where commitment and energy can be focused on mission and vision rather than time-consuming activities required to assess and verify business conduct in low trust environments. This small sample of scenarios is instructive of the value of trust and consequential damages in low trust environments.

1. Bloomberg Businessweek's website reported the world's largest online currency is Bitcoin, a decentralized network with no government or central bank banking issues independent of any commodity—besides trust (Ford, 2013) with a $1B valuation.

2. "Martha Stewart testified in court (March 5, 2013) about what motivated her to sign a deal with JCPenney when she already had an exclusive contract with Macy's, her largest contract to date, with an estimated $300 million in sales. When Stewart told CEO Terry Lundgren about her plans to do business with JCPenney, he hung up on her and quickly announced that the company was suing Martha to keep her product line off shelves" (Lutz, 2013).

3. Horsemeat has been discovered in products labeled as 100% beef and sold in Sweden, the United Kingdom and France (Cullinane, 2013). According to *The Guardian*, Tesco, the supermarket most heavily hit by

the revelations of the horsemeat scandal, is still suffering from the furor as figures show an ongoing depression in market share (para. 1).

Better Social Worlds Build Workplace Trust

Positive workplace trust experiences begin with trusting relationships across the organization. Trust is transformational in business and can be catalyzed by how humans develop—by building, creating and growing through inclusion, collaboration and relationship building in generative organizations.

The late Dr. Barnett Pearce co-developed the Coordinated Management of Meaning (CMM) theory (Pearce & Cronen, 1980) to explain what we do when we communicate with each other (CMM Institute, 2013). We can build workplace trust taking a "communication perspective" focusing on questions of what is "made" by particular instances of communication Pearce & Pearce (2003).

All business interactions occur in "social worlds". Social worlds are metaphorical spaces where people tell stories, attempt sense making, build relationships and operate within their various cultures. From our birth until our passing, "social worlds" exist and evolve in conversation as we seek meaning through our different experiences. Dr. Pearce explained social worlds in the context "how we join our actions with the actions of other people and how we make sense out of what we're doing" (personal communication, December 28, 2007). In response, we build communication habits that interpret meaning. When we ask questions or respond to another individual, we are creating conversational patterns to facilitate this interpretation. We can create better social worlds by transforming our patterns of communication.

Changing conversation patterns by asking four questions recommended by Dr. Pearce can create awareness and support trust in business social worlds (personal communication, December 28, 2007).

- What are we making together when we interact in this particular way?
- How are we making it?
- What are we becoming as we make this?
- How can we make better social worlds?

When seeking to understand a situation we can ask ourselves:

- How can I/we act in ways that prevent undesirable events and objects?
- How can I/we act in ways that intervene in and improve existing events and objects?
- How can I/we act in ways that call into being preferred events and objects (Pearce, 2007)

Parting Thoughts and Call for Action

We teetered on the abyss of financial collapse during the economic crisis of 2008. Transforming capitalism and global economies currently operating in default non-trusting communication modes to ones driven by trustworthy business dialogue and behavior will not happen overnight. It will likely take time for the pendulum of greed and untrustworthy misdeeds to swing toward positive and sustainable change. Until then, moneyed interests will continue to seek short-term gains. Building a culture of high trust by leveraging the "right" conversations as intangible assets is the antiseptic and new structure global capitalism requires.

References

Business Roundtable Institute for Corporate Ethics. Retrieved from http://www.corporate-ethics.org/initiatives/public-trust-in-business/

CMM Institute—About CMM. (2013). CMM Institute for Personal and Social Evolution. Retrieved http://www.cmminstitute.net/about-cmm.html

CoveyLink (2013). How we define trust. Retrieved from http://www.coveylink.com/about-coveylink/how-we-define-trust.php

Cullinane, S. (2013). *What's behind the horsemeat contamination scandal?* Retrieved from http://www.cnn.com/2013/02/12/world/europe/horsemeat-contamination-qanda

Ford, P. (2013). *Bitcoin May Be the Global Economy's Last Safe Haven.* Retrieved from http://www.businessweek.com/articles/2013-03-28/bitcoin-may-be-the-global-economys-last-safe-haven

Lutz, A. (2013). Martha Stewart's Court Testimony Macy's—Business Insider.Business Insider. Retrieved April 1, 2013, from http://www.businessinsider.com/martha-stewarts-court-testimony-macys-2013-3#ixzz2P7cOOMgz

Meyer, C., & Kirby, J. (2012). *Standing on the sun: how the explosion of capitalism abroad will change business everywhere.* Boston, MA: Harvard Business Press.

Pearce, W. B., & Cronen, V. (1980). *Communication, action, and meaning: The creation of social realities.* New York: Praeger.

Pearce, W. B. (2007). *Making social worlds: a communication perspective.* Malden, MA: Blackwell Pub.

Pearce, W. B., & Pearce, K. A. (2003). Retrieved from http://www.pearceassociates.com/essays/comm_perspective.htm

Street, J. (2013). Gallup: 50% believe america's best years are behind us. Retrieved from http://cnsnews.com/news/article/gallup-50-believe-america-s-best-years-are-behind-us

Telliano, S. (2013). Three key things you must know to do business in california. Retrieved from http://www.edelman.com/post/three-key-things-you-must-know-to-do-business-in-california/

Trust Across America: A New Framework For Trustworthy Business Behavior. (2013). Trust Across America: Press Center. Retrieved http://www.trustacrossamerica.com/about.shtml

Zadronzy, W. (2006, Fall). Leveraging the Power of Intangible Assets . MIT Sloan Management Review, 85-91.

Steven N. Pyser, J.D.

Steven N. Pyser, J.D., is an Assistant Professor (Teaching/Instructional Track) at the Fox School of Business at Temple University where he teaches business and legal ethics, law and public policy. A speaker, consultant and program designer, the central focus of his work is building learning communities and securing compliance with ethical and statutory mandates within corporate and regulatory environments. He can be reached at SNPyser@temple.edu.

Conclusion: Creating a Positive Deviance of Trust

By Robert Easton

Trust is an essential agent of social development and organizational sustainability. It operates in, and allows for, the intricate web of interaction between individuals, institutions, communities and society; be it a marriage or a corporate C-Suite. We use words like "the glue", "catalyst", "energizer" and "connector" to describe trust. Yet most trust dialogue in today's world is about the trust deficit, or distrust. Implicit in this depiction of the current state of affairs is that the primary goal of increasing trust and trustworthiness is for individuals, workplaces and society to return to functional levels of trust, and by doing so some level of increased individual or organizational performance and well-being will return.

What if we were to think more constructively than mere functionality of trust and trustworthiness—in other words, positive trust? This concept does not simply connote the absence of distrust, or merely the presence of a normal state of trust; rather, it focuses on creating a positive deviance of trust- a force for helping people, corporations and societies to thrive. Yes, where distrust is prevalent we have to return to normal functioning- to a state where people feel safe at home, at work and in their communities. But in a paradigm of positive trust, a mere normal level of functioning is a necessary, but not sufficient condition for trust to catalyze social change. We must encourage leaders to view trust as more than just an instrument to improve corporate profit and organizational accomplishments to one of fundamentally increasing the total positivity of the organization.

What will it take?

Imagine a world where there is no trust and no one is trustworthy. Policemen are no more trustworthy than felons and employees and business leaders are always on guard against their con-artist co-workers. In this dysfunctional world fear, hostility, and suspicion are high; as are rates of suicide, crime, workplace accidents, divorce, depression, absenteeism, sexual harassment and violence. Risk taking behavior and innovation are low to nonexistent and the prevailing state of blame, defensiveness, negativity, vigilance, stress, adrenaline and cortisol effect our short and long-term psychological and physical well-being, not to mention our health care costs. Quite simply a world of distrust is a world where individuals, organizations and society languish.

Now imagine a world where trust and trustworthiness replace all distrust. The need for time cards, keys, locksmiths, home security and even the military disappears. It is a world of belonging, cooperation and sharing, growth and prosperity, reciprocity, security, vitality, energy, compassion, forgiveness and high quality social interactions. Wow—I want to live in that world, don't you?

How can we evolve to a world characterized by high levels of trust and trustworthiness? Simply by thinking bigger. We must move beyond an attempt to solve the trust deficit to building a trusting and trustworthy society, to a world where a positive deviance of trust exists. If leaders in corporate America embrace this concept, trust could change the world. With the optimization of trust enabled positivity, we would reap the benefits of unprecedented cooperation and sharing; increased risk taking and innovation; increased productivity, profits, accomplishment, and performance; and increased meaning, positive emotions, relationships, and engagement at home and at work. Such is the power of trust.

The essays in this book provide evidence that trust matters. They also provide a foundation for understanding what trustworthy companies and their leaders look like, how they act, the culture, processes, systems and governance put in place to build and maintain trust. Across these essays a consistent set of words emerge describing the characteristics of corporations and leaders who, in practice, are trustworthy—candid, caring, competent, compassionate, credible, ethical, honest, open, and transparent.

Collectively the essays highlight how trust and distrust are an asymmetrical relationship, and. it is the leader's responsibility to be vigilant about maintaining it. Once it is damaged the costs involved in rebuilding trust skyrocket, and many times the opportunity itself disappears.

In closing, there are two enduring themes running through this book. The first is that for one to get trust, one needs to give trust. Leaders must "lead" first by being trustworthy and also by reaching out with trust. The second key theme is that trust is an enabler of transformation and change, precisely because it is an agent of positivity. Trust is a necessary condition for individuals, organizations and communities to flourish. These essays provide a sprinkle of wisdom for each of us. Think about what we individually and collectively can do to raise the bar on trust and trustworthiness within our sphere of influence. If every corporate leader accepts this challenge it will kick start a contagion of positive trust from which we will all benefit. The moon-landing goal of these essays is for every one of us to draw on the lessons and practices contained in this book, and to think about how we can contribute to building and maintaining trust. When this is achieved, economic growth, and prosperity will follow and humanity will flourish. Let's all band together and unleash the power of trust for humankind.

Robert Easton

Robert (Bob) Easton is a Senior Managing Director at Accenture, where he has been for the past 15 years. Bob specializes in managing a select few of Accenture's largest global clients within the healthcare industry. Bob has worked and lived throughout the world including: New Zealand, Australia, Singapore, Hong Kong, Taiwan, China, Germany, London and currently, the United States. He is well known for the contributions he has made to building trust based relationships. He is the creator and designer of the Ways of Working program implemented at a large Global Life Sciences company where he has personally trained hundreds of Client and Accenture people across the world.

Appendix

APPENDIX A

Global Experts Define Organizational Trust/Trustworthiness

What do we mean when we say an organization is trustworthy or exhibits high levels of trust? Does the definition change from country to country? We polled experts from around the world to find out. The responses are listed alphabetically by the last name of the contributor.

Organizational trust is a product of the "ripple effect." Every act of management has an impact in the organization. Whenever a manager retaliates against an internal "whistleblower," or ignores misconduct on his team, that creates negative ripples across the organization and destroys trust. But when another leader opens a team meeting with an "ethics moment," or takes a surprise safety tour of a plant, those positive trust-building ripples also reverberate. Add up the ripples, positive and negative, at any given time, and you have a pretty good barometer of the culture and trustworthiness of a company.

Donna Boehme is Principal, Compliance Strategists LLC. www.compliancestrategists.com (USA)

Trusted organizations create value for customers, employees, suppliers, partners, shareholders and society. They have a strong mission, clear and admirable values and a responsible business model, which together consistently inform the behavior of all their employees, suppliers and partners. When mistakes are made, they quickly acknowledge the error and take corrective action. They carefully balance the needs of all stakeholders, making responsible choices aligned with their mission and values. They listen to and consider the value of others' points of view and are willing to be convinced to change their own policies or positions when appropriate.

Roger Bolton, President, Arthur Page Society www.awpagesociety.com (USA)

When we speak about people (or organisations) being trustworthy, we express our belief that their future behaviour will be beneficial for us—even if we do not know what it will be. Thus there is no certain way in telling who is trustworthy, as we talk about the unpredictable future. However, what we tend to seek can be described as a "benevolent adaptive resilience." It is the ability of trustworthy people to remain true to core values that we share with them while adapting to new challenges that the future brings. This balancing act is not easy, but this is the only trustworthiness worth being recognised with our trust.

Dr Piotr Cofta
cofta.net (UK)

An essential component of being human is trust. It is our faith in the integrity, competency, reliability, morality, and fairness of a person or organization. Trust is difficult to acquire, and if abused, hard to salvage and regain. When trust exists in an organization, individuals are at their most creative and productive. People freely exchange information, collaborate, and explore possibilities for the greater good of the whole instead of the individual. When there is trust, there is community and no room for " the end justifies the means."

Dianne Crampton, Founder TIGERS Success Series
www.CoreValues.com (USA)

Organizational Trust is a facet of social and relationship capital; the belief and willingness to engage that an organization has developed and strives to build and protect with all its stakeholders.

Paul Druckman, Chief Executive Officer, International Integrated Reporting Council
www.theiirc.org (UK)

When defining Organizational Trust, we should refer to the following issues:

1) What are the trust major components?

   Competence—Is the organization capable of delivering its promise?

   Integrity—To what extent is the organization congruent?

   Caring—Does the organization care for the consumer interests?

2) Where is it being engendered?

   Trust is the sum of all the trust experiences the consumer has with the organization.

   Every touch point can turn to a 'Trust-Builder' by adjusting the right set of tools.

3) What steps are required in order to make trust transcend all functions?

Adjust a Trust-based Strategy in the organizational strategic layers: starting from the Business Strategy, continue to HR strategy, Marketing Strategy and ending at the Advertising Strategy.

Lilach Felner
www.TrustBasedStrategy.com (Israel)

Trust is a powerful concept. It is about having confidence in a person's or organization's character to do the right thing, no matter how inconsequential. It is about having confidence that someone will treat you as you would treat yourself. When it comes to reputation, trust is the foundation that gives companies the freedom to exist. If you trust in a company's reputation, it means that you trust them to treat their employees well, build quality products and services, disclose information in a timely manner, govern your investment in them, and take care of communities that depend on them. Trust is critical to building a good name.

Leslie Gaines-Ross, Chief Reputation Strategist Weber Shandwick
lgaines-ross@webershandwick.com (USA)

Institution where all individuals and teams are encouraged to be and are respected, valued and rewarded for being authentic, honest, transparent and concerned about how all professional and personal actions affect others inside and outside the organization. All stakeholders can count on these integrity qualities to be business drivers as consistently important to the institution as its profits, not to be sacrificed to achieve short-, mid- or long-term goals at the expense of core values.

Nadine B. Hack, CEO, beCause Global Consulting
www.beCause.net (Switzerland)

Trustworthy are those individuals or organisations whose character is perceived as fair, integer and generally caring for society. Before trustworthiness leads to the development of trust between two parties, these parties often undertake a due diligence on each other by interviewing trustworthy third parties on the trustworthiness of their counterparty. Trustworthiness has emerged into mutual trust, when both parties fully believe in the good and fair spirits of the other. Trust is the oxygen of business. Without it, no business relationship survives and no business transaction is repeated. Among all assets valuable to the business community, trust is always the most essential.

Dr. Andreas Hoepner, Lecturer in Banking & Finance, School of Management,
University of St. Andrews Academic Fellow, UN–backed Principles for Responsible
Investment, andreas.hoepner@unpri.org (Scotland)

Organizational Trust refers to the ability of the corporation to effectively and consistently honor its commitments and meet the expectations for transparency and accountability of its key stakeholders. It is at the same time a reciprocal relationship in that trust is established when these key stakeholders would also effectively and consistently honor their commitments towards the organization. Finally, organizational trust is built when both the organizations as well as their stakeholders put in place processes and procedures that inform, compensate and provide acceptable alternatives in those rare instances when honoring the commitments or meeting the expectations is no longer possible.

Prof. Ioannis Ioannou, Assistant Professor of Strategy and Entrepreneurship at London Business School, (@iioannoulbs, iioannou@london.edu) (UK)

Trust is the core issue impacting organizational, team and leadership effectiveness. Trust adds value for businesses, their customers and audiences. Trust means a commitment to truth, open communication, sharing and collaboration, and caring relationships. If trust isn't present, everything's harder. The soft stuff in trust is the hard stuff in trust: accountability, authenticity, credibility, honesty, integrity, respect and transparency. Trust in business means doing the right thing and doing things right for the good of all shareholders through the strategic alignment of values with behavior, words and actions.

Noreen J. Kelly, Chief Trust Officer, Noreen Kelly Communications, Inc. noreen@noreenkelly.com (USA)

We accrue faith in an organization by the promises it keeps and the values it lives. While any specific promise or value is debatable – a mining company and environmental protection agency will certainly differ – the willingness and ability to follow through builds reputations. Just as we do not judge a society by its laws alone, but also by the institutions that uphold them, we do not judge an organization by its mission statement or advertising; we judge it by the mechanisms through which it delivers what it espouses, and through which it identifies and corrects failures. Trustworthiness, therefore, is the will and the skill to turn words into results.

Deb Krizmanich, CEO Powernoodle Inc. www.powernoodle.com (Canada)

Organizational trustworthiness is an aura—the source and sum of all mental associations people make when thinking about the entity. Trustworthiness is rarely the product of marketing. Rather, it flows from reality, accurately reflecting the complex adaptive system arising out of the thousands of interactions that occur for the organization each day through operations, transactions, networks, communications, and supply chains—and how these are experienced and reported. Ideally, trustworthiness will operate as a halo, shedding light and drawing positive attention. The more closely the organization's systems align with each other and with principles of truth and service, the brighter the halo.

Alexandra Reed Lajoux is Chief Knowledge Officer of the
National Association of Corporate Directors, Washington DC.
arlajoux@nacdonline.org (USA)

The amount of trust in the organization is the sum of how all people in the organization serve both internal and external customers. If it is based on real trust there will be short response time to a low cost. If the serving time is long it is likely that that the cost is higher and the poor performance in itself leads to decreased profitability. The trust has to start in the top of the organization. I believe that this should be the head of the organizations primary concern, in how to give, increase and maintain trust throughout the whole organization.

Pär Larshans, Chief Sustainability Officer Max Burgers
par.larshans@max.se (Sweden)

If you run an organization, or seek to influence one, it's useful to think of trust and its payoffs on a continuum. At one end are the sine qua non, the Mechanics. You speak honestly, you do what you say, consistently, predictably. You get permission to engage. Further along, you are trusted for the Substance of who you are as an indicator of your intention. Each party experiences deep value, mutual benefit and possibly, sustained relationship. Today, the trust premium goes to businesses whose Substance reeks of their sense of humanity - and who act in congruence with it.

Elsie Maio, the founder of Humanity, Inc and The SoulBrandingSM Institute
elsiemaio@soulbranding.com (USA)

Most organizations have cultures based on power and fear, resulting in reduced effectiveness. Work processes and structures are matrixed and virtual. But our work requires greater collaboration and interdependence. Trust is the glue that binds us together and enables organizations to become more than the sum of its parts. It is based on principle-based behavior: ownership, alignment, integrity, mutual respect, responsibility and accountability. It reflects our confidence, competence, and belief in others. Trust-building is a journey that starts at the top and, with perseverance, is brought to the entire organization. With high trust comes high performance and sustainability.

Edward M. Marshall, Ph.D., President, The Marshall Group, Inc.,
dr.edwardmarshall@gmail.com (USA)

A trustworthy organization can be relied upon to be true to the image, values, goals and priorities it conveys to the outside world.

Jack Marshall, President, ProEthics, Ltd
jamproethics@verizon.net (USA)

To effectively cultivate trust in an organization we must recognize that trust is more than just a feeling. It is an assessment we make, either consciously or unconsciously, regarding the extent to which we can count on someone to honor their promises. To build, as well as restore trust that has been broken, we must be willing to reach beyond our gut feelings and mindfully make assessments about trust by considering the sincerity, ability, and integrity in a person's words and deeds over time. It is in the conversations based on these assessments that we have the power to build relationships that make the remarkable possible.

Susan Mazza, Leadership Coach, Change Agent and Motivational Speaker, www.RandomActsofLeadership.com (USA)

Organizational trust is a positive outcome of the formal and informal relationships and mechanisms that exist in an organization to create, promote and preserve goodwill, capability and integrity between people, departments and stakeholders. Extremely dynamic, it moves and changes among people and groups and has extraordinary generative capacity to build on itself - positively or negatively. Beyond psychological elements of interpersonal trust, organizational trust is created and supported by policies and practices that promote fairness, collaboration, transparent communications and more. It requires equality and vulnerability and is shaped by culture, norms and expectations which determine the behaviours that are rewarded and that shape the organization's reputation.

Dominique O'Rourke, Accolade Communications accoladecommunications.wordpress.com (Canada)

There is no magic formula to build organizational trust, nor a silver bullet to restore it. Trust is hard fought, hard earned & hard won everyday. It remains forever complex and fragile. Trusted leaders are those with vision; are transparent & accountable; democratic & empowering; transformational and with a transition plan; judged by what they do, not what they say.

Robert Phillips - Co-founder Jericho Chambers; Visiting Professor, Cass Business School; robert@robertphillips.me.uk (UK)

Organizational Trust results when people at all levels practice behaviors that contribute to three dimensions of Transactional Trust®: Contractual, Communication, and Competence Trust.

- Contractual Trust establishes how people work together; how they manage expectations, establish boundaries, encourage mutually serving intentions, keep agreements and are consistent in behavior.
- Communication Trust defines how information flows; how people share information, tell the truth, admit mistakes, give and receive constructive feedback, maintain confidentiality, speak with good purpose.
- Competence Trust identifies how people leverage their skills and abilities to achieve results; allow people to make decisions, seek their input and help them learn new skills.

Dr. Dennis Reina, a Principal of Reina, a Trust Building Consultancy
www.ReinaTrustBuilding.com (USA)

A contextual view of trust sees it happening in our environment, making it possible for us to trust. An agency view of trust sees a person trusting "self" to handle a situation no matter what happens. The agency view of trust suggests organizations foster internal locus of control and agency by design. To bring about changes in social and planetary imperatives, increasing personal agency and internal locus of control is paramount.

The organization has a role in trust. It is not "trusting" the organization but building the capability of each individual to trust themselves, to count on and take responsibility for their own experiences and action and designing work to foster this.

Carol Sanford, Founder and Executive Director of
The Responsible Entrepreneur Institute,
www.TheResponsibleBusiness.com (USA)

"Trust is an essential intangible asset and skill in organizations and leadership. It creates and facilitates cooperation in workplaces. Trust forms an intellectual resource and influential force for leaders and enables them to build trustful workplace relationships and organizational climate. Leadership by trust is an invaluable skill and tool to develop and sustain human intellectual capital for the vitality, innovativeness and competitiveness of organizations. Through openness and mutual interaction individuals may build stable relationships and bonds that cannot be easily broken. In the e-era trust building creates added value benefiting the entire organization, as competitive advantages strongly rest on creating and sharing knowledge.

Taina Savolainen, Professor of Management and Leadership, University of Eastern Finland, Business School; Leader of the research group of Trust within Organizations www.linkedin.com/pub/taina-savolainen/1a/778/ba4 (Finland)

Organizational trust begins with credibility, with developing the necessary integrity, intent, capabilities and performance to make us believable, to us and to others.

Second, trust must be given. We have to give our trust to get trust.

Third, trust is built through behavior. Relationship trust is built through thinking, speaking and acting with integrity, through empathy, humanity and respect, through transparency, through humility, through standing up for what is right and keeping commitments, through confronting reality, through clarifying expectations, through loyalty, through practicing accountability, through results and through our willingness to continuous learning, improvement and change.

Karin Sebelin, Leadership Expert
de.linkedin.com/in/karinsebelin/en (Germany)

Organizational trustworthiness is the confidence and enthusiasm that arises from employees, customers, suppliers, investors and the wider community after

the organization commits to, and consistently delivers on, the conscious alignment of all stakeholder interests over the short, medium and long-term. It is
what facilitates the ability and eagerness for each group to co-operate, add value
and create growth.

Omer Soker is the CEO of The Ethics of Success Corporation.
omer@ethicsofsuccess.com.au (Australia)

Trust in organizations is both a responsibility and an opportunity. Ethical leaders
know that it doesn't just happen, and must be carefully tended. Building trust
through responsible leadership also brings out the best in people and organizations.
It is positive and proactive, building strong working relationships and productive
groups. It enables shared success and creates a strong foundation for collaboration,
innovation and creativity. High trust groups find that work is easier, more
meaningful, and more fun. Building trust and being worthy of trust are important
leadership roles, and they also bear fruit – high-trust organizations have a
tangible business advantage.

Linda Fisher Thornton, CEO, Leading in Context® LLC
www.LeadinginContext.com (USA)

Organizational trust is the social license to operate granted to the organization by
its stakeholders. Organizational trust is built by consistently meeting or exceeding
stakeholders' expectations across four dimensions of sustainability and responsibility:
value creation, good governance, societal contribution and environmental integrity.
Organizations earn this trust by ensuring positive responses by interested and
affected parties to the following questions. Does this organization: 1) Create and
share economic value fairly? 2) Operate ethically and transparently? 3) Listen and
respond to community needs, and 4) Protect ecosystems and conserve resources?

Wayne Visser, PhD. Director of Kaleidoscope Futures and
Founder of CSR International.
www.waynevisser.com. (UK)

"Trust is a double-edged sword, resilient when carefully constructed but fragile in the face of crisis. The key to building up robust trust is to focus all activities and decisions around the needs of stakeholders. An in-depth understanding of their needs set against the company's overarching business objectives is a priority. This understanding in the arena of digitalized communications, the front line of crisis management, necessitates greater importance and awareness placed on transparency, consistency and flexibility. Furthermore, as people become more skeptical towards authority but lean towards 'someone like me', selection of the right endorser is paramount to creating a trusted company."

Kevin Wang, Managing Director, Edelman Public Relations
Kevin.Wang@edelman.com (Beijing, China.)

APPENDIX B

Examples of Vision and Values Statements

Does your organization have a clearly articulated vision and values statement governing what you do, for who you do it and how you (plan to) excel? Clearly articulated values combined with workable goals will drive an organization's culture.

Every year Trust Across America—Trust Around the World evaluates, through its FACTS® Framework, the trustworthiness of the largest 2000+ publicly traded US companies. This appendix pulls most of its examples from the mission, vision and values statements of the Top 100 Most Trustworthy Public Companies in 2012, representing over one dozen business sectors. These examples go beyond what LJ Rittenhouse describes in her earlier essay "*Choosing Candor: The Language of Trust*" as "Just Talk" towards "Transforming Talk."

The following examples may be useful in creating vision and values for your organization, and serve as a tool to build trust.

Autos/Trucks

The **safety** of our associates is our number-one value and priority. The company and its associates will continually strive to eliminate incidents and injuries throughout all operations.

It is only through total and complete **customer satisfaction** that we will survive and thrive as a business. We will achieve this through excellence in providing world-class product quality, reliable on-time delivery, and best-in-class service.

We owe it to our **shareholders** to deliver positive results that will promote increased value of our business.

Our **Associates** are central to our success. We will assist them in their development, both professionally and personally, by providing continued training opportunities, and empowering them to be successful.

Continuous **improvement** in all aspects of our business must be at the core of our very being.

Achieving and maintaining a position as a **low-cost producer** is paramount to our long-term viability and success.

Communications are at the core of most problems. We ill make effective and thorough communications a key focal point in everything we do.

As a leading employer, we willingly accept the responsibility to be **good corporate citizens** and will actively engage and support the communities in which we reside.

Business Services

We care about people and the role of work in their lives. We respect people as individuals, trusting them, supporting them, enabling them to achieve their aims in work and in life.

We help people develop their careers through planning, work, coaching and training.

We recognize everyone's contribution to our success - our staff, our clients and our candidates. We encourage and reward achievement. We share our knowledge, our expertise and our resources, so that everyone understands what is important now and what's happening next in the world of work - and knows how best to respond.

Conglomerates

Our personal integrity, our shared values and our ethical business conduct form the basis of ██████████'s reputation around the world. When combined with the quality and performance of our products, those elements create an incredibly powerful platform for business success for the company and professional growth for all of us.

- We all have an ongoing responsibility to share and live our corporate values:
- Act with uncompromising honesty and integrity in everything we do
- Satisfy our customers with innovative technology and superior quality, value and service
- Provide our investors an attractive return through sustainable, global growth
- Respect our social and physical environment around the world
- Value and develop our employees' diverse talents, initiative and leadership
- Earn the admiration of all those associated with ██████████ worldwide

Our everyday behavior and decision- making must be grounded in these values, and our adherence to ▮▮▮▮▮▮▮ Business Conduct Policies is essential to our success.

Construction

From our forward-looking forestry practices of a century ago, to the new products and strategies of today, ▮▮▮▮▮▮▮ seeks to set the standard for sustainability. Although the bar is set higher each year, we are well equipped to meet the challenge. Evidence of our successes can be seen in the following awards, organized by our three sustainability pillars:

- Performance
- People
- Planet

Consumer Products

▮▮▮▮▮▮▮ purpose is to create the ultimate coffee experience in every life it touches from tree to cup – transforming the way the world views business. ▮▮▮▮▮▮▮ operates with the belief that the continued success of the Company is an enabler for continued investment in a just and sustainable future—whether through sales of Fair Trade Certified™ coffee, energy and waste reduction programs, awareness building campaigns, new product development, employee benefits, projects in supply-chain communities, volunteerism, grants or product donations.

Energy

Our vision is to be the premier low-cost supplier of transportation fuels in our markets, providing value for our customers while delivering industry leading returns for our shareholders and conducting ourselves responsibly in the communities in which we operate.

Strategic Priorities:

- Operational efficiency and effectiveness
  - Safety and reliability
  - Cost leadership
  - System improvements
- Commercial excellence
- Financial discipline

- Value-driven growth
- High-performing culture

Finance

██████████ has a tradition of strong corporate governance. Well before the adoption of the Sarbanes-Oxley Act of 2002 and related rules, we had implemented many of the governance features that companies are now expected to have.

For example:

- ██████████ has had (and continues to have) a board comprised almost entirely of independent directors, as well as audit, compensation and governance committees comprised entirely of independent directors;
- ██████████ already had implemented, formally or informally, many of the items now included in its Corporate Governance Guidelines; and
- ██████████ has had a code of ethics for many decades because it believes ethical behavior is essential to good corporate governance.

██████████ Values Integrity and Trustworthiness

We value integrity and trustworthiness in our employees and our directors, since we feel those characteristics lead to honest, responsible business conduct. We are committed to serving our shareholders and believe that our shareholders deserve and expect ethical business practices.

Healthcare

Integrity

██████████ employees make decisions, both big and small, with a focus on what is ethically right. Above all, we are committed to the greater good —for our company, our customers and the health care industry.

Customer-First

Our commitment to our customers sets us apart. We hear time and again from our customers that they choose ██████████ for our follow-through and customer-focused service. Our customers are at the center of everything we do, and our success comes from their success.

Accountability

████████ employees make personal commitments—to their customers, vendors, colleagues and jobs. We hold ourselves accountable for keeping those promises, and we take individual responsibility for the decisions we make to get results for our customers. We build trust with our customers by delivering on our promises.

Industrial Products

Over the past 175 years, ████████ has seen a great many changes in its business, its products, its services. Change always comes with opportunity. And ████████ has always been ready and willing to embrace it. Yet, through it all, ████████ is still dedicated to those who are linked to the land – farmers and ranchers, landowners, builders. And ████████ has never outgrown, nor forgotten, its founder's original core values: integrity, quality, commitment and innovation. Those values determine the way we work, the quality we offer, and the unsurpassed treatment you get as a customer, investor, employee.

Insurance

How we conduct our business is just as important as what we do. Our core values are the principles that guide us daily in helping our customers achieve financial prosperity and peace of mind. At all times, we strive to distinguish ████████ as an admired multinational financial services leader and trusted brand that is differentiated by top talent and innovative solutions for all stages of life.

- **Worthy of Trust:** We keep our promises and are committed to doing business the right way.
- **Customer Focused:** We provide quality products and services that meet our customers' needs.
- **Respect for Each Other:** We are inclusive and collaborative, and individuals with diverse backgrounds and talents can contribute and grow.
- **Winning:** We are passionate about becoming the unrivaled industry leader by achieving superior results for our customers, shareholders, and communities.

Medical

As committed as we are to clinical accomplishment, we are equally committed to our patient support, which is a guiding principle at ████████. We believe all who can benefit from our discoveries should have the opportunity to do so. ███████ puts patients first with industry-leading programs that provide information, support and access to our innovative therapies.

Technology

What are ███████ core values? There are three core values: honesty and integrity; company without doors; and customers count on us. ███████ value of honesty and integrity means that employees take a personal ownership to uphold the company's reputation. As such, employees choose to do the right thing and tell it like it is. The company without doors value focuses on open and candid discussions. This reinforces that when all the cards are on the table and all information is available to everyone - the right decisions can be made. Customers count on us means the company is doing whatever it takes to satisfy the customer. We go the extra mile to do what's right for the customer, because ultimately, that customer is counting on us to come through for them..... We place a very low value on bureaucracy and the typical corporate perks like special executive offices and dining rooms. Those things just get in the way of doing what's right for the customer.

Transportation

At ███████ our Mission Statement has always governed the way we conduct our business. It highlights our desire to serve our Customers and gives us direction when we have to make service-related decisions. It is another way of saying, "we always try to do the right thing!" Our Mission Statement has also led the way to the airline industry's best cumulative consumer satisfaction record, according to statistics accumulated and published by the U.S. Department of Transportation. That is why we are sharing it with you. In keeping with the spirit and intent of our Mission Statement, and as evidence of our wish to continually meet the expectations of our valued Customers, ███████ wants you to have a basic understanding of how we operate. We want you to have confidence in our airline and Employees, and we want you to be aware that there are, or may be, circumstances that can have an impact on your travel plans, purchase decisions, or your overall expectations.

APPENDIX C

Call to Action

Shortly after the 2008 Global Financial Crisis, a small group of experts convened in New York to discuss topics ranging from interpersonal to organizational trust and trustworthiness. We recognized that history repeats itself. The 2008 crisis was not the first time trust had been tested.

In the early 1980s, many people lost faith in Corporate America and believed that America was "broken" and could not effectively compete with Japan. Malcolm Baldrige, Secretary of Commerce, had a vision—to canvass companies across America and identify "best in breed" practices. President Ronald Reagan and Congress named the prestigious Malcolm Baldrige National Quality Award in his honor. The awards remain an important annual event thirty years later.

Trust Across America- Trust Around the World's (TAA-TAW) mission is to help enhance trustworthy behavior in organizations. We like to think of ourselves as social innovators. We are neither a non-profit nor a profit-seeking entity – rather, we seek to be self-supporting through modest and voluntary fees for some of our services. We are not trying to build a business around trust – we are trying to help organizations become more trustworthy.

Most of what we do is "open source" and our work cuts across organizational and disciplinary boundaries. We unite previously separate individuals and organizations under the common cause of furthering organizational trust.

In early 2013, TAA-TAW embarked on a **Campaign for Trust** and formed a global group of diverse professionals and organizations called the **Alliance of Trustworthy Business Experts** that has grown to several hundred members from over twenty countries. Through collaboration, we have identified five first initiatives that will be rolled out over the next two years.

- **Community Ambassadors:** Increasing the Global Dialogue on Organizational Trust
- **Trust Talks™:** Delivering Expert Speakers and Panels on the Topic of Organizational Trust

- **Constructing a Framework for Trust:** A General Framework with Customized Components for Specific Organizational Needs
- **Making the Case for Trust:** Proving the Correlation Between Trustworthy Behavior & Organizational Leadership Success
- **Generational and Cultural Trust:** Exploring Generational and Cultural Trust Synergies and Differences

If you are interested in learning more about organizational trust, we hope you will visit our website at www.trustacrossamerica.com where you will find resources ranging from books, blogs, workshops, radio interviews, company reports, top thought leaders and examples of trustworthy organizations. You may also choose to join our Alliance and become involved in one of our initiatives.

By reading this book, you have shown an interest in building trustworthy organizations.

We hope you will choose to translate your interest into action both personally and professionally. Share your knowledge with organizations in which you play a role. Together we can build a more trustworthy world.

Index

A

ABCD Trust Model, 93–94, 96
accountability
    collaborative innovation and, 79
    deserved trust and, 101
    increased emphasis on, 50, 195
adaptation, importance of, 219
Adobe, 219
affection, leadership and, 123, 124
Africa, 67–70
AIG
    familiarity and favorability scores, 37
    trustworthiness ranking, 26
airline industry
    Boeing 787 Dreamliner, 27
    Continental, 99–100
    high-trust companies, 17
    United Airlines' reputation, 185
Allen, Sharon, 16
Alliance of Trustworthy Business Experts, 267
Amazon
    Carbon Disclosure Project, 63
    corporate social responsibility, 61
AMD, shareholder letter example, 46
American Express, 1, 2–3
and/both strategy, 82
apologizing
    in crisis situations, 205, 206
    repair of damaged trust, 95, 206
    as trustworthy behavior, 141, 143
Apple
    Carbon Disclosure Project, 62–63
    corporate social responsibility, 61
    emphasis on transparency, 59–60, 215
    employee trust, 153
    familiarity and favorability scores, 36
    Supplier Responsibility Report, 60
    supply chain management, 27, 215
Aronson, Elliot, 144
Arup, 232
The Athena Doctrine (Gerzema and D'Antonio), 69
audits
    need for, 14
    See also regulation
authority

dispersion of, 214
employee decision-making autonomy, 131, 164
pyramid of, 216, 218
See also leadership
automobile industry
bailout, 71–72
consumers, treatment of, 76
example vision and values statement, 261–262
high-trust companies, 17
Japanese manufacturers, 72–73, 74, 77, 78–79
labor relations, 75
suppliers, treatment of, 72–75

B
Babson College, 148
Baird, Chip, 134
Baldrige, Malcolm, 267
banking industry. *See* financial services industry
Bank of America, 186, 219
Beam, Aaron, 49–50
behaviors
of distrust, 140
impact on trust, 258
leader behaviors for building trust, 168–172, 197, 198
promoting trust, 141, 198
trust busters, 130
believability, as element of trust, 93, 95
Bell, Alexander Graham, 1
benevolent adaptive resilience, 250
Bennis, Warren, 18, 98
Berkshire Hathaway
avoidance of moral risk, 41
extending trust, 100–101
Owner's Manual, 47
Best Buy, 232
Bethune, Gordon, 99–100
Bitcoin, 238
blame
in crisis situations, 205
Ford Explorer litigation, 76
not placing as leadership quality, 72–73, 80, 106
public focus on, 190, 196, 205
as reaction to genetically modified food, 190–191
boards. *See* governance
Boehme, Donna, 249

Boeing
    Nairobi visit, 70
    787 Dreamliner, 27
Bohnet, Iris, 203
Bolea, Alain, 179
Bolton, Roger, 249
BP
    familiarity and favorability scores, 36
    increase in business costs, 186
    investment in trust, 25
    losses, 160
brand building
    benefits of, 33
    case studies, 36–37
    earning trust points, 33–35
    measuring brand trust, 35
    negative versus positive experiences, 35
    social media and, 160, 180, 189, 205
    strategies, 37–40
breakdowns in trust. *See* distrust; restoring/repairing trust
Breen, Ed, 132
Buffett, Warren
    avoidance of moral risk, 41
    commitment to candor, 47–48
    extending trust, 100–101
building trust
    behaviors promoting trust, 141
    branding and, 37–40
    Coordinated Management of Meaning (CMM) theory, 239–240
    going first, 155–156
    inclusive management strategy, 217–220
    leader behaviors, 168–172
    as ongoing process, 155–157
    in partnering relationships, 29–30
    ratchet effect, 170–172
    stewards/stewardship of trust, 131–135
    strategies, 20–22, 29–30, 62–64, 178–183, 197–198
    triple crown leadership components, 130–131
    Trust-based Strategy Model, 180–181, 251
    trust fall activity, 153–155
    See also extending trust; restoring/repairing trust; trust
Business Advisors Network, 179
Business Roundtable Institute for Corporate Ethics, 237
business services, example vision and values statement, 262

C

call to action, 267–268

Campaign for Trust (Trust Across America), 267

candor
  in business communication, 41–48
  as leadership strategy, 169–170, 171–172
  versus transparency, 46

capitalism, shifts in, 236

Carbon Disclosure Project (CDP), 62–63

caring. *See* concern and caring

Carroll, Dave, 185

carrot and stick approach, 162–163

Catholic Relief Services, 67

CDP. *See* Carbon Disclosure Project (CDP)

CEOs
  communication examples, 41–43
  executive life, length of, 196
  expectations for, 197
  misbehavior and scandals, 49–50, 193–194, 198–199
  perceived ethical standards of, 49
  resignations and firings, 198
  setting core values, 51–53
  trust responsibilities, 133

China
Africa and, 70
response to Foxconn riots, 28

Chrysler, 71–72, 74

Citizens Financial Group, 207

civil sector
  collaboration with public and private sectors, 222–225
  See also consumers

Cleveland, Jill, 153

Clinton, Hillary, 70

Closing the Engagement Gap (Bennis), 18

Coca-Cola, valuation of, 159

coffee industry, example vision and values statement, 263

Cofta, Piotr, 250

collaboration. *See* partnering relationships

collaborative innovation, 78–80

Collins, Jim, 228

commitment
  compared to compliance, 109
  creating, 110
  disengagement of employees, 15–16, 91–92, 129, 161

communication

about corporate values, 30, 52–53

brand building and, 35, 37–38

candor in, 41–48, 169–172

CEO examples, 41–43

changing patterns of, 239–240

of competence and concern, 125–126

Coordinated Management of Meaning (CMM) theory, 239–240

credibility of, 28–29

levels of business conversations, 44–47

rapidity of, 160, 161, 195

rebuilding trust, 207

recommended content in crisis situations, 189

with small groups, 207

top-down, shift away from, 214, 216, 217–219

transactional trust and, 257

of trustworthy companies, 27

community

    corporate social responsibility and, 61, 62

    pyramid of, 216, 218

Community Ambassadors initiative, 267

compassion, organizational, 64

    See also concern and caring; corporate social responsibility (CSR)

competence

    as component of leadership, 123–126

    as element of trust, 93, 105, 251

    transactional trust and, 257

compliance, compared to commitment, 109

concern and caring

    for consumers, 188–189

    heart, leading from, 105–107

    as leadership component, 123–126

    teamwork and, 142

    as trust component, 251

conglomerates, example vision and values statement, 262–263

connection, as element of trust, 93–94, 105–106

Conscious Capitalism, 177–178

consistency, as element of trust, 106–107

Constructing a Framework for Trust initiative, 268

construction industry, example vision and values statement, 263

consumers

    buying behavior, 17

    enlisting feedback of, 219

    expectations of, 187–188

    public trust, 17, 160, 180, 236

    restoring trust of, 180–181, 217–220

sustainability, emphasis on, 63
use of social media, 160, 180, 189, 205
Continental Airlines, 99–100
continuous improvement
    collaborative innovation and, 80
    as core value, 53–54
contractual trust, 257
control, fear of losing, 100
conversation
    changing patterns of, 239–240
    levels of, 44–47
    See also communication
Cook, Tim, 59, 215
Coordinated Management of Meaning (CMM) theory, 239–240
Corporate Branding Index, 35
corporate social innovation (CSI), 230–233
corporate social responsibility (CSR)
    building, 62–64
    compared to corporate social innovation (CSI), 230–231
    desired practices, 2
    limitations of, 227–228
    measuring, 60–61
CoveyLink, 237
Covey, Stephen M. R., 129, 170, 182
Crampton, Dianne, 250
credibility
    of earnings estimates, 28–29
    as element of trust, 106, 188, 258
Crews, Clyde Wayne, 14
crime
    costs of, 14
    criminal actions of CEOs, 193–194, 198–199
    See also scandals
criminal justice system, 13
CRISIS OF CHARACTER: Building Corporate Reputation in the Age of Skepticism
    (Firestein), 29–30
crisis situations
    communication during, 189
    denial and blame, 204–206
    preparation for, 30
CSI. *See* corporate social innovation (CSI)
CSR. *See* corporate social responsibility (CSR)
CSRHub, 61–62
customer service
    of trustworthy companies, 27

United Airlines, 185
Zappos.com, 131
See also consumers

D
da Silva, Jo, 232
DataProm, 229
daycare centers, fee assessments, 163
Deepwater Horizon disaster. *See* BP
Dell, 61, 232
denial, in crisis situations, 204–206
dependability, as element of trust, 94
deserved trust, 101
Detroit, Michigan, 78
diabetes, social initiatives, 228–229
diamond of influence, 216, 218
distrust
    among team members, 142
    of auto industry, 71–78
    business consequences of, 14–15, 98, 104–105, 191, 238
    conditioning of, 139–140
    contagious nature of, 156–157
    employee disengagement and, 15–16, 91–92, 129, 161
    factors producing/trust busters, 130, 140
    of financial services industry, 71, 201–204
    leadership and, 123, 124, 195–197
    productivity and, 129, 182
    in public and private sectors, 221–222, 237
    regulations, need for, 100, 147, 186
    social consequences of, 13–14, 98, 203–204, 238, 243–244
    See also building trust; restoring/repairing trust
diversity, of board members, 30
Dow Chemical, 231
DreamWorks, 131
Drive (Pink), 162, 163
Druckman, Paul, 250
Durkheim, Émile, 100

E
earnings estimates, credibility of, 28–29
Eastman Kodak, 167–168
Eaton Corporation, shareholder letter example, 47
eBay, 178
ecomagination initiative, 224
Edelman Trust Barometer, 186, 214, 217, 222, 237

EILEEN FISHER (EF), 112–114
emotions
    fear, 100, 170, 198
    financial services meltdown, reactions to, 189–190
    genetically modified food, reactions to, 190–191
    reputation and trust based on, 185–188
empathy
    expressing for consumers, 188–189, 190, 191
    as leadership quality, 124–125, 197
    perceptions about, 69
employees
    brand training, 38, 39
    corporate social responsibility and, 61, 62
    decision-making autonomy, 131, 164
    disengagement of, 15–16, 91–92, 129, 161
    earning trust of, 18, 39
    health and well-being, 92
    inclusion and collaboration with, 51–52, 81–86, 164, 217–220
    motivating, 161–165
    positive effects of trust, 16, 18
    reasons for leaving, 125–126
    soliciting input from about values, 51, 52
    trusting, 100–101, 153
    trust responsibilities, 134–135
energy industry, example vision and values statement, 263–264
engagement
    of employees, 15–16, 91–92, 129, 161, 238
    importance of to stakeholders, 214
Enron, 50
environment
    corporate social responsibility and, 61, 63–64
    emphasizing shared interests in, 29–30
    social innovation initiatives, 229–230
equity analysts, importance of credibility to, 28–29
Ericsson, 229
Esty, Daniel, 62
ethics
    consumer expectations, 187–188
    conveying in communications, 43–47
    as core value, 53
    decline in public perception of, 217
    employee perceptions of, 15
    essential elements of, 118–119
    ethical leadership and coaching, 117–120
    "Giving Voice to Values" approach, 148–151

perceived standards of executives, 49
Ethics and Workplace Survey, 91
excellence, collaborative innovation and, 80
executives. *See* CEOs
expertise
    as element of trust, 93
    See also competence
extending trust
    Buffet approach to, 100–101
    going first, 97–98, 155–156
    as leadership quality, 98, 104, 245, 258
    pros and cons of, 97–102, 155–156, 245
    reluctance, 103–104, 139–140
    risks associated with, 98, 100, 156
    See also building trust; trust

F
FACTS Framework, 18–19, 261
fairness
    collaborative innovation and, 79
    consumer expectations, 187–188
    as element of trust, 93
    perceptions about, 15, 69
farmers, 224
FARTHEST principles, 79–80
fear
    financial services meltdown, reaction to, 189–190
    genetically modified food, reaction to, 190–191
    incompatibility with trust, 170, 198
    of losing control, 100
FedEx, 70
Felner, Lilach, 180–181, 251
financial services industry
    distrust of, 71, 201–204
    example vision and values statement, 264
    reactions to 2008 crisis, 189–190, 236
    rebuilding trust, options for, 206–208
    recent headlines about, 201
Firestone, 76
first impressions, brand trust and, 37
Fombrun, Charles, 160
Ford
    Explorer litigation, 76
    industry bailout and, 71–72
    suppliers, treatment of, 74, 75

Fortune, 100 Best Companies to Work For, 16–17, 92
Four C's, 105–107, 123–126
Foxconn, 28, 215
Friedman, Milton, 1

G
Gaines-Ross, Leslie, 251
Garcia, Fred, 204
GDP, transaction costs and, 15
GE, 224
genealogy of trust, 101–102
Generally Accepted Accounting Principles (GAAP), 38
General Motors
    bailout, 71–72
    suppliers, treatment of, 72–75
Generational and Cultural Trust initiative, 268
genetically modified food, emotional reactions to, 190–191
Gentile, Mary, 16
Gerzema, John, 159
Gilbert, Dan, 164
"Giving Voice to Values" approach, 148–151
Glanz, James, 63
Gneezy, Uri, 163
Google, 61
governance
    board member trust responsibilities, 30, 132–133
    corporate social responsibility and, 61, 62
    diversity of board members, 30
government
    collaboration with private and civil sectors, 222–225
    lack of trust in, 222, 237
Graham, John, 162
Great Places to Work Institute, 92
Greenpeace, 63
Greenspan, Alan, 178
Grieg Shipping Group, 225

H
Hack, Nadine B., 252
Halliburton, 25
handshake, practice of, 222
Harvey, Paul, 164
healthcare industry, example vision and values statement, 264–265
HealthSouth, 49
heart, leading from, 105–107

See also concern and caring
Henke, John, 77
Hewlett-Packard, 61
high trust
    competitive advantage and, 79, 165, 191
    creating culture of, 97–102, 238
    customer perceptions and, 17, 27
    employee engagement and, 18, 27, 191
    as foundation of collaborative innovation, 78–80
    indicators of, 18–19, 26–27
    productivity and, 126, 129, 182
    profitability and, 16–18, 25–26, 92, 104
    social benefits of, 203, 244
    team effectiveness and, 141
    See also building trust; trust
Hoepner, Andreas, 252
Honda, 72–74, 78
honesty. *See* candor; integrity
honorable purpose, collaborative innovation and, 79–80
horsemeat scandal, 238–239
"how" mandate, 214–215
How the Mighty Fall (Collins), 228
HOW: Why HOW We Do Anything Means Everything . . . in Business (and in Life)
    (Seidman), 144
Hsieh, Tony, 131

I
IBM, 232
IMA. *See* Institute of Management Accountants (IMA)
inclusive management, 217–220
industrial products industry, example vision and values statement, 265
influence, diamond of, 216, 218
innovation
    collaborative, 78–80
    as core value, 53–54
    corporate social innovation (CSI), 228–233
Institute of Management Accountants (IMA), 50, 52, 53
insurance industry, example vision and values statement, 265
intangibles
    communication as, 239–240
    company value based on, 159
    defined, 238
    trust as, 258
integrity
    as component of trust, 251

    decline in, 195
    importance of to stakeholders, 214–215
    as leadership quality, 197
    qualities of, 252
Intel, 61, 229–230
international markets, trust issues, 69–70
intrinsic motivation, 163–164
investment industry. *See* financial services industry
Ioannou, Ioannis, 252–253
Iwata, John, 161

J
Japanese automobile manufacturers, 72–73, 74, 77, 78–79
JCPenney, 238
Johnson & Johnson, trustworthiness ranking, 25–26
Justice Department, leaked memo, 213
"Just Talk" communication, 45, 46

K
Kelly, Noreen J., 253
Ken Blanchard Companies, 93
Kenya, 67–69
KickStart, 232
Kilpatrick, Kwame, 78
Kimmel, Barbara, FACTS Framework, 18–19
kindness, perceptions about, 69
King, Brett, 205
Komen Foundation, 186, 214
Korngold, Alice, 4
Kramer, Mark, 232
Krizmanich, Deb, 253
Krol, John, 132

L
labor relations
    automobile industry, 75
    distrust and, 71
Lajoux, Alexandra Reed, 254
Lanberg, Chris, 70
Larcker, David F., 100
Larshans, Pär, 254
leadership
    candor, reinforcing, 169–170, 171–172
    carrot and stick approach, 162–163
    characteristics of leaders, 124–126, 197–198

definition of leader, 126
dispersion of authority, 214
emphasis on profit, 162, 177
employee disengagement, impact on, 15–16, 91–92, 161–162
enabling actions, 169
Four C's, 105–107, 123–126
"Giving Voice to Values" approach, 148–151
inclusive management, 217–220
lack of trust in, 91–92, 103–105, 217, 237
leaders as ethical coaches, 117–120
leading from the heart, 105, 107
learning from mistakes, 110–114
motivational strategies, 163–164
non-operational issues, emphasis on, 196
productivity, impact on, 126
public declaration of intentions, 197
shifting roles and activities, 91, 195–196
short-termism, 162
table stakes, 168–169
triple crown components, 130–131
trust as element of, 20, 103–105, 124–126
See also CEOs; communication; extending trust
Lebar, Edward, 159
legacy of trust, 101–102
Leveraging the Power of Intangible Assets (Zadrozny), 238
Lincoln, Abraham, tree metaphor, 159, 165
Lindblom, Dawn, 155–156
litigation, cost of, 14
lockbox savings clubs, 67–69
Lockheed Martin, shareholder letter example, 47
Lopez, Ignatio, 75
low trust. *See* building trust; distrust; high trust; restoring/repairing trust
LRN, 144
Lubin, David, 62
Lundgren, Terry, 238
Lynch, Robert Porter, 17

M
Macy's, 238
Maio, Elsie, 254–255
Making the Case for Trust initiative, 268
Malcolm Baldrige National Quality Award, 267
managers
trust responsibilities, 133–134
See also CEOs

Managing with a Conscience (Sonnenberg), 18
marketing, budgeting considerations, 38–39
Marshall, Edward M., 255
Marshall, Jack, 255
Mazza, Susan, 255–256
McGovern, Gail, 155–156
media
 effect on reputation, 160, 185
 rapidity of news exposure, 160, 195
 See also social media
medical industry, example vision and values statement, 265–266
Megatrends 2010: The Rise of Conscious Capitalism (Aburdene), 177
Menasha Packaging Corp (MPC), 81–86
Merten, Greg, 182
Microsoft
 Carbon Disclosure Project, 63
 corporate social responsibility, 61
misbehavior of CEOs, 49–50, 193–194, 198–199
mistakes, learning from, 110–114
Mistakes Were Made (But Not By Me) (Tavris and Aronson), 144
mistrust. *See* distrust
Morales, La Rita, 76
morality
 avoiding moral risk, 41
 conveying in communications, 43–47
 decline in public perception of, 217
 definition, 43
 as leadership quality, 197
 moral competence, 148
 See also ethics; scandals
motivation
 carrot and stick approach, 162–163
 as intangible asset, 238
 intrinsic, 163–164
MPC. *See* Menasha Packaging Corp (MPC)
Munger, Charlie, 101

N
National Basketball Association, 71
National Hockey League, 71
Navran, Frank, 204
Nelson, Dave, 72–74
Nike, corporate social responsibility, 61
Nissan, 72, 74, 78
Nokia, 232

North Castle Partners, 134
Novo Nordisk, 228–229

O
Occupy Wall Street, 177
Olympics (1992), 167–168
Omidyar, Pierre, 178
openness. *See* transparency
organizational trust. *See* trust; trustworthiness
O'Rourke, Dominique, 256

P
packaging industry. *See* Menasha Packaging Corp (MPC)
Parker, Mark, 61
Parks, Judi McLean, 165
partnering relationships
    automobile industry suppliers, 72–75
    building trust, 29–30
    collaborative innovation, 78–80
    cross-sector collaboration, 222–225
    Menasha Packaging Corp, 81–86
    positive effects of trust on, 18
    See also teamwork
passion for serving, as core value, 53
Patagonia, 131
Pearce, Barnett, 239
peer coaching, 150–151
people first mentality, 94
Phillips, Robert, 256
Pink, Daniel, 162, 163
Porath, Christine, 164, 165
Porter, Michael, 22, 232
private sector
    collaboration with public and civil sectors, 222–225
    lack of trust in, 221–222
profits. *See* revenue and profits
promises, keeping, 93, 253
Proposition 37, California, 190–191
public sector
    collaboration with private and civil sectors, 222–225
    lack of trust in, 222, 237
public trust. *See* consumers
pyramids of authority/community, 216, 218

R

"Real Talk" communication, 45–46, 47
reciprocity of trust, 97–102, 207, 252–253
Recognition Equipment, 129, 134
Red Cross, 155–156
reflection, questions for, 143–144, 239–240
regulation
    consequences of, 100, 186
    cost of, 14
    as reaction to distrust, 147, 186
    self-regulation, 132
Reina, Dennis, 257
reliability, as element of trust, 94
reputation
    building from within, 30
    crises in, 186
    emotional responses to, 185–186
    employee impact on, 159–165
    as factor in valuation, 159–160
    relationship to trust, 25–27, 159–160, 165, 251
    strategies for building, 29–30
respect
    collaborative innovation and, 79
    as core value, 53
    leadership and, 123, 124
restoring/repairing trust
    communication, 207
    financial services industry, 206–208
    inclusive management strategy, 217–220
    strategies, 94–95, 157–158, 206–208
    Trust-based Strategy Model, 180–181, 251
    See also building trust
revenue and profits
    distrust and, 14–15, 98, 104–105, 191, 238
    emphasis on, 162, 177
    high trust and, 16–18, 22, 25–26, 92, 104
    Menasha Packaging Corp example, 81–86
    productivity, 126, 129, 182
    reputational crisis and, 186
Rindova, Violina, 160
risks/risk taking
    extending trust, 98, 155–156
    need for safety and, 179
    reputational risk, 160
Rittenhouse, LJ, 261

Rittenhouse Rankings, 43–44, 46
Rosier, Grady, 100–101
Rowe, Jack, 164
Rustichini, Aldo, 163

S
safety
    collaborative innovation and, 80
    as prerequisite for trust, 179
Sanford, Carol, 257
Sarbanes-Oxley Act, 50
savings clubs, 67–69
Savolainen, Taina, 258
scandals
    consequences of, 50
    criminal actions, 49–50, 193–194, 198–199
    HealthSouth, 49–50
    horsemeat scandal, 238–239
    Tyco, 132
    See also ethics; morality
Schultz, Howard, 218–219
Scripps Health, 111–112
Scrushy, Richard, 49
Sebelin, Karin, 258
Seidman, Dov, 144
self-organized teams, 83
self-regulation, 132
sensitivity
    ethical, 118, 119
    as leadership quality, 197
shared value, 232–233
short-termism, 162
Shrivastava, Sonia, 229–230
Simons, Tony, 165
Smart Trust (Covey), 129
social issues
    corporate social innovation (CSI), 228–233
    emphasis on, 227, 259
    social world concept, 239
    societal costs of low trust, 13–14, 98, 203–204
    sustainability, 62–64, 229–230, 259
    technology, influence of, 235–236
    See also corporate social responsibility (CSR)
social media
    consumer feedback via, 189

corporate social innovation and, 232
  impact on public opinion, 161, 205
  power of, 180, 213–214
Soker, Omer, 259
Sonnenberg, Frank, 18
Southwest Airlines, 131
The Speed of Trust (Covey), 129, 182
Spreitzer, Gretchen, 164, 165
stakeholders. *See* consumers; employees
Standing on the Sun: How the Explosion of Capitalism Abroad Will Change Business
      (Meyer and Kirby), 236
Starbucks, 218–219
steel industry, high-trust companies, 17
stewardship, culture of, 131–135
Stewart, Martha, 238
strategic plan development, Menasha Packaging Corp, 81–86
Studio Moderna, 232
suicides, at Foxconn plants, 28
Sull, Don, 228
Supplier Responsibility Report (Apple), 60
Susan G. Komen Foundation, 186, 214
sustainability
  building culture of, 62–64
  consumer expectations, 63, 259
  initiatives, 229–230
  natives, 63

T
TAA. *See* Trust Across America (TAA)
table stakes, 168–169
Tavris, Carol, 144
Tayan, Brian, 100
teamwork
  as core value, 54
  effectiveness surveys, 141–142
  factors producing distrust, 140
  high trust, characteristics of, 141–143
  low trust, characteristics of, 142
  Menasha Packaging Corp, 81–86
  questions for reflection, 143–144, 239–240
  self-organized teams, 83
  trustworthiness in, 21
  See also partnering relationships
technology
  industry vision and values statements, 266

influence of, 235–236
See also social media
Telefónica, 229
"The Ten Thousand Commandments," 14
Tesco, 238–239
Thornton, Linda Fisher, 259
thoughtfulness, trustworthiness and, 22
Toyota, 72, 74, 78
Transactional Trust, 257
transaction costs, 14–15
"Transforming Talk" communication, 45, 46, 47
Transocean, 25
transparency
 Apple's emphasis on, 59–60, 215
 availability of information and, 195, 213–214
 building culture of, 62–64
 versus candor, 46
 collaborative innovation and, 80
 in cross-sector collaboration, 223–225
 definition, 21
 lack of in leadership, 15
 social media and, 213–214
transportation industry, vision and values statements, 266
Triscendance Trust Assessment of Leadership Teams survey, 141–142
trust
 ABCD Trust Model, 93–94
 bank account analogy, 170–171
 brand trust, 33–40
 characteristics of trusted companies, 26–28
 consumer buying behavior, impact on, 17
 correlation to increased returns, 17, 22, 92, 104
 decline in, 13, 195, 236
 definitions of, 198, 249–260
 deserved trust, 101
 as emotional construct, 185–188
 factors affecting, 130, 140
 as foundation of collaborative innovation, 79–80
 four basic elements of, 93–94
 as glue for collaboration, 221, 222, 225
 international markets, 69–70
 investing in, 25–26
 legacy of, 101–102
 need for and importance of, 103, 147, 153
 paradoxical nature of, 22, 25
 positive deviance of, creating, 243–245

power of, 178, 244

prerequisites of, 179

public trust, 17, 160, 180, 236

ratchet effect, 170–172

as social glue, 203

See also building trust; distrust; extending trust; high trust; leadership; restoring/repairing trust; trustworthiness

Trust Across America (TAA)

call to action, 268

collaborative initiatives, 267–268

FACTS Framework, 18–19, 261

mission, 267

"Trust Barometer" survey, 13

trust busters, 130

Trusted to Lead (Lynch), 17

trust fall activity, 153–155

Trust Matters: New Links to Employee Retention and Well-Being report, 91

Trust Talks initiative, 267

trustworthiness

ABCD Trust Model, 93–94

characteristics and indicators of, 18–19, 26–28

Four C's, 105–107, 123–126

influence on business, 13, 17, 22, 92, 95, 104

low trust, costs of, 13–16

rehearsal of, 148, 150

reputation development, 25–27

strategies for achieving, 20–22, 29–30, 62–64

Top Ten list, 20–22

See also high trust; leadership; trust

truth-telling

collaborative innovation and, 79

as leadership principle, 112–113

trustworthiness and, 21

TSA airport security program, cost of low trust, 13

Tyco, 132

U

Uganda Department of Meteorology, 229

Unilever, 223–224, 229

unions, distrust and, 71, 75

United Airlines, 185

United States, decline in public trust, 236

See also government

V

values
 American Express, 3
 example vision and values statements, 261–266
 "Giving Voice to Values" approach, 148–151
 importance of establishing, 29, 53
 need for, 50
 setting and reinforcing, 51–53
 shared values, 233
Van Gorder, Chris, 111–112
Vanmeenen, Guy, 67–69
vision
 creating and sharing, 218–219
 example vision and values statements, 261–266
Visser, Wayne, 259
Vivo, 229

W

Waite, Mike, 81–86
Wall Street, credibility of communication with, 28–29
Walmart, Nairobi visit, 70
Wang, Kevin, 260
workplace climate
 disengagement of employees, 15–16, 91–92, 129, 161
 managers' impact on, 164–165
 See also employees; leadership
WorldCom, 50
World Diabetes Foundation, 229
World Meteorological Organization, 229

Y

Yamaguchi, Kristi, 168

Z

Zane's Cycles, 99
Zappos.com, 131